Project Planning and Control

Project Planning and Control

Fourth Edition

Eur Ing Albert Lester, CEng, FICE, FIMechE, FIStructE, FAPM

ELSEVIER
BUTTERWORTH
HEINEMANN

AMSTERDAM BOSTON HEIDELBERG LONDON NEW YORK OXFORD
PARIS SAN DIEGO SAN FRANCISCO SINGAPORE SYDNEY TOKYO

Elsevier Butterworth-Heinemann
Linacre House, Jordan Hill, Oxford OX2 8DP
200 Wheeler Road, Burlington MA 01803

First published by Butterworth & Co (Publishers) Ltd 1982
Second edition published by Butterworth-Heinemann 1991
Third edition 2000
Fourth edition 2003

British Library Cataloguing in Publication Data
A catalogue record for this book is available from the British Library

Library of Congress Cataloguing in Publication Data
A catalogue record for this book is available from the Library of Congress

ISBN 0 7506 5843 6

> For information on all Butterworth-Heinemann publications
> visit our website at www.bh.com

Composition by Genesis Typesetting, Rochester, Kent
Printed and bound in Great Britain by MPG Books Ltd, Bodmin, Cornwall

Contents

Preface to the fourth edition

About a year ago I was asked by a firm of insurance loss adjusters to investigate the possibility of reducing the anticipated overrun caused by an explosion at a power station. Based on previous experience of similar problems, I asked the contractors (a firm of international design and build constructors) to let me examine the critical path network which formed the basis of the computer-generated bar charts previously sent to the loss adjusters. My objective was to see whether the original sequence of construction activities could be rescheduled to mitigate the inevitable delays caused by long lead times of replacements and in some cases redesign of the damaged components.

To my dismay, I discovered that there was no network. The planners inputted the data straight into the computer, based on very detailed established modular packages. These packages contained the sequences, interrelationships and durations of the constituent activities.

It is a fact that most commercial computer programs recommend such a procedure. The planner can then see the program on the screen in bar chart form as he/she proceeds, but will only obtain a network printout (in precedence format) *after* the data has been processed. In other words the network has become virtually redundant as it has not been used to develop the structure of the project before the data was inputted.

This procedure turns network analysis on its head and does not give a project team the ability to discuss and refine the interrelationships to give the optimum results in terms of time and cost. The very act of communally drafting and developing the network generates not only an understanding and appreciation of the problems, but also enables the overall time to be reduced to an acceptable level by maximizing parallel working without necessarily increasing resources and costs. It is for this reason that I have retained the chapter setting out the case for manual analysis. Even in this age of the universal use of the PC for just about every management and operational function of an organization, the thinking process, i.e. the basic planning and sequencing of a project cannot be left to a machine.

One of the by-products of computerization was the introduction of precedence or AoN (activity on node) networks. These types of networks seem to militate against manual drafting for large projects, because drawing and filling in of the many node boxes is very time consuming, when compared to the drafting of arrow or AoA (activity on arrow) diagrams.

However, the big advantage of the AoN diagram is the substitution of node numbers by activity numbers. This clearly simplifies the numbering system and enables activities to be added or changed without affecting the numbers of the other activities. Indeed most computer programs add the activity numbers automatically as the data is entered.

There is no reason therefore why a simplified form of AoN network cannot be used in the manual drafting process to give the same benefit as an arrow diagram. A selected number of the arrow (AoA) diagram examples given in Chapters 12 and 18 have therefore been augmented by these simplified precedence diagrams, in the hope that the important part of network analysis, the initial drafting, will be carried out. Unfortunately the description of the activities will have to be written into the nodes, which will usually reduce the number of activities that can be accommodated on a sheet of paper when compared with an arrow diagram. A 'marriage' of the two methods, called the 'Lester' diagram is given in Chapter 13.

At the time of writing, Earned Value Analysis (EVA) has still not been fully embraced by certain sections of industry. One reason for this may be the jargon associated with this technique. When we developed our own EVA system at Foster Wheeler as far back as 1978 we used the simple terms of Actual Cost, Planned Cost and Earned Value. Unfortunately the American CSCSC system introduced such terms as ACWP, BCWS and BCWP which often generated groans from students and rejection from practitioners. It is gratifying to note therefore that the campaign to eradicate these abbreviations has prompted the British Standards Institution and the Association for Project Management to give prominence to the original English words. To encourage this welcome trend, the terms used in EVA methods in this book are in English instead of jargon.

Since publication of the third edition, the APMP examination has undergone a number of changes. In order to meet the new requirements for paper 2 of the examination, some new topics have been included in this edition and a number of topics have been enhanced. However, no attempt has been made to include the 'soft' topics such as team building and motivation, which, while important, are really part of good general management and are certainly not exclusive to project management.

A number of chapters have been rewritten and their order rearranged to reflect as far as possible the sequence in which the various techniques are carried out when managing a project.

A. Lester

Preface to the third edition

The shortest distance between two points is a straight line

Euclid

The longest distance between two points is a shortcut

Lester

The first two editions of this book dealt primarily with producing planning networks and control systems for all types of projects, whether large or small, complex or simple.

In the last two paragraphs of the second edition, reference was made to other project management skills, emphasizing that planning and monitoring systems were only part of the project manager's armoury. The purpose of this book, therefore, is to explain what some of these other parts are. It was not, however, the intention to produce a comprehensive book on project management, but merely to update the previous edition, adding such sections as were considered to be more closely related to project management than general management.

An examination of courses on project management will reveal that they cover two types of skills:

1 *Soft skills* such as investment appraisal, communication, team selection, team building, motivation, conflict management, meetings, configuration management and quality management.
2 *Hard skills* such as project organization, project evaluation, project planning, cost control, monitoring, risk management and change management.

As the first two editions already contained such hard skills as project planning and cost control, it seemed logical to only add those skills which would virtually turn the book into a Hard Skill Manual. This, it is hoped, will be of maximum value to readers who have learnt the soft skills through past experience or from the more general management courses including the outward-bound management courses, so popular with up and coming managers.

The original text has been updated where considered necessary, including the list of the currently available project management software programs, which are however being themselves updated constantly. One important change is the substitution of the description of the Primavera P3 program by the Hornet Windmill program. The reason for this change is that while Primavera P3 is still an excellent project tool, the Hornet Windmill now includes an integrated SMAC cost control system which can accept and print both precedence and arrow diagrams and update progress on them directly and automatically from the SMAC returns. Unfortunately, the stipulated book size did not allow space for both, especially as the chapter on MS Project had to be included, simply because after being 'bundled' with Microsoft Office, it is now, despite its limitations, so widely used.

When the first edition was written in 1982, the use of arrow diagrams or Activity on Arrow (AoA) diagrams was the generally used method of drafting networks. By the time the second edition was published, precedence diagrams or Activity on Node (AoN) diagrams were already well established, mainly due to the proliferation of relatively inexpensive so called project management computer programs. While AoN has a number of advantages over AoA, it still has two serious drawbacks:

1 When producing the first draft of the network by hand, (something which should always be done, especially on large projects), the AoN takes up considerably more space and therefore restricts the size of network which can be drawn on one sheet of A1 or A0 paper (the standard size of a CP network).
2 When the network is subsequently reproduced by the computer, the links, which are often drawn either horizontally or vertically to miss the node boxes, are sometimes so close together, that they merge into a thick line from which it is virtually impossible to establish where a dependency comes from or where it goes. As tracing the dependencies is the heart of network analysis, this reduces the usefulness of the network diagram.

Because of these disadvantages, the AoA method was generally retained for this third edition, especially as the new 'Lester' diagram described in

Chapter 2 enables the advantages of both the AoA and AoN configuration to be combined to give the best of both worlds. After absorbing the fascinating capabilities of the various computer programs, there is one important message that the author would like to 'bring across'. This is, that in all cases the network should be roughed out *manually* with the project team *before* using the computer. The thinking part of project planning cannot be left to a machine.

A. Lester

Acknowledgements

The author and publishers would like to make acknowledgement to the following for their help and cooperation in the preparation of this book.

The National Economic Development Office for permission to reproduce the relevant section of their report 'Engineering Construction Performance Mechanical & Electrical Engineering Construction, EDC, NEDO December 1976'.

Foster Wheeler Power Products Limited for assistance in preparing the text and manuscripts and permission to utilize the network diagrams of some of their contracts.

Mr P. Osborne for assistance in producing some of the computerized examples.

Claremont Controls Limited, Suite 43, Wansbeck Business Centre, Rotary Parkway, Ashington, Northumberland NE63 8QZ, for the description and diagrams of their Hornet Windmill project management software.

Microsoft Ltd. for permission to use some of the screen dumps of MS Project 98.

Extracts from BS 6079: 1996 are reproduced with the permission of BSI under licence No. 2003DH0199. Complete editions of the standards are obtainable by post from BSI Customer Services, 389 Chiswick High Road, London W4 4AL. Tel. 44(0)20 8996 9001.

WPMC for some of the diagrams.

A. P. Watt for permission to quote the first verse of Rudyard Kipling's poem, 'The Elephant's Child'.

Daimler Chrysler for permission to use their diagram of the Mercedes-Benz 190 car.

Automobile Association for the diagram of an engine.

1

Project definition

Project definition

Many people and organizations have defined what a project is, or should be, but probably the most authoritative definition is that given in BS 6079 'Guide to Project Management'.

This states that a project is:

> 'A unique set of co-ordinated activities, with definite starting and finishing points, undertaken by an individual or organization to meet specific objectives within defined schedule, cost and performance parameters.'

The next question that can be asked is 'Why does one need project management?' What is the difference between project management and management of any other business or enterprise? Why has project management taken off so dramatically in the last twenty years?

The answer is that project management is essentially management of change, while running a functional or ongoing business is managing a continuum or 'business-as-usual'.

Project management is not applicable to running a factory making sausage pies, but it will be the right system when there is a requirement to relocate the factory, build an extension, or produce a different product requiring new machinery, skills, staff training and even marketing techniques.

As stated in the definition, a project has a definite starting and finishing point and must meet certain specified objectives.

Broadly these objectives, which are usually defined as part of the business case and set out in the project brief, must meet three fundamental criteria:

1 The project must be completed on time;
2 The project must be accomplished within the budgeted cost;
3 The project must meet the prescribed quality requirements.

These criteria can be graphically represented by the well-known project triangle (Figure 1.1). Some organizations like to substitute the word 'quality' with 'performance', but the principle is the same – the operational requirements of the project must be met, and met safely.

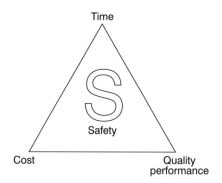

Figure 1.1

In certain industries like airlines, railways and mining etc. the fourth criterion, safety, is considered to be equally, if not more important. In these organizations, the triangle can be replaced by a diamond now showing the four important criteria (Figure 1.2).

The order of priority given to any of these criteria is not only dependent on the industry, but also on the individual project. For example, in designing and constructing an aircraft, motor car or railway carriage, safety must be paramount. The end product may cost more than budgeted, may be late in going into service and certain quality requirements in terms of comfort may

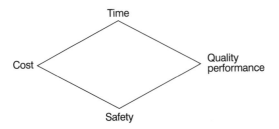

Figure 1.2

have to be sacrificed, but under no circumstances can safety be compromised. Aeroplanes, cars and railways *must* be safe under all operating conditions.

The following (rather obvious) examples show where different priorities on the project triangle (or diamond) apply.

Time bound project

A scoreboard for a prestigious tennis tournament must be finished in time for the opening match, even if it costs more than anticipated and the display of some secondary information, such as the speed of the service, has to be abandoned. In other words, cost and performance may have to be sacrificed to meet the unalterable starting date of the tournament.

(In practice, the increased cost may well be a matter of further negotiation and the temporarily delayed display can usually be added later during the non-playing hours.)

Cost bound project

A local authority housing development may have to curtail the number of housing units and may even overrun the original construction programme, but the project cost cannot be exceeded, because the housing grant allocated by central government for this type of development has been frozen at a fixed sum. Another solution to this problem would be to reduce the specification of the internal fittings instead of reducing the number of units.

Performance (quality) bound project

An armaments manufacturer has been contracted to design and manufacture a new type of rocket launcher to meet the client's performance specification in terms of range, accuracy and rate of fire. Even if the delivery has to be delayed to carry out more tests and the cost has increased, the specification must be met. Again if the weapons were required during a war, the specification might be relaxed to get the equipment into the field as quickly as possible.

Safety bound project

Apart from the obvious examples of public transport given previously, safety is a factor that is required by law and enshrined in the Health & Safety at Work Act.

Not only must safe practices be built into every project, but constant monitoring is an essential element of a safety policy. To that extent it could be argued that *all* projects are safety bound, since if it became evident after an accident that safety was sacrificed for speed or profitability, some or all of the project stakeholders could find themselves in real trouble, if not in jail.

A serious accident which may kill or injure people will not only cause anguish among the relatives, but, while not necessarily terminating the project, could very well destroy the company. For this reason the 'S' symbol when shown in the middle of the project management triangle gives more emphasis of its importance (see Figure 1.1).

It can be seen therefore that the priorities can change with the political or commercial needs of the client even within the life cycle of the project, and the project manager has to constantly evaluate these changes to determine the new priorities. Ideally, all the main criteria should be met (and indeed on many well-run projects, this is the case), but there are times when the project manager, with the agreement of the sponsor or client, has to take difficult decisions to satisfy the best interests of most, if not all, the stakeholders.

2

Business case

Before embarking on a project, it is clearly necessary to show that there will be a benefit either in terms of money or service or both. The document which sets out the main advantages and parameters of the project is called the *Business Case* and is (or should be) produced by either the client or the sponsor of the project who in effect becomes the owner of the document.

A business case in effect outlines the 'why' and 'what' of the project as well as making the financial case by including the investment appraisal.

As with all documents, a clear procedure for developing the business case is highly desirable and the following headings give some indication of the subjects to be included:

1 Why is the project required?
2 What are we trying to achieve?
3 What are the deliverables?
4 What is the anticipated cost?
5 How long will it take to complete?
6 What quality standards must be achieved?
7 What are the performance criteria?
8 What are Key Performance Indicators (KPI)?

9 What are the main risks?

10 What are success criteria?

12 Who are the main stakeholders?

In addition any known information such as location, key personnel, resource requirements etc. should be included so that the recipients, usually a board of directors, are in a position to accept or reject the case for carrying out the project.

Investment appraisal

The investment appraisal, which is part of the business case, will, if properly structured, improve the decision-making process regarding the desirability or viability of the project. It should have examined all the realistic options before making a firm recommendation for the proposed case. The investment appraisal must also include a cost/benefit analysis and take into account all the relevant factors such as:

Capital costs, operating costs, overhead costs
Support and training costs
Dismantling and disposal costs
Expected residual value (if any)
Any cost savings which the project will bring
Any benefits which cannot be expressed in monetary terms

To enable some of the options to be compared, the payback, return on capital, net present value and anticipated profit must be calculated. In other words, the project viability must be established.

Project viability

1 Return on investment (ROI)

The simplest way to ascertain whether the investment in a project is viable is to calculate the return on investment (ROI).

If a project investment is £10 000, and gives a return of £2000 per year over 7 years,

$$\text{the average return/year} = \frac{(7 \times £2000) - £10\,000}{7}$$

$$= \frac{£4000}{7} = £571.4.$$

The return on the investment, usually given as a percentage, is the average return over the period considered × 100, divided by the original investment, i.e.

$$\text{return on investment \%} = \frac{\text{average return} \times 100}{\text{investment}}$$

$$= \frac{£571.4 \times 100}{£10\,000} = 5.71\%.$$

This calculation does not, however, take into account the cash flow of the investment which in a real situation may vary year by year.

2 Net Present Value

As the value of money varies with time due to the interest it could earn if invested in a bank or other institution, the actual cash flow must be taken into account to obtain a realistic measure of the profitability of the investment.

If £100 were invested in a bank earning an interest of 5%
The value in 1 year would be £100 × 1.05   = £105
The value in 2 years would be £100 × 1.05 × 1.05   = £110.25
The value in 3 years would be £100 × 1.05 × 1.05 × 1.05 = £115.76

It can be seen therefore that, today, to obtain £115.76 in 3 years it would cost £100. In other words, the present value of £115.76 is £100.

Another way of finding the present value (PV) of £115.76 is to divide it by 1.05 × 1.05 × 1.05 or 1.157, for

$$\frac{115.76}{1.05 \times 1.05 \times 1.05} = \frac{115.76}{1.157} = £100.$$

If instead of dividing the £115.76 by 1.157, it is multiplied by the inverse of 1.157, one obtains the same answer, since

$$£115.76 \times \frac{1}{1.157} = £115.76 \times 0.8638 = £100.$$

The 0.8638 is called the discount factor or Present Value Factor and can be quickly found from discount factor tables, a sample of which is given in Figure 2.1.

Years Hence	1%	2%	4%	6%	8%	10%	12%	14%	15%	16%	18%	20%	22%	24%	25%	26%	28%	30%	35%	40%	45%	50%
1	0.990	0.980	0.962	0.943	0.926	0.909	0.895	0.877	0.870	0.862	0.847	0.833	0.820	0.806	0.800	0.794	0.781	0.769	0.741	0.714	0.690	0.667
2	0.980	0.961	0.925	0.890	0.857	0.826	0.797	0.769	0.756	0.743	0.718	0.694	0.672	0.650	0.640	0.630	0.610	0.592	0.549	0.510	0.476	0.444
3	0.971	0.942	0.889	0.840	0.794	0.751	0.712	0.675	0.658	0.641	0.609	0.579	0.551	0.524	0.512	0.500	0.477	0.455	0.406	0.364	0.328	0.296
4	0.961	0.924	0.855	0.792	0.735	0.683	0.636	0.592	0.572	0.552	0.516	0.482	0.451	0.423	0.410	0.397	0.373	0.350	0.301	0.260	0.226	0.198
5	0.951	0.906	0.822	0.747	0.681	0.621	0.567	0.519	0.497	0.476	0.437	0.402	0.370	0.341	0.328	0.315	0.291	0.269	0.223	0.186	0.136	0.132
6	0.942	0.888	0.790	0.705	0.630	0.564	0.507	0.456	0.432	0.410	0.370	0.335	0.303	0.275	0.262	0.250	0.227	0.207	0.165	0.133	0.108	0.088
7	0.933	0.871	0.760	0.665	0.583	0.513	0.452	0.400	0.376	0.354	0.314	0.279	0.249	0.222	0.210	0.198	0.178	0.159	0.122	0.095	0.074	0.059
8	0.923	0.853	0.731	0.627	0.540	0.467	0.404	0.351	0.327	0.305	0.266	0.233	0.204	0.179	0.168	0.157	0.139	0.123	0.091	0.068	0.051	0.039
9	0.914	0.837	0.703	0.592	0.500	0.424	0.361	0.308	0.284	0.263	0.225	0.194	0.167	0.144	0.134	0.125	0.108	0.094	0.067	0.048	0.035	0.026
10	0.905	0.820	0.676	0.558	0.463	0.386	0.322	0.270	0.247	0.227	0.191	0.162	0.137	0.116	0.107	0.099	0.085	0.073	0.050	0.035	0.024	0.017
11	0.896	0.804	0.650	0.527	0.429	0.350	0.287	0.237	0.215	0.195	0.162	0.135	0.112	0.094	0.086	0.079	0.066	0.056	0.037	0.025	0.017	0.012
12	0.887	0.788	0.625	0.497	0.397	0.319	0.257	0.208	0.187	0.168	0.137	0.112	0.092	0.076	0.069	0.062	0.052	0.043	0.027	0.018	0.012	0.008
13	0.879	0.773	0.601	0.469	0.368	0.290	0.229	0.182	0.163	0.145	0.116	0.093	0.075	0.061	0.055	0.050	0.040	0.033	0.020	0.013	0.008	0.005
14	0.870	0.758	0.577	0.442	0.340	0.263	0.205	0.160	0.141	0.125	0.099	0.078	0.062	0.049	0.044	0.039	0.032	0.025	0.015	0.009	0.006	0.003
15	0.861	0.743	0.555	0.437	0.345	0.239	0.183	0.140	0.123	0.108	0.084	0.065	0.051	0.040	0.035	0.031	0.025	0.020	0.011	0.005	0.004	0.002
16	0.853	0.728	0.534	0.394	0.292	0.218	0.163	0.123	0.107	0.093	0.071	0.054	0.042	0.032	0.028	0.025	0.019	0.015	0.008	0.005	0.003	0.002
17	0.844	0.714	0.523	0.371	0.270	0.198	0.146	0.108	0.093	0.080	0.060	0.045	0.034	0.026	0.023	0.020	0.015	0.012	0.006	0.003	0.002	0.001
18	0.836	0.700	0.494	0.350	0.250	0.180	0.130	0.095	0.081	0.069	0.051	0.038	0.028	0.021	0.018	0.016	0.012	0.009	0.005	0.002	0.001	0.001
19	0.828	0.686	0.475	0.331	0.232	0.164	0.116	0.083	0.070	0.060	0.043	0.031	0.023	0.017	0.014	0.012	0.009	0.007	0.003	0.002	0.001	
20	0.820	0.673	0.456	0.312	0.215	0.149	0.104	0.073	0.061	0.051	0.037	0.026	0.019	0.014	0.012	0.010	0.007	0.005	0.002	0.001	0.001	
21	0.811	0.660	0.439	0.294	0.199	0.135	0.095	0.064	0.053	0.044	0.031	0.022	0.015	0.011	0.009	0.008	0.006	0.004	0.002	0.001		
22	0.803	0.647	0.422	0.278	0.184	0.123	0.083	0.056	0.046	0.038	0.026	0.018	0.013	0.009	0.007	0.006	0.004	0.003	0.001	0.001		
23	0.795	0.634	0.406	0.262	0.170	0.112	0.074	0.049	0.040	0.035	0.022	0.015	0.010	0.007	0.006	0.005	0.003	0.002	0.001			
24	0.788	0.622	0.390	0.247	0.158	0.102	0.066	0.043	0.035	0.028	0.019	0.013	0.008	0.006	0.005	0.004	0.003	0.002	0.001			
25	0.780	0.610	0.375	0.235	0.146	0.092	0.059	0.038	0.030	0.024	0.016	0.010	0.007	0.005	0.004	0.003	0.002	0.001	0.001			
26	0.772	0.598	0.361	0.220	0.135	0.084	0.053	0.033	0.026	0.021	0.014	0.009	0.006	0.004	0.003	0.002	0.002	0.001				
27	0.764	0.586	0.347	0.207	0.125	0.076	0.047	0.029	0.023	0.018	0.011	0.007	0.005	0.003	0.002	0.002	0.001	0.001				
28	0.757	0.574	0.333	0.196	0.116	0.069	0.042	0.026	0.020	0.016	0.010	0.006	0.004	0.002	0.002	0.002	0.001	0.001				
29	0.749	0.563	0.321	0.185	0.107	0.063	0.037	0.022	0.017	0.014	0.008	0.005	0.003	0.002	0.002	0.001	0.001	0.001				
30	0.742	0.552	0.308	0.174	0.099	0.057	0.033	0.020	0.015	0.012	0.007	0.004	0.003	0.002	0.001	0.001	0.001	0.001				
40	0.672	0.453	0.208	0.097	0.046	0.022	0.011	0.005	0.004	0.003	0.001	0.001										
50	0.608	0.372	0.241	0.054	0.021	0.009	0.005	0.004	0.001	0.001												

Figure 2.1

It will be noticed from these tables that 0.8638.5 is the PV factor for a 5% return after 3 years. The PV factor for a 5% return after 2 years is 0.9070 or

$$\frac{1}{1.05 \times 1.05} = \frac{1}{1.1025} = 0.9070.$$

In the above example the income (5%) was the same every year. In most projects, however, the projected annual net cash flow (income minus expenditure) will vary year by year and to obtain a realistic assessment of the Net Present Value (NPV) of an investment, the net cash flow must be discounted separately for every year of the projected life.

The following example will make this clear.

Year	Income £	Discount rate	Discount factor	NPV £
1	10 000	5%	$1/1.05 = 0.9523$	$10\,000 \times 0.9523 = 9\,523.8$
2	11 000	5%	$1/1.05^2 = 0.9070$	$10\,000 \times 0.9070 = 9\,070.3$
3	12 000	5%	$1/1.05^3 = 0.8638$	$12\,000 \times 0.8638 = 10\,365.6$
4	12 000	5%	$1/1.05^4 = 0.8227$	$12\,000 \times 0.8227 = 9\,872.4$
Total	45 000			39 739.1

One of the main reasons for finding the NPV is to be able to compare the viability of competing projects or different repayment modes. Again an example will demonstrate the point.

A company decides to invest £12 000 for a project which is expected to give a total return of £24 000 over the 6 years. The discount rate is 8%.

There are two options of receiving the yearly income.

1 £6000 for years 1 & 2 = £12 000	2 £5000 for years 1, 2, 3 & 4 = £20 000	
£4000 for years 2 & 3 = £8 000	£2000 for years 5 & 6 = £4 000	
£2000 for years 5 & 6 = £4 000		
Total £24 000	£24 000	

The DCF method will quickly establish which is the most profitable option to take as will be shown in the following table.

Year	Discount factor	Cash flow A £	NPV A £	Cash flow B £	NPV B £
1	$1/1.08 = 0.9259$	6 000	5 555.40	5 000	4 629.50
2	$1/1.08^2 = 0.8573$	6 000	5 143.80	5 000	4 286.50
3	$1/1.08^3 = 0.7938$	4 000	3 175.20	5 000	3 969.00
4	$1/1.08^4 = 0.7350$	4 000	2 940.00	5 000	3 675.00
5	$1/1.08^5 = 0.6806$	2 000	1 361.20	2 000	1 361.20
6	$1/1.08^6 = 0.6302$	2 000	1 260.40	2 000	1 260.40
Total		24 000	19 437.00	24 000	19 181.50

Clearly A gives the better return and after deducting the original investment of £12 000, the net discounted return for A = £7437.00 and for B = £7181.50.

The mathematical formula for calculating the NPV is as follows:

If NPV = Net Present Value

r = the interest rate

n = number of years the project yields a return

B1, B2, B3 etc. = the annual net benefits for years 1, 2 and 3 etc.

NPV for year 1 = $B1/(1 + r)$

for year 2 = $B1/(1 + r) + B2/(1 + r)^2$

for year 3 = $B1/(1 + r) + B2/(1 + r)^2 + B3/(1 + r)^3$ and so on

If the annual net benefit is the same for each year for n years, the formula becomes

NPV = $B/(1 + r)^n$

As explained previously, the discount rate can vary year by year, so that the rate relevant to the year for which it applies must be used when reading off the discount factor table.

Two other financial calculations need to be carried out to enable a realistic decision to be taken as to the viability of the project.

3 Payback

Payback is the period of time it takes to recover the capital outlay of the project, having taken into account all the operating and overhead costs during

Return this card today and enter £100 book draw

Select the subjects you'd like to receive information about, enter your email and mail address and freepost it back to us.

TECHNOLOGY

☐ **Architecture and Design:**
History of architecture ○
Landscape ○
Urban design ○
Sustainable architecture ○
Planning and design ○

☐ **Building and Construction**

☐ **Computing: Professional:**
Communications ○
Data Management ○
Enterprise Computing ○
IT Management ○
Operating Systems ○

☐ **Computing: Beginner:**
Computing ○
Programming ○

☐ **Conservation and Museology**

☐ **Engineering:**
Aeronautical Engineering ○
Automotive Engineering ○
Chemical Engineering ○

Health & Safety ○
Environmental Engineering ○
Plant / Maintenance / Manufacturing ○
Marine Engineering ○
Materials Science & Engineering ○
Mechanical Engineering ○
Petroleum Engineering ○
Quality ○

☐ **Electronics and Electrical Engineering:**
Electrical Engineering ○
Electronic Engineering ○
Radio, Audio and TV Technology ○
Computer Technology ○

☐ **Film, Television, Video & Audio:**
Audio/Radio ○
Post Production ○
Lighting ○
Theatre Performance ○
Photography/Imaging ○
Radio ○

TV ○
Film/TV/Video Production ○
Journalism ○
Multimedia ○
Computer Graphics/ Animation ○
Broadcast Management & Theory ○
Broadcast & Communications Technology ○

☐ Security ○

MANAGEMENT
☐ Finance and Accounting
☐ Hospitality, Leisure and Tourism
☐ HR and Training
☐ Pergamon Flexible Learning
☐ Knowledge Management
☐ Management
☐ Marketing
☐ IT Management

Name:

Email address:

Mail address:

Postcode _____ Date _____

Please keep me up to date by ☐ email ☐ post ☐ both

Science & Technology Books, Elsevier Ltd., Registered Office: The Boulevard, Langford Lane, Kidlington, Oxon OX5 1GB. Registered number: 1982084

Jo Blackford

Data Co-ordinator

Elsevier

FREEPOST - SCE5435

Oxford

Oxon

OX2 8BR

this period. Usually this is based on the undiscounted cash flow. A knowledge of the payback is particularly important when the capital must be recouped as quickly as possible as would be the case in short-term projects or projects whose end products have a limited appeal due to changes in fashion, competitive pressures or alternative products. Payback is easily calculated by summating all the net incomes until the total equals the original investment, e.g. if the original investment is £600 000, and the net income is £75 000 per year for the next ten years, the payback is £600 000/£75 000 = 8 years.

4 Internal Rate of Return (IRR)

It has already been shown that the higher the discount rate (usually the cost of borrowing) of a project, the lower the Net Present Value (NPV). There must therefore come a point at which the discount rate is such that the NPV becomes zero. At this point the project ceases to be viable and the discount rate at this point is the Internal Rate of Return (IRR). In other words it is the discount rate at which the NPV is 0.

While it is possible to calculate the IRR by trial and error, the easiest method is to draw a graph as shown in Figure 2.2.

The horizontal axis is calibrated to give the discount rates from 0 to any chosen value, say 20%. The vertical axis represents the NPVs which are + above the horizontal axis and − below.

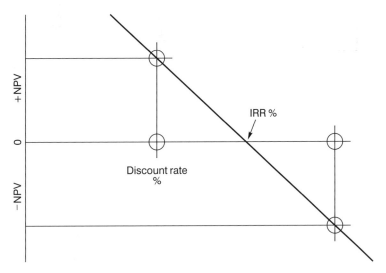

Figure 2.2 Internal Rate of Return (IRR) graph

By choosing two discount rates (one low and one high) two NPVs can be calculated for the same envisaged net cash flow. These NPVs (preferably one +ve and one –ve) are then plotted on the graph and joined by a straight line. Where this line cuts the horizontal axis, i.e. where the NPV is zero, the IRR can be read off.

The basic formulae for the financial calculations are given in Figure 2.3.

Investment appraisal definitions

NPV (Net Present Value)   = Summation of PV's – Original Investment

Net Income   = Incoming moneys – Outgoing moneys

Payback Period   = No. of years it takes for Net Income to equal Original Investment

Profit   = Total Net Income – Original Investment

$$\text{Average Return/Annum} = \frac{\text{Total Net Income}}{\text{No. of years}}$$

$$\text{Return on Investment \%} = \frac{\text{Average Return} \times 100}{\text{Investment}}$$

$$= \frac{\text{Net Income} \times 100}{\text{No. of years} \times \text{Investment}}$$

IRR (Internal Rate of Return) = % Discount Rate for NPV = 0

Cost/benefit analysis

Once the cost of the project has been determined, an analysis has to be carried out which compares these costs with the perceived benefits. The first cost/benefit analysis should be carried out as part of the business case investment appraisal, but in practice such an analysis should really be undertaken at the end of every phase of the life cycle to ensure that the project is still viable. The phase interfaces give management the opportunity to proceed with, or alternatively, abort the project if there is an unacceptable escalation in costs or a diminution of the benefits due to changes in market conditions such as a reduction in demand caused by political, economic, climatic, demographic or a host of other reasons.

It is relatively easy to carry out a cost/benefit analysis where there is a tangible deliverable producing a predictable revenue stream. Provided there is an acceptable NPV, the project can usually go ahead. However, where the deliverables are intangible, such as better service, greater customer satisfaction, lower staff turnover, higher staff morale etc., there may be considerable difficulty in quantifying the benefits. It will be necessary in such cases to run a series of tests and reviews and assess the results of interviews and staff reports.

Similarly while the cost of redundancy payments can be easily calculated, the benefits in terms of lower staff costs over a number of years must be partially offset by lower production volume or poorer customer service. Where the benefits can only be realized over a number of years, a benefit profile curve as shown in Figure 2.3 should be produced, making due allowance for the NPV of the savings.

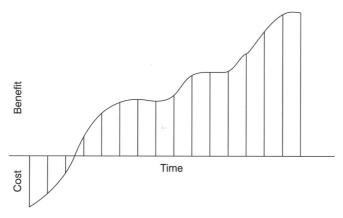

Figure 2.3

The following lists some of the benefits which have to be considered, from which it will be apparent that some will be very difficult to quantify in monetary terms.

Financial
Statutory
Economy
Risk reduction
Productivity
Reliability
Staff morale
Cost reduction

Safety
Flexibility
Quality
Delivery
Social

Stakeholder analysis

Almost anyone associated with a project can be termed a *stakeholder*. It is important therefore for the project manager to analyse this list of stakeholders and as far as possible categorize them into two main groups:

1   Direct stakeholders

This group includes the sponsor, client, project manager, the project team, construction or installation team, contractors and subcontractors, suppliers, consultants etc. In other words people or organizations directly involved or have a vested interest in all or some of the various phases of the project.

2   Indirect stakeholders

This group includes the support staff of an organization such as the accounts department, HR department, secretariat, management levels not directly involved in the project, environmental and political pressure groups and of course the families of the members of the project team and construction/installation team. On environmentally sensitive projects, the general public could be termed as indirect stakeholders.

Each group can then be split further into positive and negative stakeholders.

Positive stakeholders are concerned with the design and implementation of the project with the object of completing the project within the specified parameters of time, cost and quality/performance. They therefore include the sponsor, project manager and the project and construction/installation teams.

Negative stakeholders are those who either try to modify or delay the project or indeed prevent it from even starting. These are usually environmental or political pressure groups, trade unions or sections of the media who, though they may seen to be disruptive, must nevertheless be considered and given an opportunity to state their case. In some situations, statutory/regulatory authorities or even government agencies who have the power to issue or withhold permits, access, wayleaves or other consents can be considered as negative stakeholders. The negotiations with such organizations and the subsequent agreements reached are an essential part of stakeholder analysis, but it must be borne in mind that any compromises reached must be approved by the client or sponsor.

All stakeholders, whether positive or negative, must be analysed to assess their contribution, influence or disruptive capabilities on the project and this will help the project manager to prioritize their needs and decide whether they should be embraced or treated with caution. Diplomacy and tact are essential when negotiating with potentially disruptive organizations and it is highly advisable to enlist experts in the discussion process. Most large organizations employ labour and public relations experts as well as lawyers well versed in dealing with difficult stakeholders and their services can be of enormous help to the project manager.

3

Organization structures

To manage a project, a company or authority has to set up a project organization, which can supply the resources for the project and service it during its life cycle.

There are three main types of project organizations:

1 Functional;
2 Matrix;
3 Project or task force.

Functional organization

This type of organization consists of specialist or functional departments each with their own departmental manager responsible to one or more directors. Such an organization is ideal for routine operations where there is little variation of the end product. Functional organizations are usually found where items are mass produced, whether they are motor cars or sausages. Each department is expert at its function and the interrelationship between them is well established. In this sense a functional organization is not a project-type organization at all and is only included because when small, individual, one-off projects have to be carried out, they may be given to a particular department to manage. For projects of any reasonable size or complexity, it will be necessary to set up one of the other two types of organizations.

Matrix organization

This is probably the most common type of project organization, since it utilizes an existing functional organization to provide the human resources without disrupting the day-to-day operation of the department.

The personnel allocated to a particular project are responsible to a project manager for meeting the three basic project criteria, time, cost and quality. The departmental manager is, however, still responsible for their 'pay and rations' and their compliance with the department's standards and procedures, including technical competence and conformity to company quality standards. The members of this project team will still be working at their desks in their department, but will be booking their time to the project. Where the project does not warrant a full-time contribution, only those hours actually expended on the project will be allocated to it.

The advantages of a matrix organization are:

1 Resources are employed efficiently, since staff can switch to different projects if held up on any one of them;
2 The expertize built up by the department is utilized and the latest state-of-the-art techniques are immediately incorporated;
3 Special facilities do not have to be provided and disrupting staff movements are avoided;
4 The career prospects of team members are left intact;
5 The organization can respond quickly to changes of scope;
6 The project manager does not have to concern himself with staff problems.

The disadvantages are:

1 There may be a conflict of priorities between different projects;
2 There may be split loyalties between the project manager and the departmental manager due to the dual reporting requirements;
3 Communications between team members can be affected if the locations of the departments are far apart;
4 Executive management may have to spend more time to ensure a fair balance of power between the project manager and the department manager.

All the above problems can, however, be resolved if there is a good working relationship between the project manager and the department heads. At times both sides may have to compromize in the interests of the organization as a whole.

Project organization (task force)

From a project manager's point of view this is the ideal type of project organization, since with such a set up he has complete control over every aspect of the project. The project team will usually be located in one area which can be a room for a small project or a complete building for a very large one.

Lines of communication are short and the interaction of the disciplines reduces the risk of errors and misunderstandings. Not only are the planning and technical functions part of the team but also the project cost control and project accounting staff. This places an enormous burden and responsibility on the project manager, who will have to delegate much of the day-to-day management to special project coordinators whose prime function is to ensure a good communication flow and timely receipt of reports and feedback information from external sources.

On large projects with budgets often greater than £0.5 billion, the project manager's responsibilities are akin to those of a managing director of a medium-size company. Not only is he concerned with the technical and commercial aspects of the project, but has also to deal with the staff, financial and political issues, which are often more difficult to delegate.

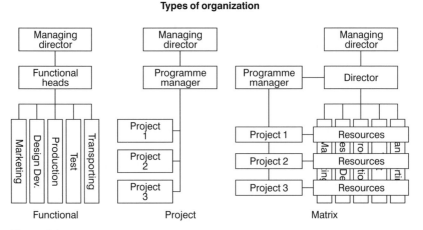

Types of organization

Figure 3.1

There is no doubt that for large projects a task force type of project organization is essential, but as with so many areas of business, the key to success lies with the personality of the project manager and his ability to inspire the project team to regard themselves as personal stakeholders in the project.

One of the main differences between the two true project organizations (matrix and task force) and the functional organization is the method of financial accounting. For the project manager to retain proper cost control during the life of the project, it is vital that a system of project accounting is instituted, whereby all incomes and expenditures, including a previously agreed overhead allocation and profit margin, are booked to the project as if it were a separate self-standing organization. The only possible exceptions are certain corporate financial transactions such as interest payments on loans taken out by the host organization and interest receipts on deposits from a positive cash flow.

Figure 3.1 shows a diagrammatic representation of the three basic project management organizations, Functional, Project (or Task Force) and Matrix.

4

Project life cycles

Most, if not all, projects go through a life cycle which varies with the size and complexity of the project. On medium to large projects the life cycle will generally follow the pattern which has been set out in BS 6079. This is:

1 Concept	Basic ideas, business case, statement of requirements, scope;
2 Feasibility	Tests for technical, commercial and financial viability, technical studies, investment appraisal, DCF etc.;
3 Evaluation	Application for funds, stating risks, options, TCQ criteria;
4 Authorization	Approvals, permits, conditions, project strategy;
5 Implementation	Development design, procurement, fabrication, installation, commissioning;
6 Completion	Performance tests, handover to client, post project appraisal;
7 Operation	Revenue earning period, production, maintenance;
8 Termination	Close-down, decommissioning, disposal.

Items 7 and 8 are not usually included in a project life cycle where the project ends with the issue of an acceptance certificate after the performance tests have been successfully completed. Where these two phases are included, as, for example, with defence projects, the term *'extended project life cycle'* is often used.

The project life cycle of an IT project may be slightly different as the following list shows:

1 Feasibility	Definition, cost benefits, acceptance criteria, time and cost estimates;	
2 Evaluation	Definitions of requirements, performance criteria, processes;	
3 Function	Functional and operational requirements, interfaces, system design;	
4 Authorization	Approvals, permits, firming up procedures;	
5 Design and build	Detail design, system integration, screen building, documentation;	
6 Implementation	Integration and acceptance testing, installation, training;	
7 Operation	Data loading, support set-up, hand-over.	

Running through the period of the life cycle are control systems and decision stages at which the position of the project is reviewed. The interfaces of the phases of the life cycle form convenient milestones for progress payments and reporting progress to top management, who can then make the decision to abort or provide further funding. In some cases the interface of the phases overlap, as in the case of certain design and construct contracts, where construction starts before the design is finished. This is known as concurrent engineering and is often employed to reduce the overall project programme.

As the word 'cycle' implies, the phases may have to be amended in terms of content, cost and duration as new information is fed back to the project manager and sponsor. Projects are essentially dynamic organizations which are not only specifically created to effect change, but are also themselves subject to change.

On some projects it may be convenient to appoint a different project manager at a change of phase. This is often done where the first four stages are handled by the development or sales department, who then hand the project over to the operations department for the various stages of the implementation, and completion phases.

When the decommissioning and disposal is included, it is known as an extended life cycle, since these two stages could occur many years after commissioning and could well be carried out by a different organization.

Figure 4.1 shows three typical life cycles prepared by three different organizations. The first example from BS 6079 is a very simple generic life cycle consisting of only five basic phases. Some of these phases are subdivided in the next (APM) life cycle where 'implementation', shown in BS 6079, has been replaced by 'design, contract & implementation'. The third life cycle shown as formulated by the Ministry of Defence clearly shows the phases required for a typical weapons system, where concept, feasibility and project definition are the responsibility of the MoD, design, development and production are carried out by the manufacturer, and in-service and disposal are the phases when the weapon is in the hands of the armed forces.

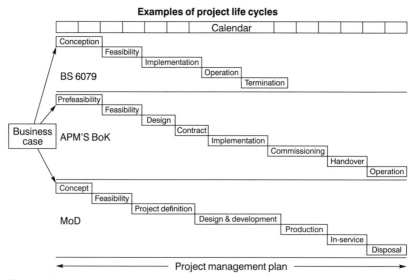

Figure 4.1

The diagram also shows a calendar scale over the top. While this is not strictly necessary, it can be seen that if the lengths of the bars representing the phases are drawn proportional to the time taken by the phases, such a presentation can be used as a high level reporting document, showing which

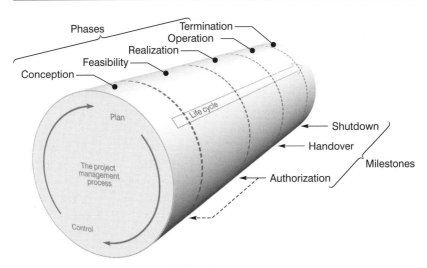

Figure 4.2 Project management life cycle

phases are complete or partially complete in relation to the original schedule.

The important point to note is that each organization should develop its own life cycle diagram to meet its particular needs. Where the life cycle covers all the phases from cradle to grave as it were, it is often called a *programme life cycle*, since it spans over the full programme of the deliverable. The term *project life cycle* is then restricted to those phases which constitute a project within the programme, e.g. the design, development and manufacturing periods.

Figure 4.2 shows how decision points or milestones (sometimes called trigger points or go, no-go gates) relate to the phases of a life cycle.

Figure 4.3 shows how the life cycle of the MoD project shown in Figure 4.1 could be split into the *Project life cycle*, i.e. the phases under the control of the Project Team (conception to production), the *Product life cycle*, the phases of

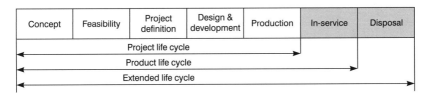

Figure 4.3 Life cycle of MoD project

23

interest to the sponsor, which now includes the in-service performance, and lastly the *Extended life cycle*, which includes disposal. From the point of view of the contractor, the *Project life cycle* may only include design and development and production. It can be seen therefore that there are no hard and fast rules where the demarcation points are as each organisation will define its own phases and life cycles to suit its method of working.

5

Work breakdown structures (WBS)

Before any meaningful programme can be produced, it is essential that careful thought is given to the number and size of networks required. Not only is it desirable to limit the size of network, but each 'block' of networks should be considered in relation to the following aspects:

1 The geographical location of the various portions or blocks of the project;
2 The size and complexity of each block;
3 The systems in each block;
4 The process or work being carried out in the block when the plant is complete;
5 The engineering disciplines required during the design and construction stage;
6 The erection procedures;
7 The stages at which individual blocks or systems have to be completed, i.e. the construction programme;
8 The site organization envisaged;
9 Any design or procurement priorities.

For convenience, a block can be defined as a *geographical process area within a project*, which can be easily identified, usually because it serves a specific function. The importance of choosing the correct blocks, i.e. drawing the demarcation lines in the most advantageous way, cannot be overemphasized. This decision has an effect not only on the number and size of planning networks but also on the organization of the design teams and, in the case of large projects, on the organizational structure of the site management set-up.

Because of its importance, a guide is given below which indicates the type of block distribution which may be sensibly selected for various projects. The list is obviously limited, but it should not be too difficult to abstract some firm guidelines to suit the project under consideration.

1 Pharmaceutical factory

Block A Administration block (offices and laboratories)
Block B Incoming goods area, raw material store
Block C Manufacturing area 1 (pills)
Block D Manufacturing area 2 (capsules)
Block E Manufacturing area 3 (creams)
Block F Boiler house and water treatment
Block G Air-conditioning plant room and electrical distribution control room
Block H Finished goods store and dispatch

For planning purposes, general site services such as roads, sewers, fencing and guard houses can be incorporated into Block A or, if extensive, can form a block of their own.

2 New housing estate

Block A Low-rise housing area – North
Block B Low-rise housing area – East
Block C Low-rise housing area – South
Block D Low-rise housing area – West
Block E High-rise – Block 1
Block F High-rise – Block 2
Block G Shopping precinct
Block H Electricity substation

Obviously, the number of housing areas or high-rise blocks can vary with the size of the development. Roads and sewers and statutory services are part of their respective housing blocks unless they are constructed earlier as a separate contract, in which case they would form their own block or blocks.

3   Portland cement factory

Block A Quarry crushing plant and conveyor
Block B Clay pit and transport of clay
Block C Raw meal mill and silos
Block D Nodulizer plant and precipitators
Block E Preheater and rotary kiln
Block F Cooler and dust extraction
Block G Fuel storage and pulverization
Block H Clinker storage and grinding
Block I Cement storage and bagging
Block J, Administration, offices, maintenance workshops, lorry park

Here again, the road and sewage system could form a block on its own incorporating the lorry park.

4   Oil terminal

Block A Crude reception and storage
Block B Stabilization and desalting
Block C Stabilized crude storage
Block D NGL separation plant
Block E NGL storage
Block F Boiler and water treatment
Block G Effluent and ballast treatment
Block H Jetty loading
Block J Administration block and laboratory
Block K Jetty 1
Block L Jetty 2
Block M Control room 1
Block N Control room 2
Block P Control room 3

Here roads, sewers and underground services are divided into the various operational blocks.

5   Multistorey block of offices

Block A Basement and piling work
Block B Ground floor
Block C Plant room and boilers

Block D Office floors 1–4
Block E Office floors 5–8
Block F Lift well and service shafts
Block G Roof and penthouse
Block H Substation
Block J Computer room
Block K External painting, access road and underground services

Clearly, in the construction of a multistorey building, whether for offices or flats, the method of construction has a great bearing on the programme. There is obviously quite a different sequence required for a block with a central core – especially if sliding formwork is used – than with a more conventional design using reinforced concrete or structural steel columns and beams. The degree of precasting will also have a great influence on the split of the network.

6 Colliery surface reconstruction

Block A Headgear and airlocks
Block B Winding house and winder
Block C Mine car layout and heapstead building
Block D Fan house and duct
Block E Picking belt and screen building
Block F Wagon loading and bunkering
Block G Electricity substation, switch room and lamp room
Block H Administration area and amenities
Block J Baths and canteen (welfare block)

Roads, sewers and underground services could be part of Block J or be a separate block.

7 Bitumen refinery

Block A Crude line and tankage
Block B Process unit
Block C Effluent treatment and oil/water separator
Block D Finished product tankage
Block E Road loading facility, transport garage and lorry park
Block F Rail loading facility and sidings
Block G Boiler house and water treatment
Block H Fired heater area

Block J Administration building, laboratory and workshop
Block K Substation
Block L Control room

Depending on size, the process unit may have to be subdivided into more blocks but it may be possible to combine K and L. Again, roads and sewers may be separate or part of each block.

8 Typical manufacturing unit

Block A Incoming goods ramps and store
Block B Batching unit
Block C Production area 1
Block D Production area 2
Block E Production area 3
Block F Finishing area
Block G Packing area
Block H Finished goods store and dispatch
Block J Boiler room and water treatment
Block K Electrical switch room
Block L Administration block and canteen

Additional blocks will, of course, be added where complexity or geographical location dictates this.

It must be emphasized that these typical block breakdowns can, at best, be a rough guide, but they do indicate the splits which are possible. When establishing the boundaries of a block, the main points given on page 25 must be considered.

The interrelationship and interdependence between blocks during the construction stage is, in most cases, remarkably small. The physical connections are usually only a number of pipes, conveyors, cables, underground services and roads. None of these offer any serious interface problems and should not, therefore, be permitted to unduly influence the choice of blocks. Construction restraints must, of course, be taken into account but they too must not be allowed to affect the basic block breakdown.

This very important point is only too frequently misunderstood. On a refinery site, for example, a delay in the process unit has hardly any effect on the effluent treatment plant except, of course, right at the end of the job.

In a similar way, the interrelationship at the design stage is often overemphasized. Design networks are usually confined to work in the various engineering departments and need not include such activities as planning and financial approvals or acceptance of codes and standards. These should preferably be obtained in advance by project management. Once the main flowsheets, plot plans and piping and instrument diagrams have been drafted (i.e. they need not even have been completed), design work can proceed in each block with a considerable degree of independence. For example, the tank farm may be designed quite independently of the process unit or the NGL plant, etc., and the boiler house has little effect on the administration building or the jetties and loading station.

In the case of a single building being divided into blocks, the roof can be designed and detailed independently of the other floors or the basement, provided, of course, that the interface operations such as columns, walls, stairwell, lift shaft and service ducts have been located and more or less finalized. In short, therefore, the choice of blocks is made as early as possible, taking into account all or most of the factors mentioned before, particular attention being given to design and construction requirements.

This split into blocks or work areas is, of course, taking place in practice in any design office or site, whether the programme is geared to it or not. One is, in effect, only formalizing an already well-proven and established procedure. Depending on size, most work areas in the design office are serviced by squads or teams, even if they only consist of one person in each discipline who looks after that particular area. The fact that on a small project the person may look after more than one area does not change the principle; it merely means that the team is half an operator instead of one.

On-site, the natural breakdown into work areas is even more obvious. Most disciplines on a site are broken down into gangs, with a ganger or foreman in charge, and, depending again on size and complexity, one or more gangs are allocated to a particular area or block. On very large sites, a number of blocks are usually combined into a complete administrative centre with its own team of supervisors, inspectors, planners, subcontract administrators and site engineers, headed by an area manager.

No difficulty should, therefore, be experienced in obtaining the cooperation of an experienced site manager when the type, size and number of blocks are proposed. Indeed, this early discussion serves as an excellent opportunity to involve the site team in the whole planning process, the details of which are added later. By that time, the site team is at least aware of the principles and a potential communication gap, so frequently a problem with construction people, has been bridged.

Generic work breakdown structure

While such a breakdown into blocks is suitable for an engineering contract, a similar system can be used for any other type of project. By breaking the project down into discrete components or tasks, we create what is known as a work breakdown structure or WBS.

The choice of tasks incorporated in the WBS is best made by the project team drawing on their combined experience or engaging in a brainstorming session.

Once the main tasks have been decided upon, they can in turn can be broken down into subtasks, which should be coded to fit in with the project cost coding system. This will greatly assist in identifying the whole string of relationships from overall operational areas down to individual tasks. For this reason the WBS is the logical starting point for subsequent planning networks. Another advantage is that a cost allocation can be given to each task in the WBS and, if required, a risk factor can be added. This will assist in building up the total project cost and creates a risk register for a subsequent, more rigorous risk assessment.

The object of all this is to be able to control the project by allocating resources (human, material and financial) and giving time constraints to each task. It is always easier to control a series of small entities which make up a whole, than trying to control the whole enterprize as one operation. What history has proven to be successful for armies, which are divided into divisions, regiments, battalions, companies and platoons, or corporations which have area organizations, manufacturing units and sales territories, is also true for projects, whether they are large or small, sophisticated or straightforward.

The tasks will clearly vary enormously with the type of project in both size and content, but by representing their relationship diagramatically, a clear graphical picture can be created. This, when distributed to other members of the project team, becomes a very useful tool for disseminating information as well as a reporting medium to all stakeholders. As the main tasks are in effect the major project milestones, the WBS is an ideal instrument for reporting progress upwards to senior management and for this reason it is essential that the status of each task is regularly updated.

Table 5.1

Project risks			
Organization	**Environment**	**Technical**	**Financial**
Management	Legislation	Technology	Financing
Resources	Political	Contracts	Exchange rates
Planning	Pressure groups	Design	Escalation
Labour	Local customs	Manufacture	Financial stability of
Health and safety	Weather	Construction	(a) project
Claims	Emissions	Commissioning	(b) client
Policy	Security	Testing	(c) suppliers

As the WBS is produced in the very early stages of a project, it will probably not reflect all the tasks which will eventually be required. Indeed the very act of draughting the WBS often throws up the missing items or work units, which can then be formed into more convenient tasks. As these tasks are decomposed further, they may be given new names such as unit or work package It is then relatively easy for management to allocate task owners to each task or group of tasks, who have the responsibility for delivering this task to the normal project criteria of cost, time and quality/performance.

Although the WBS may have been built up by the project team, based on their collective experience or by brainstorming, there is always the risk that a stage or task has been forgotten. An early review then opens up an excellent opportunity to refine the WBS and carry out a risk identification for each task, which can be the beginning of a risk register. At a later date a more rigorous risk analysis can then be carried out. The WBS does in effect give everyone a better understanding of the risk assessment procedure.

Indeed a further type of breakdown structure is the Risk Breakdown Structure. Here the main risks are allocated to the WBS or PBS in either financial or risk rating terms, giving a good overview of the project risks.

In another type of Risk Breakdown Structure the main areas of risk are shown in the first level of the Risk Breakdown Structure and the possible risk headings are listed below. See Table 5.1.

The abbreviation WBS is a generic term for a hierarchy of stages of a project. However, some methodologies like PRINCE call such a hierarchical diagram a Product Breakdown Structure (PBS). The difference is basically what part of speech is being used to describe the stages. If the words used are *nouns*, it is

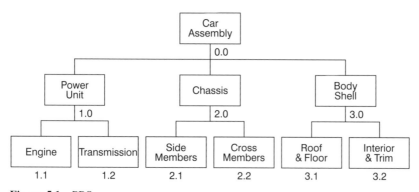

Figure 5.1 PBS

strictly speaking a Product Breakdown Structure (PBS), because we are dealing with products or things. If on the other hand we are describing the work which has to be performed on the nouns and use *verbs*, we call it a Work Breakdown Structure (WBS). Frequently, a diagram starts as a PBS for the first three or four levels and then becomes a WBS as more detail is being introduced.

Despite this unfortunate lack of uniformity of nomenclature in the project management fraternity, the principles of subdividing the project into manageable components are the same.

It must be pointed out, however, that the work breakdown structure is *not* a programme, although it looks like a precedence diagram. The interrelationships shown by the link lines do not necessarily imply a time dependence or indeed any sequential operation.

Figure 5.1, which is a Product Breakdown Structure, shows the process as: Car assembly, Power unit, Chassis, Body shell etc. Giving numbers to the tasks, enables a logical costing system to be built up as shown in Figure 5.3.

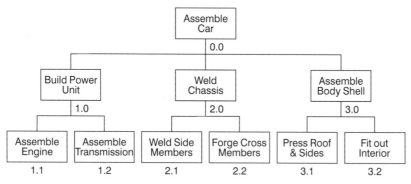

Figure 5.2 WBS

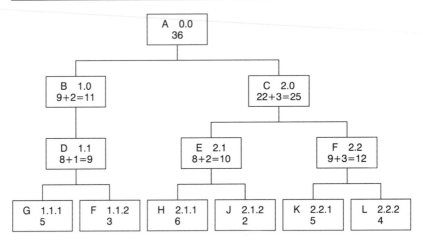

Figure 5.3

The corresponding Work Breakdown Structure shown in Figure 5.2 uses verbs and the descriptions of the packages or tasks then become: *Assemble* car, *build* power unit, *weld* chassis, *press* body shell etc.

It can be seen that a WBS is a powerful tool which can show clearly and graphically who is responsible for a task, how much it should cost and how it relates to the other tasks in the project. It was stated earlier that the WBS is not a programme, but once it has been accepted as a correct representation of the project tasks, it will become a good base for drawing up the network diagram. The interrelationships of the tasks will have to be shown more accurately and the only additional items of information to be added are the durations.

The degree to which the WBS needs to be broken down before a planning network can be drawn, will have to be decided by the project manager, but there is no reason why a whole family of networks cannot be produced to reflect each level of the WBS.

Once the WBS (or PBS) has been drawn, a bottom-up cost estimate can be produced starting at the lowest branch of the family tree. In this method, each work package is costed and arranged in such a way that the total cost of the packages on any branch must add up to the cost of the package of the parent package on the branch above. If the parent package has a cost value of its own, this must clearly be added before the next stage of the process. This is shown in Figure 5.3, which not only explains the bottom-up estimating process, but also shows how the packages can be coded to produce a project cost coding system that can be carried through to network analysis and earned value analysis.

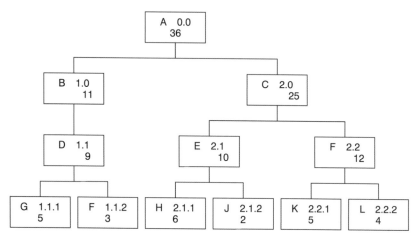

Figure 5.4 Top-down cost allocation

An alternative to the *bottom-up* cost allocation is the *top-down* cost allocation. In this method, the cost of the total project (or subproject) has been determined and is allocated to the top package of the WBS (or PBS) diagram. The work packages below are then forced to accept the appropriate costs so that the total cost of each branch cannot exceed the total cost of the package above. Such a top-down approach is shown in Figure 5.4

In practice both methods may have to be used. For example, the estimator of a project may use the bottom-up method on a WBS or PBS diagram to calculate the cost. When this is given to the project manager, he/she may break this total down into the different departments of an organization and allocate a proportion to each, making sure that the sum total does not exceed the estimated cost. Once names have been added to the work packages of a WBS or PBS it becomes an Organization Breakdown Structure or OBS.

It did not take long for this similarity to be appreciated, so that another name for such an organization diagram became 'Organization Breakdown'. This is the family tree of the organization in the same way that the WBS is in effect the family tree of the project. It is in fact more akin to a family tree or organization chart (organogram).

Figure 5.5 shows a typical OBS for a manufacturing project such as the assembly of a prototype motor car. It can be seen that the OBS is not identical in layout to the WBS, as one manager or task owner can be responsible for more than one task.

35

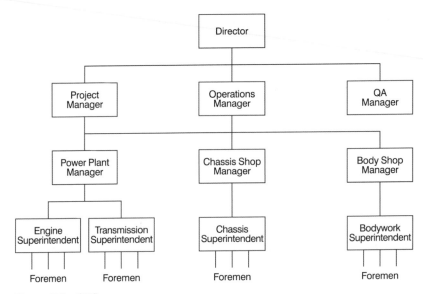

Figure 5.5 OBS

The OBS shown is typical of a matrix-type project organization where the operations manager is in charge of the actual operating departments for 'pay and rations', but each departmental head (or his designated project leader) also has a reporting line to the project manager. If required, the OBS can be expanded into a responsibility matrix to show the responsibility and authority of each member of the organization or project team.

	Director	Project Manager	Operations Manager	QA Manager	Power Plant Manager	Chassis Shop Manager	Body Shop Manager	Engine Superintendent	Transmission Superintendent	Chassis Superintendent	Bodywork Superintendent
Car Assembly	A	B	A	B							
Power Unit	A	B	A	B	C						
Chassis	A	B	A	B		C					
Body Shell	A	B	A	B			C				
Engine		B	A	B	C			C			
Transmission		B	A	B	C				C		
Side Members		B	A	B		C				C	
Cross Members		B	A	B		C				C	
Roof & Floor		B	A	B			C				C
Interior & Trim		B	A	B			C				C

Figure 5.6

The quality assurance (QA) manager reports directly to the director to ensure independence from the operating and projects departments. He will, however, assist all operating departments with producing the quality plans and give ongoing advice on QA requirements and procedures as well as pointing out any shortcomings he may discover.

Responsibility matrix

By combining the WBS with the OBS it is possible to create a Responsibility Matrix. Using the car assembly example given in Figures 5.1 and 5.5, the matrix is drawn by writing the WBS work areas vertically and the OBS personnel horizontally as shown in Figure 5.6.

By placing a suitable designatory letter into the intersecting boxes, the level of responsibility for any work area can be recorded on the matrix.

A = Receiving monthly reports
B = Receiving weekly reports
C = Daily supervision

6

Estimating

Allocation of costs to the WBS or PBS requires of course that these costs are known. Unfortunately in only a few situations are these costs available in a form for simply slotting into the work package boxes. It is necessary therefore to produce realistic estimates of each package and indeed the entire project before a meaningful cost allocation can be carried out.

Estimating the costs of a project requires a structured approach, but whichever method is used, the first thing is to decide the level of accuracy required. This depends on the status of the project and the information available. In many cases a client or sponsor requires only an approximate or 'ball park' figure before deciding whether to proceed to the next stage. An estimate in such a situation does not have to be as accurate as an estimate for the final contract cost to which one is then committed.

Estimating is an essential part of project management, since it becomes the baseline for subsequent cost control. If the estimate for a project is too low, a company may well lose money in the execution of the work. If the estimate is high, the company may well lose the contract due to overpricing.

There are a number of estimating methods in use, varying from the very approximate to the very accurate. Most organizations have their own estimating norms, developed over the years and updated regularly to reflect changes in operating methods and systems. In addition the variations in labour rates, material costs and exchange rates will have to be built into the estimate.

The four main types of estimating techniques, each giving different degrees of accuracy, are:

1   Subjective

With this method the estimator relies on his experience of similar projects to give a cost indication based largely on very subjective 'feel' or 'hunch'. Geographical and political factors have to be taken into account as well as the more obvious labour and material content. Frequently such estimates are required to be given with little notice so that the accuracy may well be in the order of ±40%. Such an approximate method of estimating is therefore often called 'guesstimating'.

2   Parametric

By using well-known empirical formulae or ratios in which costs can be related to specific characteristics of known sections or areas of the project, it is possible to produce a good estimate on which firm decisions can be based. Clearly such estimates require to be qualified to enable external factors to be separately assessed. For example, an architect will be able to give a parametric estimate of a new house once he is given the cube (height × length × depth) of the proposed building and the standard of construction or finish. The estimate will be in £/cubic metre of structure. Similarly, office blocks are often estimated in £/square metre of floor space. The qualifications would be the location, ground conditions and costs of the land etc. Another example of a parametric estimate is when a structural steel fabricator gives the price of fabrication in £/ton of steel depending on whether the steel sections are heavy beams and columns or light lattice work. In both cases the estimate may or may not include the cost of the steel itself.

Such parametric estimates can vary in accuracy between ±10% and 20%.

3   Comparative

When a new project is very similar to another project recently completed, a quick comparison can be made of the salient features. Making due allowance for the inevitable minor differences and inflation or other cost escalation, a good comparative estimate can be produced with a degree of error of only ±10%. An example of such a comparative estimate is the installation of a new computer system in a building when an almost identical (and proven) system was installed 6 months earlier in another building nearby. It must be stressed that such an estimate does not require detailed cost breakdowns.

4 Analytical

As the name implies, this is the most accurate estimating method, but it requires the project to be broken down into sections, subsections and finally individual components. Each component must then be given a cost value including both the material and labour content. The values, which are sometimes referred to as 'norms', are usually extracted from a database or company archives and must be individually updated or factored to reflect the present day political and environmental situation.

Examples of analytical estimates are the norms used by the petrochemical industry where a value exists for the installation of piping depending on pipe diameter, wall thickness, material composition, height from ground level and whether flanged or welded. The norm is given as a cost/linear metre which is then multiplied by the metreage including an allowance for waste. Contingencies, overheads and profit are then added to the total sum.

Quantity surveyors will cost a building or structure by measuring the architect's drawings and applying a cost to every square metre of wall or roof, every door and window, and such systems as heating, plumbing and electrics etc. Such estimates are known as bills of quantities and together with a schedule of rates for costing variations form the basis of most building and civil engineering contracts. The accuracy of such estimates are better than ±5% depending on the qualifications accompanying the estimate. The rates used in bills of quantities (when produced by a contractor) are usually inclusive of labour, materials, plant, overheads and anticipated profit, but when produced by an independent quantity surveyor the last two items may have to be added by the contractor.

It must be emphasized that such detailed estimating is not restricted to the building or engineering industry. Every project, given sufficient time, can be broken down into its labour, material and overhead content and costed very accurately.

Whatever type of estimating method has been used in preparing the base estimate, extra sums must be added to cover overheads, profit and contingencies based on a risk assessment of the project. This total is then the price, i.e. what the customer is being asked to pay.

Often the estimate produced by the estimator is drastically changed by senior management to reflect market conditions, the volume of work in the company and the strength of the perceived competition. However, from a control point of view, such changes to the final price should be ignored, as they normally fall in the profit/overhead bracket and while they should be realized, they are usually outside the control of the project manager.

7

Project management plan

As soon as the project manager has received his brief or project instructions, he must produce a document which distils what is generally a vast amount of information into a concise, informative and well-organized form that can be distributed to all members of the project team and indeed all the stakeholders in the project. This document is called a project management plan (PMP), but is also sometimes just called a project plan, or in some organizations a coordination procedure.

The PMP is one of the key documents required by the project manager and his/her team. It lists the phases and encapsulates all the main parameters, standards and requirements of the project in terms of time, cost and quality/performance by setting out the '*Why*', '*What*', '*When*', '*Who*', '*Where*' and '*How*' of the project. In some organizations the PMP also includes the '*How much*', that is the cost of the project. There may, however, be good commercial reasons for restricting this information to key members of the project team.

The contents of a PMP vary depending on the type of project. While it can run to several volumes for a large petrochemical project, it need not be more than a slim binder for a small, unsophisticated project.

There are, however, a number of areas and aspects which should always feature in such a document. These are set out very clearly in Table 1 of BS 6079-1-2002. With the permission of the British Standards Institution, the main headings of what is termed the *Model Project Plan* are given below, but augmented and rearranged in the sections given above.

General

1 Foreword
2 Contents, distribution and amendment record
3 Introduction
3.1 Project diary
3.2 Project history

The Why

4 Project aims and objectives
4.1 Business case

The What

5 General description
5.1 Scope
5.2 Project requirement
5.3 Project security and privacy
5.4 Project management philosophy
5.5 Management reporting system

The When

6 Programme management
6.1 Programme method
6.2 Program software
6.3 Project life cycle
6.4 Key dates
6.5 Milestones and milestone slip chart
6.6 Bar chart and network if available

The Who

7 Project organization
8 Project resource management
9 Project team organization
9.1 Project staff directory

9.2   Organizational chart
9.3   Terms of reference (TOR)
      (a) for staff
      (b) for the project manager
      (c) for the committees and working group

The Where

10   Delivery requirements
10.1 Site requirements and conditions
10.2 Shipping requirements
10.3 Major restrictions

The How

11   Project approvals required and authorization limits
12   Project harmonization
13   Project implementation strategy
13.1 Implementation plans
13.2 System integration
13.3 Completed project work
14   Acceptance procedure
15   Procurement strategy
15.1 Cultural and environmental restraints
15.2 Political restraints
16   Contract management
17   Communications management
18   Configuration management
18.1 Configuration control requirements
18.2 Configuration management system
19   Financial management
20   Risk management
20.1 Major perceived risks
21   Technical management
22   Tests and evaluations
22.1 Warranties and guarantees
23   Reliability management (see also BS 5760: Part 1)
23.1 Availability, reliability and maintainability (ARM)
23.2 Quality management
24   Health and safety management
25   Environmental issues
26   Integrated logistic support (ILS) management
27   Close-out procedure

The numbering of the main headings should be standardized for all projects in the organization. In this way the reader will quickly learn to associate a clause number with a subject. This will not only enable him/her to find the required information quickly, but will also help the project manager when he/she has to write the PMP. The numbering system will in effect serve as a convenient checklist. If a particular item or heading is not required, it is best simply to enter 'not applicable' (or NA), leaving the standardized numbering system intact.

Apart from giving all the essential information about the project between two covers, for quick reference, the PMP serves another very useful function. In many organizations the scope, technical and contractual terms of the project are agreed in the initial stages by the proposals or sales department. It is only when the project becomes a reality that the project manager is appointed. By having to assimilate all these data and write such a PMP (usually within two weeks of the hand-over meeting), the project manager will inevitably obtain a thorough understanding of the project requirements as he/she digests the often voluminous documentation agreed with the client or sponsor.

Clearly not every project requires the exact breakdown given in this list and each organization can augment or expand this list to suit the project. If there are any subsequent changes, it is essential that the PMP is amended as soon as changes become apparent so that every member of the project team is immediately aware of the latest revision. These changes must be numbered on the amendment record at the front of the PMP and annotated on the relevant page and clause with the same amendment number or letter.

The contents of the project management plan are neatly summarized in the first verse of the little poem from the *Elephant's Child* by Rudyard Kipling:

I keep six honest serving-men
(They taught me all I knew);
Their names are What and Why and When,
And How and Where and Who.

8

Risk management

Every day we take risks. If we cross the street we risk being run over. If we go down the stairs, we risk missing a step and tumbling down. Taking risks is such a common occurrence, that we tend to ignore it. Indeed, life would be unbearable if we constantly worried whether we should or should not carry out a certain task or take an action, because the risk is, or is not, acceptable.

With projects, however, this luxury of ignoring the risks cannot be permitted. By their very nature, because projects are inherently unique and often incorporate new techniques and procedures, they are risk prone and risk has to be considered right from the start. It then has to be subjected to a disciplined regular review and investigative procedure known as risk management.

Before applying risk management procedures, many organizations produce a *Risk Management Plan*. This is a document produced at the start of the project which sets out the strategic requirements for risk assessment and the whole risk management procedure. In certain situations the risk management plan should be produced at the estimating or contract tender stage to ensure that adequate provisions are made in the cost build-up of the tender document.

The Project Management Plan (PMP) should include a résumé of the Risk Management Plan, which will first of all define the scope and areas to which risk management applies, particularly the risk types to be investigated. It will also specify which techniques will be used for risk identification and assessment, whether SWOT (Strengths, Weaknesses, Opportunities and Threats) analysis is required and which risks (if any) require a more rigorous quantitative analysis such as Monte Carlo methods.

The Risk Management Plan will set out the type, content and frequency of reports, the roles of risk owners and the definition of the impact and probability criteria in qualitative and/or quantitative terms covering cost, time and quality/performance.

The main contents of a Risk Management Plan are as follows:

General introduction explaining the need for the risk management process;
Project description. Only required if it is a stand-alone document and not part of the PMP;
Types of risks. Political, technical, financial, environmental, security, safety, programme etc.;
Risk processes. Qualitative and/or quantitative methods, max. nos of risks to be listed;
Tools and techniques. Risk identification methods, size of P-I matrix, computer analysis etc.;
Risk reports. Updating periods of Risk Register, exception reports, change reports etc.;
Attachments. Important project requirements, dangers, exceptional problems etc.

The Risk Management Plan of an organization should follow a standard pattern in order to increase its familiarity (rather like standard conditions of contract) but each project will require a bespoke version to cover its specific requirements and anticipated risks.

Risk management consists of the following five stages, which, if followed religiously, will enable one to obtain a better understanding of those project risks which could jeopardize the cost, time, quality and safety criteria of the project. The first three stages are often referred to as *qualitative analysis* and are by far the most important stages of the process.

Stage 1   Risk awareness
This is the stage at which the project team begins to appreciate that there are risks to be considered. The risks may be pointed out by an outsider, or the

47

team may be able to draw on their own collective experience. The important point is that once this attitude of mind has been achieved, i.e. that the project, or certain facets of it, are at risk, it leads very quickly to . . .

Stage 2   Risk identification
This is essentially a team effort at which the scope of the project, as set out in the specification, contract and WBS (see Chapter 5) (if drawn) is examined and each aspect investigated for a possible risk.

To get the investigation going, the team may have a brainstorming session and use a prompt list (based on specific aspects such as legal or technical problems) or a checklist compiled from risk issues from similar previous projects. It may also be possible to obtain expert opinion or carry out interviews with outside parties. The end product is a long list of activities which may be affected by one or a number of adverse situations or unexpected occurrences. The risks which generally have to be considered may be:

Technical	New technology or materials. Test failures;
Environmental	Unforeseen weather conditions. Traffic restrictions;
Operational	New systems and procedures. Training needs;
Cultural	Established customs and beliefs. Religious holidays;
Financial	Freeze on capital. Bankruptcy of stakeholder. Currency fluctuation;
Legal	Local laws. Lack of clarity of contract;
Commercial	Change in market conditions or customers;
Resource	Shortage of staff, operatives or materials;
Economic	Slow-down in economy, change in commodity prices;
Political	Change of government or government policy.
Security	Safety. Theft. Vandalism.

The following list gives the advantages and disadvantages of the more usual risk identification methods:

Brainstorming
Advantages:	Wide range of possible risks suggested for consideration;
	Involves a number of stakeholders.
Disadvantages:	Time consuming;
	Requires firm control by facilitator.

Prompt list

Advantages: Gives benefit of past problems;
Saves time by focusing on real possibilities;
Easy to discuss.

Disadvantages: Restricts suggestions to past experience;
Past problems may not be applicable.

Checklist

Advantages: Similar to prompt list; Company standards

Disadvantages: Similar to prompt list.

Work breakdown structure

Advantages: Focused on specific project risks;
Quick and economical.

Disadvantages: May limit scope of possible risks.

Delphi technique

Advantages: Offers wide experience of experts;
Can be wide ranging.

Disadvantages: Time consuming if experts are far away;
Expensive if experts have to be paid;
Advice may not be specific enough.

Asking experts

Advantages: As Delphi.

Disadvantages: As Delphi.

At this stage it may be possible to identify who is best to manage each risk. This person becomes the *risk owner*.

To reduce the number of risks being seriously considered from what could well be a very long list, some form of screening will be necessary. Only those risks which pass certain criteria need be examined more closely, which leads to the next stage...

Stage 3   Risk assessment

This is the qualitative stage at which the two main attributes of a risk, *probability* and *impact*, are examined.

The *probability* of a risk becoming a reality has to be assessed using experience and/or statistical data such as historical weather charts or close-out reports from previous projects. Each risk can then be given a probability rating of HIGH, MEDIUM or LOW.

In a similar way, by taking into account all the available statistical data, past project histories and expert opinion, the *impact* or effect on the project can be rated as SEVERE, MEDIUM or LOW.

A simple matrix can now be drawn up which identifies whether a risk should be taken any further. Such a matrix is shown in Figure 8.1.

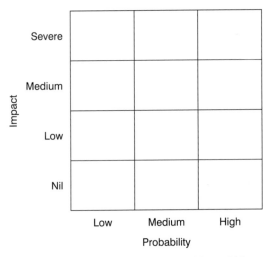

Figure 8.1 Probability versus impact table. Such a table could be used for each risk worthy of further assessment, and to assess, for example, all major risks to a project or programme

Each risk can now be given a *risk number*, so that it is now possible to draw up a simple chart which lists all the risks so far considered. This chart will show the risk number, a short description, the risk category, the probability rating, the impact rating (in terms of high, medium or low) and the *risk owner* who is charged with monitoring and managing the risk during the life of the project.

Figure 8.2 shows the layout of such a chart.

A *quantitative analysis* can now follow. This is known as ...

Stage 4   Risk evaluation
It is now possible to give comparative values, often on a scale 1 to 10, to the probability and impact of each risk and by drawing up a matrix of the risks,

	Risk Summary Chart			
Risk No.	Description	Probability rating	Impact rating	Risk owner

Figure 8.2

an order of importance or priority can be established. By multiplying the *impact rating* by the *probability rating*, the *exposure rating* is obtained. This is a convenient indicator which may be used to reduce the list to only the top dozen that require serious attention, but an eye should nevertheless be kept on even the minor ones, some of which may suddenly become serious if unforeseen circumstances arise.

An example of such a matrix is shown in Figure 8.3. Clearly the higher the value, the greater the risk and the more attention it must receive to manage it.

Another way to quantify both the impact and probability is to number the ratings as shown in Figure 8.4 from 1 for very low to 5 for very high. By multiplying the appropriate numbers in the boxes, a numerical (or quantita-

Exposure table							
			Probability				
	Rating		Very low	Low	Medium	High	Very high
		Value	0.1	0.2	0.5	0.7	0.9
	Very high	0.8					
	High	0.5					
Impact	Medium	0.2					
	Low	0.1					
	Very Low	0.05					

Figure 8.3

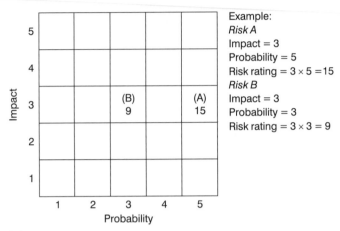

Example:
Risk A
Impact = 3
Probability = 5
Risk rating = 3 × 5 = 15
Risk B
Impact = 3
Probability = 3
Risk rating = 3 × 3 = 9

Figure 8.4

tive) exposure rating is obtained, which gives a measure of seriousness and hence importance for further investigation.

For example, if the impact is rated 3 (i.e. medium) and the probability 5 (very high), the exposure rating is 3 × 5 = 15.

Further sophistication in evaluating risks is possible by using some of the computer software developed specifically to determine the probability of occurrence. These programs use sampling techniques like 'Monte Carlo simulations' which carry out hundreds of iterative sampling calculations to obtain a probability distribution of the outcome.

One application of the Monte Carlo simulation is determining the probability to meet a specific milestone (like the completion date) by giving three time estimates to every activity. The program will then carry out a great number of iterations resulting in a frequency/time histogram and a cumulative 'S' curve from which the probability of meeting the milestone can be read off (see Figure 8.5)

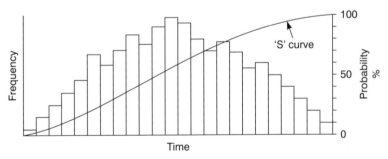

Figure 8.5

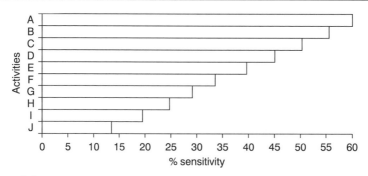

Figure 8.6

At the same time a *Tornado* diagram can be produced, which shows the sensitivity of each activity as far as it affects the project completion (see Figure 8.6).

Other techniques such as sensitivity diagrams, influence diagrams and decision trees have all been developed in an attempt to make risk analysis more accurate or more reliable. It must be remembered, however, that any answer is only as good as the initial assumptions and input data, and the project manager must give serious consideration as to the cost effectiveness of theses methods for his/her particular project.

Stage 5   Risk management

Having listed and evaluated the risks and established a table of priorities, the next stage is to decide how to manage the risks. In other words what to do about them and who should be responsible for managing them. For this purpose it is advisable to appoint a *risk owner* for every risk which has to be monitored and controlled. A risk owner may, of course, be responsible for a number or even all the risks. There are a number of options available to the project manager when faced with set of risks. These are:

avoidance
reduction
sharing
transfer
deference
mitigation

contingency
insurance
acceptance

These options are perhaps most easily explained by a simple example.

A owner of a semi-detached house decides to replace part of his roof with solar panels to save on his hot water heating bill. The risks in carrying out this work this are as follows:

Risk 1 The installer may fall off the roof;
Risk 2 The roof may leak after completion;
Risk 3 The panels may break after installation;
Risk 4 Birds may befoul the panels;
Risk 5 The electronic controls may not work;
Risk 6 The heat recovered may not be sufficient to heat the water on a cold day;
Risk 7 It may not be possible to recover the cost if the house is sold within 2–3 years;
Risk 8 The cost of the work will probably never pay for itself;
Risk 9 The cost may escalate due to unforeseen structural problems.

These risks can all be managed by applying one or several of the above options:

Risk 1	Transfer	Employ a builder who is covered by insurance;
Risk 2	Transfer	Insist on a two-year guarantee for the work (at least two season cycles);
Risk 3	Insurance	Add the panel replacement to the house insurance policy;
Risk 4	Mitigation	Provide access for cleaning (this may increase the cost);
Risk 5	Reduction	Ensure a control unit is used which has been proven for a number of years;
Risk 6	Contingency	Provide for an electric immersion heater for cold spells;
Risk 7	Deference	Wait 3 years before selling the house;
Risk 8	Acceptance	This is a risk one must accept if the work goes ahead, or
Risk 8	Avoidance	Don't go ahead with the work;
Risk 9	Sharing	Persuade the neighbour in the adjoining house to install a similar system at the same time.

Monitoring

To keep control of the risks, a *risk register* should be produced which lists all the risks and their method of management. Such a list is shown in Figure 8.7.

Figure 8.7

Where risk owners have been appointed, these will be identified on the register. The risks must be constantly monitored and at preset periods, the register must be reassessed and if necessary amended to reflect the latest position. Clearly as the project proceeds, the risks reduce in number, so that the contingency sums allocated to cover the risk of the completed activities can be allocated to other sections of the budget. These must be recorded in the register under the heading of *risk closure*.

The summary of the risk management procedure is then as follows:

1 Risk awareness;
2 Risk identification (checklists, prompt lists, brainstorming);
3 Risk owner identification;
4 Qualitative assessment;
5 Quantification of probability;
6 Quantification of impact (severity);
7 Exposure rating;
8 Mitigation;
9 Contingency provision;
10 Risk register;
11 Software usage (if any);
12 Monitoring and reporting.

To aid the process of risk management, a number of software tools have been developed. The must commonly used ones are *Riskman*, *@Risk*, *Predict*, *Pandora* and *Plantrac Marshal*, but no doubt new ones will be developed in the future.

9

Quality management

Quality (or performance) forms the third corner of the time–cost–quality triangle which is the basis of project management.

Quality management can be divided into quality assurance (QA), quality control (QC) and quality standards.

Quality assurance is the process that ensures that adequate systems, procedures and control documents are in place to meet the quality criteria set by management. The basic principle of QA is to get it right first time, and every time after that.

To ensure that the necessary quality processes are in place, quality management systems (QMS), which may well cover the whole spectrum of an organization, have to be established and regularly monitored. Guidelines for quality management and quality assurance standards are published by BSI in the ISO 9000, 9001 and 9004 series of standards. ISO 10006 are guidelines for quality in project management and ISO 10007 are guidelines for configuration management.

Quality is an attitude of mind which should permeate right through an organization from the board of directors down to the operatives on the shop floor or the site. Ideally everybody should be responsible for ensuring that his or her work meets the quality standards set down. To ensure that these standards are met, quality assurance requires checks and audits to be carried out on a regular basis.

Quality control is essentially the process of measuring the preset levels of accuracy or performance of a component, system, process or procedure and making sure that these levels are achieved. The methods used to control quality include dimensional checks, material tests, non-destructive tests, pressure tests, leak tests, performance tests, documentation control etc. Most organizations have their own test procedures and standards as well as having to comply with clients' requirements and a quality control system must be in place to meet all these criteria.

The tools of quality management are

1 The quality manual (policy manual);
2 Operational procedures;
3 The quality plan;
4 Quality reviews and audits;
5 Cause and effect analysis;
6 Failure mode analysis;
7 Pareto analysis;
8 Recording quality problems in a project history;
9 A documentation folder containing all the test results, checks and test certificates.

Apart from the quality standards developed by an organization, the following British, European and International standards must generally be complied with:

BS 4778 Quality vocabulary
BS 5760 Reliability of systems equipment & components
BS 5750 Guide to quality management & quality systems now replaced by
BS EN ISO 9000 Series, Quality management & quality assurance standards
BS ISO 10006 Quality management – Guide to quality in project management
ISO 10007 Quality management – Guidelines for configuration management

10

Change and configuration management

There are very few projects which do not change in some way during their life cycle. Equally there are very few changes which do not affect in some way either (or all) the time, cost or quality aspects of the project. For this reason it is important that all changes are recorded, evaluated and managed to ensure that the effects are appreciated by the originator of the change, and the party carrying out the change is suitably reimbursed where the change is a genuine extra to the original specification or brief.

In cases where a formal contract exists between the client and the contractor, an equally formal procedure of dealing with changes (or variations) is essential to ensure that:

1 No unnecessary changes are introduced;
2 The changes are only issued by an authorized person;
3 The changes are evaluated in terms of cost, time and performance;
4 The originator is made aware of these implications before the change is put into operation. In practice this may not always be possible if the extra work has to be carried out urgently for

safety or security reasons. In such a case the evaluation and report of the effect must be produced as soon as possible;

5 The contractor is compensated for the extra costs and given extra time to complete the contract.

Unfortunately clients do not always appreciate what effect even a minor change can have on a contract. For example, a client might think that by eliminating an item of equipment such as a small pump, a few weeks into the contract would reduce the cost. He might well find, however, that the changes in the design documentation, data sheets, drawings, bid requests etc. will actually cost more than the capital value of the pump, so that the overall cost of the project will increase! The watchwords must therefore be: *is the change really necessary.*

In practice as soon as a change or variation has been requested either verbally or by a change order, it must be confirmed back to the originator with a statement to the effect that the cost and time implications will be advised as soon as possible.

A Change of Contract Scope Notice must then be issued to all departments who may be affected to enable them to assess the cost, time and quality implications of the change.

A copy of such a document is shown in Figure 10.1, which should contain the following information:

Project or contract no.
Change of scope no.
Issue date
Name of originator of change
Method of transmission (letter, fax, telephone e-mail etc.)
Description of change
Date of receipt of change order or instruction

When all the affected departments have inserted their cost and time estimates, the form is sent to the originator for permission to proceed or for advice of the implications if the work has had to be started before the form could be completed. The method of handling variations will probably have been set out in the contract documentation but it is important to follow the agreed procedures, especially if there are time limitations for submitting the claims at a later stage.

As soon as a change has been agreed, the cost and time variations must be added to the budget and programme respectively to give the revised target values against which costs and progress will be monitored.

FOSTER WHEELER POWER PRODUCTS LTD. HAMSTEAD ROAD LONDON NW1 7QN	ADVICE OF CHANCE OF CONTRACT SCOPE
	DEPARTMENT: ENGINEERING No 82

To: Contract Management Department

☑ Please note that the scope of the subject contact has been altered due to the change(s) detailed below.To: Contract Management Department

☐ The following is a statement of the manhours and expenses incurred due to Contract Variation Notice

reference _____ dated _____ 17 Dec. 1982

ICI BILLINGHAM
2-32-07059

BRIEF DESCRIPTION OF CHANGE AND EFFECT ON DEPARTMENTAL WORK

The provision of an 'Air to Igniters' control valve.
Scope of work includes purchasing and adding to drawings.
The clients preferred - specified vendor for control valves is Fisher Controls.

Manhour requirements are as follows:-

Dept 1104-63 manhours   (1104 Split)

Dept 1102- 8 manhours   Req. 60
                         Drg.   2
Dept 1105-38 manhours   MH.   1
                               ___
                                63

CHANGE NOTIFIED BY		MANHOURS AND COSTS INCURRED IN	
☐ Minutes of Meeting with client	Date of Meeting : ___ Subject of Meeting : ___ Minute Number : ___	Department No.	1104, 1102, 1105
☐ Client's telex	Date of Telex : ___ Reference : ___ Signed by : ___	☐ Increase ☐ Decrease	
		Engineering	69 Manhours
		Design/drghtg	37 Manhours
☒ Client's letter	Date of Letter : 10.12.1992 Reference : SGP 3641 Signed by : B. Francis	Tech clerks	3 Manhours
		TOTAL	109 Manhours
☐ Client's request by telephone	Date of Call : ___ Name of Contact : ___	COSTS	£ T.B.A. Manhours
☐ Client's Variation Order	V.O.Ref. : ___ Date of V.O. : ___	Remarks	
NOTES 1. The 'change notified by' section need not be completed if form is used to advise manhours and costs only.		Initiated by N. Smith	Date 17.12.82
2. This form to be completed IMMEDIATELY ON RECEIPT of definite instructions.		Checked by MWN	Date 22.12.82
3. Manhours MUST BE REALISTIC. Make FULL ALLOWANCE for all additional and re-cycle work. Take into account 'chain reaction' affect throughout department.		Approved by	Date
4. Submit copy of this form to Manager Engineering if manhours involved exceed 250.			

Figure 10.1

The accurate and timely recording and managing of changes could make the difference between a project making a profit or losing money.

Change management must not be confused with *management of change*, which is the art of changing the culture or systems of an organization and managing the human reactions. Such a change can have far-reaching repercussions on the lives and attitudes of all the members of the organization, from the board level to the operatives on the shop floor. The way such changes are handled and the psychological approaches used to minimize stress and resistance are outside the scope of this book.

Document control

Invariably a change to even the smallest part of a project requires the amendment of one or more documents. These may be programmes, specifications, drawings, instructions and of course financial records. The amendment of each document is in itself a change and it is vital that the latest version of the document is issued to *all* the original recipients. In order to ensure that this takes place, a document control, or version control procedure must be part of the project management plan.

In practice a document control procedure may be either a single page of A4 or several pages of a spreadsheet as part of the computerized project management system. The format should, however, feature the following columns:

Document number
Document title
Originator of document
Original issue date
Issue code (general or restricted)

Name of originator (or department) of revision
Revision (or version) number
Date of revision (version)

The sheet should include a list of recipients.

A separate sheet records the date the revised document is sent to each recipient and the date of acknowledgement of receipt.

Where changes have been made to one or more pages of a multi-page document, such as a project management plan, it is only necessary to issue the revised pages under a page revision number. This requires a discrete version control sheet for this document with each clause listed and its revision and date of issue recorded.

Configuration management

Although in the confined project management context configuration management is often assumed to be synonymous with version control of documentation or software, it is of course very much more far reaching in the total project environment. Developed originally in the aerospace industry, it has been created to ensure that changes and modifications to physical components, software, systems and documentation are recorded and identified in such a way that replacements, spares and assembly documentation has conformed to the version in service. It also has been developed to ensure that the design standards and characteristics were reflected accurately in the finished product.

It can be seen that when projects involve complex systems as in the aerospace, defence or petrochemical industry, configuration management is of the utmost importance as the very nature of these industries involves development work and numerous modifications not only from the original concept or design but also during the whole life cycle of the product.

Keeping track of all these changes to specifications, drawings, support documentation and manufacturing processes is the essence of configuration management which can be split into the following five main stages:

1 *Configuration management and planning.* This covers the necessary standards, procedures, support facilities, resources and training and sets out the scope, definitions, reviews, milestones and audit dates.
2 *Configuration identification.* This encompasses the logistics and systems and procedures. It also defines the criteria for selection in each of the project phases.
3 *Configuration change management.* This deals with the proposed changes and their investigation before acceptance. At this stage changes are compared with the configuration baseline including defining when formal departure points have been reached.
4 *Configuration status accounting.* This records and logs the accepted (registered) changes and notification as well as providing traceability of all baselines.
5 *Configuration audit.* This ensures that all the previous stages have been correctly applied and incorporated in the organization. The output of this stage is the audit report.

In all these stages resources and facilities must always be considered and arrangements must be made to feed back comments to the management stage.

Essentially the process of identification, evaluation and implementation of changes requires accurate monitoring and recording and subsequent dissemination of documentation to the interested parties. This is controlled by a Master Record Index (MRI). An example of such an MRI for controlling documents is shown in Figure 10.2.

Master record index

| Document Title | Reference number | Documents | | Responsibility | Distribution |
		Issue	Date		
Business Case	Rqmt SR 123	Draft A	14/6/86	Mr Sponsor	PM, Line Mgmt
		Draft B	24/7/86		
		Issue 1	30/7/86		
		Issue 2	30/9/86		
Project Mgmt Plan	PMP/MLS/34	Draft A	28/7/86	Ms MLS PM	All Stakeholders
		Issue 1	30/9/86		
WBS	WBS/PD1	Draft A	30/7/86	Mr MLS Deputy PM	IPMT (Project Team)
		Issue 1	2/8/86		
Risk Mgmt Plan etc.	RMP/MLS/1				

Figure 10.2

On large, complex and especially multinational projects, where the design and manufacture are carried out in different countries, great effort is required to ensure that product configuration is adequately monitored and controlled. To this end a *Configuration Control Committee* is appointed to head up special *Interface Control Groups* and *Configuration Control Boards* which investigate and, where accepted, approve all proposed changes.

11

Basic network principles

It is true to say that whenever a process requires a large number of separate but integrated operations, a critical path network can be used to advantage. This does not mean, of course, that other methods are not successful or that CPM is a substitute for these methods – indeed, in many cases network analysis can be used in conjunction with traditional techniques – but if correctly applied CPM will give a clearer picture of the complete programme than other systems evolved to date.

Every time we do anything, we string together, knowingly or unknowingly, a series of activities which make up the operation we are performing. Again, if we so desire, we can break down each individual activity into further components until we end up with the movement of an electron around a nucleus. Clearly, it is ludicrous to go to such a limit but we can call a halt to this successive breakdown at any stage to suit our requirements. The degree of the breakdown depends on the operation we are performing or intend to perform.

In the UK it was the construction industry which first realized the potential of network analysis and most of, if not all, the large construction, civil engineering and building firms now use CPM regularly for their larger contracts. However, a contract does not have to be large before CPM can be usefully employed. If any process can be split into twenty or more operations or 'activities', a network will show their interrelationship in a clear and logical manner so that it may be possible to plan and rearrange these interrelationships to produce either a shorter or a cheaper project, or both.

Network analysis

Network analysis, as the name implies, consists of two basic operations:

1 Drawing the network and estimating the individual activity times
2 Analysing these times in order to find the critical activities and the amount of float in the non-critical ones.

The network

Basically the network is a flow diagram showing the sequence of operations of a process. Each individual operation is known as an activity and each meeting point or transfer stage between one activity and another is an event or node. If the activities are represented by straight lines and the events by circles, it is very simple to draw their relationships graphically, and the resulting diagram is known as the network. In order to show which activity has to be performed before its neighbour, arrow heads are placed on the straight lines, but it must be explained that the length or orientation of these lines is quite arbitrary.

It can be seen, therefore, that each activity has two nodes or events, one at the beginning and one at the end (Figure 11.1). Thus events 1 and 2 in the figure show the start and finish of activity A. The arrow head indicates that 1 comes before 2, i.e. the operation flows towards 2.

Figure 11.1

We can now describe the activity in two ways:

1 By its activity title (in this case, A)
2 By its starting and finishing event nodes 1–2.

For analysis purposes, the second method must be used.

Basic rules

Before proceeding further it may be prudent at this stage to list some very simple but basic rules for network presentation, which must be adhered to rigidly:

1 Where the starting node of an activity is also the finishing node of one or more other activities, it means that *all* the activities with this finishing node must be completed before the activity starting from that node can be commenced. For example, in Figure 11.2, 1–3(A) and 2–3(B) must be completed before 3–4(C) can be started.

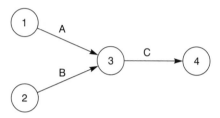

Figure 11.2

2 Each activity must have a different set of starting and finishing node numbers. This poses a problem when two activities start and finish at the same event node, and means that the example shown in Figure 11.3 is incorrect. In order to apply this rule, therefore, an artificial or 'dummy' activity is introduced into the network (Figure 11.4). This 'dummy' has a duration of zero time and thus does not affect the logic or overall time of the project. It can be seen that activity A still starts at 1 and takes 7 units

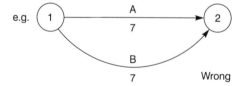

Figure 11.3

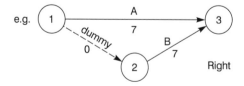

Figure 11.4

of time before being completed at event 3. Activity B also still takes 7 units of time before being completed at 3 but it starts at node 2. The activity between 1 and 2 is a timeless dummy.

3 When two chains of activities are inter-related, this can be shown by joining the two chains either by a linking activity or a 'dummy' (Figure 11.5). The dummy's function is to show that all the activities preceding it, i.e. 1–2 (A) and 2–3 (B) shown in Figure 11.5, must be completed before activity 7–8 (F) can be started. Needless to say, activities 5–6(D), 6–7(E) as well as 2–6(G) must also be completed before 7–8(F) can be started.

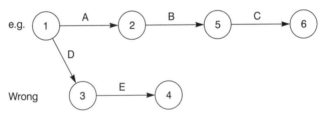

Figure 11.5

4 Each activity (except the last) must run into another activity. Failure to do so creates a loose end or 'dangle' (Figure 11.6). Dangles create premature 'ends' of a part of a project, so that the relationship between this end and the actual final completion node cannot be seen. Hence the loose ends must be joined to the final node (in this case, node 6 in Figure 11.7) to enable the analysis to be completed.

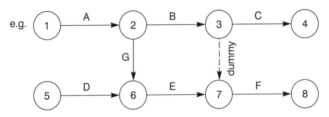

Figure 11.6

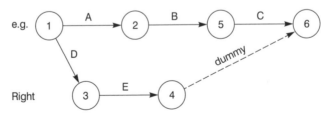

Figure 11.7

5 No chain of activities must be permitted to form a loop, i.e. such a sequence that the last activity in the chain has an influence on the first. Clearly, such a loop makes nonsense of any logic since, if one considers activities 2–3(B), 3–4(C), 4–5(E) and 5–2(F) in Figure 11.8, one finds that B, C and E must precede F, yet F must be completed before B can start. Such a situation cannot occur in nature and defies analysis.

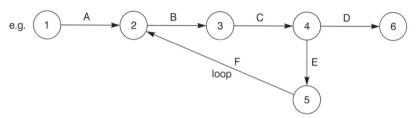

Figure 11.8

Apart from strictly following the basic rules 1 to 5 set out above, the following points are worth remembering to obtain the maximum benefit from network techniques.

1 Maximize the number of activities which can be carried out in parallel. This obviously (resources permitting) cuts down the overall programme time.
2 Beware of imposing unnecessary restraints on any activity. If a restraint is convenient rather than imperative, it should best be omitted. The use of resource restraints is a trap to be particularly avoided since additional resources can often be mustered – even if at additional cost.
3 Start activities as *early* as possible and connect them to the rest of the network as *late* as possible (Figures 11.9 and 11.10). This avoids unnecessary restraints and gives maximum float.

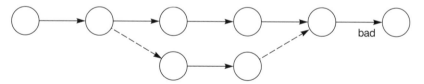

Figure 11.9

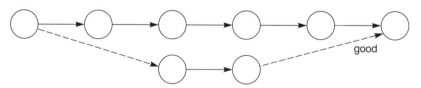

Figure 11.10

4 Resist the temptation to use a conveniently close node point as a 'staging post' for a dummy activity used as a restraint. Such a break in a restraint could impose an additional unnecessary restraint on the succeeding activity. In Figure 11.11 the intent is to restrain activity E by B and D and activity G by D. However, because the dummy from B uses node 6 as a staging post, activity G is also restrained by B. The correct network is shown in Figure 11.12. It must be remembered that the restraint on G may have to be added at a later stage, so that the effect of B in Figure 11.11 may well be overlooked.

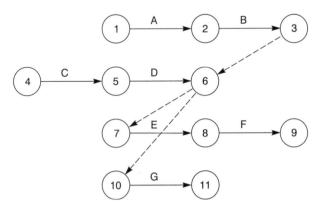

Figure 11.11

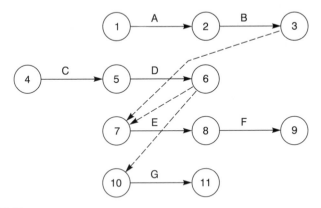

Figure 11.12

5 When drawing ladder networks (see page 75) beware of the danger of trying to economize on dummy activities as described later (Figures 11.24 and 11.25).

Durations

Having drawn the network in accordance with the logical sequence of the particular project requirements, the next step is to ascertain the duration or time of each activity. These may be estimated in the light of experience, in the same manner that programme times are usually ascertained, but it must be remembered that the shorter the duration, the more accurate they are.

The times are then written against each activity in any convenient unit but this must, of course, be the same for every activity. For example, referring to Figure 11.13, if activities 1–2(A), 2–5(B) and 5–6(C) took 3, 2 and 7 days, respectively, one would show this by merely writing these times under the activity.

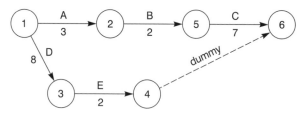

Figure 11.13

Numbering

The next stage of network preparation is numbering the events or nodes. Depending on the method of analysis, the following systems shown in Figure 11.14 can be used.

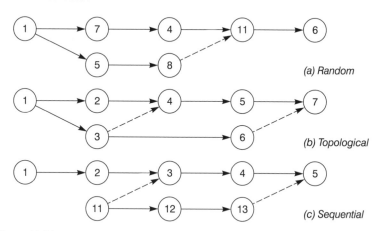

Figure 11.14

Random

This method, as the name implies, follows no pattern and merely requires each node number to be different. All computers (if used) can, of course, accept this numbering system, but there is always the danger that a number may be repeated.

Topological

This method demands that the starting node of an activity must be smaller than the finishing node of that activity. If this law is applied throughout the network, the node numbers will increase in value as the project moves towards the final activity. It has some value for beginners using network analysis since loops are automatically avoided. However, it is very time consuming and requires constant back-checking to ensure that no activity has been missed. The real drawback is that if an activity is added or changed, the whole network has to be renumbered from that point onwards. Clearly, this is an unacceptable restriction in practice.

Sequential

This is a random system from an analysis point of view, but the numbers are chosen in blocks so that certain types of activities can be identified by the nodes. The system therefore clarifies activities and facilitates recognition. The method is quick and easy to use, and should always be used whatever method of analysis is employed. Sequential numbering is usually employed when the network is banded (see Chapter 21). It is useful in such circumstances to start the node numbers in each band with the same prefix number, i.e. the nodes in band 1 would be numbered 101, 102, 103, etc., while the nodes in band 2 are numbered 201, 202, 203, etc. Figure 21.1 would lend itself to this type of numbering.

Coordinates

This method of activity identification can only be used if the network is drawn on a gridded background. In practice, thin lines are first drawn on the *back* of the translucent sheet of drawing paper to form a grid. This grid is then given coordinates or map references with letters for the vertical coordinate and numbers for the horizontal (Figure 11.15). The reason for drawing the lines on the back of the paper is, of course, to leave the grid

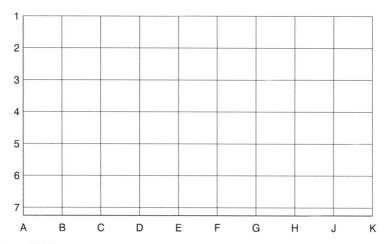

Figure 11.15

intact when the activities are changed or erased. A fully drawn grid may be confusing to some people, so it may be preferable to draw a grid showing the intersections only (Figure 11.16).

When activities are drawn, they are confined in length to the distance between two intersections. The node is drawn on the actual intersection so that the coordinates of the intersection become the node number. The number may be written in or the node left blank, as the analyst prefers.

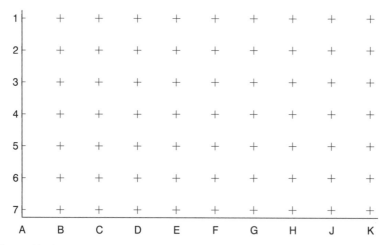

Figure 11.16

As an alternative to writing the grid letters on the nodes, it may be advantageous to write the letters *between* the nodes as in Figure 13.5. This is more fully described on pages 89 and 90.

Figure 11.17 shows a section of a network drawn on a gridded background representing the early stages of a design project. As can be seen, there is no need to fill in the nodes, although, for clarity, activities A1–B1, B1–B2, A3–B3, A3–B4 and A5–C5 have had the node numbers added. The node numbers for 'electrical layout' would be B4–C4, and the map reference principle helps to find the activity on the network when discussing the programme on the telephone or quoting it on email.

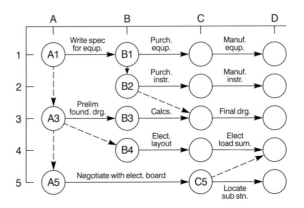

Figure 11.17

There is no need to restrict an activity to the distance between two adjacent intersections of coordinates. For example, A5–C5 takes up two spaces. Similarly, any space can also be used as a dummy and there is no restriction on the length or direction of dummies. It is, however, preferable to restrict activities to horizontal lines for ease of writing and subsequent identification.

When required, additional activities can always be inserted in an emergency by using suffix letters. For example, if activity 'preliminary foundation drawings' A3–B3 had to be preceded by, say, 'obtain loads', the network could be redrawn as shown in Figure 11.18.

Identifying or finding activities quickly on a network can be of great benefit and the above method has considerable advantages over other numbering systems. The use of coordinates is particularly useful in minimizing the risk

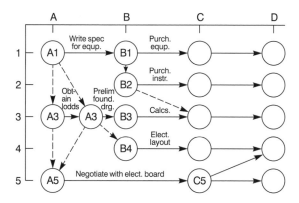

Figure 11.18

of duplicating node numbers in a large network. Since each node is, as it were, prenumbered by its coordinates, the possibility of double numbering is virtually eliminated.

Unfortunately, if the planner enters any number twice on a computer input sheet the results can be disastrous, since the machine will, in many instances, interpret the error as a logical sequence. The following example shows how this is possible. The intended sequence is shown in Figure 11.19. If the planner by mistake enters a number 11 instead of 15 for the last event of activity d, the sequence will, in effect, be as shown in Figure 11.20, but the computer will interpret the error as in Figure 11.21. Clearly, this will give a wrong analysis. If this little network had been drawn on a grid with coordinates as node numbers, it would have appeared as in Figure 11.22. Since the planner knows

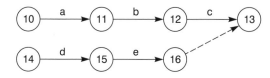

Figure 11.19

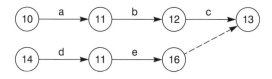

Figure 11.20

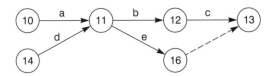

Figure 11.21

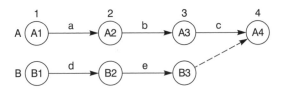

Figure 11.22

that all activities on line B must start with a B, the chance of the error occurring is considerably reduced. Furthermore, to make the computer program foolproof, one could programme it *not* to accept activities with different node letters *and* having a duration other than zero. In this way, only dummy activities can cross the grid lines.

Hammocks

When a number of activities are in series, they can be summarized into one activity encompassing them all. Such a summary activity is called a *Hammock*. It is assumed that only the first activity is dependent on another activity outside the hammock and only the last activity affects another activity outside the hammock.

On bar charts, hammocks are frequently shown as summary bars above the constituent activities and can therefore simplify the reporting document for a higher management who are generally not concerned with too much detail. For example, in Figure 11.22, activities A1 to A4 could be written as one hammock activity since only A1 and A4 are affected by work outside this activity string.

Ladders

When a string of activities repeats itself, the set of strings can be represented by a configuration known as a ladder. For a string consisting of, say, four activities relating to two stages of excavation, the configuration is shown in

Figure 11.23. This pattern indicates that, for example, hand trim of Stage II can only be done if

1 Hand trim of Stage I is complete
2 Machine excavation of Stage II is complete.

This, of course, is what it should be.

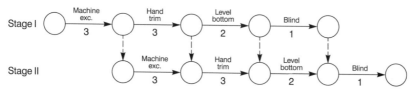

Figure 11.23

However, if the work were to be divided into three stages, the ladder could, on the face of it, be drawn as shown in Figure 11.24. Again, in Stage II all the operations are shown logically in the correct sequence, but closer examination of Stage III operations will throw up a number of logic errors which the inexperienced planner may miss.

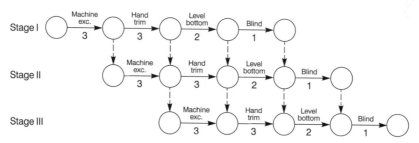

Figure 11.24

What we are trying to show in the network is that Stage III hand trim cannot be performed until Stage III machine excavation is complete and Stage II hand trim is complete. However, what the diagram says is that, in addition to these restraints, Stage III hand trim cannot be performed until Stage I level bottom is also complete.

Clearly, this is an unnecessary restraint and cannot be tolerated. The correct way of drawing a ladder therefore when more than two stages are involved is as in Figure 11.25. We must, in fact, introduce a dummy activity in Stage II

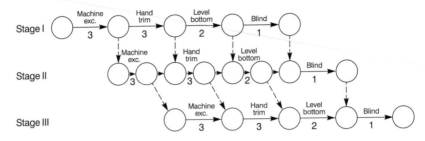

Figure 11.25

(and any intermediate stages) between the starting and completion node of every activity except the last. In this way, the Stage III activities will not be restrained by Stage I activities except by those of the same type.

An examination of Figure 11.25 shows a new dummy between the activities in Stage II, i.e.

i.e.

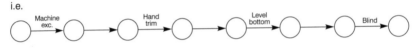

Figure 11.26

This concept led to the development of a new type of network presentation called the 'Lester' diagram, which is described more fully in Chapter 13. This has considerable advantages over the conventional arrow diagram and the precedence diagram, also described later.

Once the network has been numbered and the times or durations added, it must be analysed. This means that the earliest starting and completion dates must be ascertained and the floats or 'spare times' calculated. There are three main types of analysis:

1 Arithmetical;
2 Graphical;
3 Computer.

Since these three different methods (although obviously giving the same answers) require very different approaches, a separate chapter has been devoted to each technique (Chapters 15, 16 and 17).

Dependency

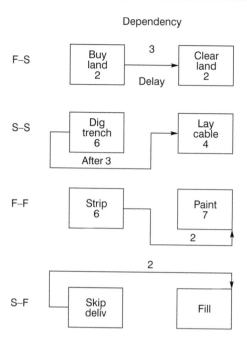

Figure 11.27

By far the most common logical constraint of a network is as given in the examples on the previous pages, i.e. 'Finish to Start' or activity B can only start when activity A is complete. However, it is possible to configure other restraints. These are: Start to Start, Finish to Finish and Start to Finish. Figure 11.27 shows these less usual constraints which are sometimes used when a lag occurs between the activities. Analysing a network manually with such restraints can be very confusing and should there be a lag or delay between any two activities, it is better to show this delay as just another activity. In fact all these three less usual constraints can be redrawn in the more conventional Finish to Start mode as shown in Figure 11.28

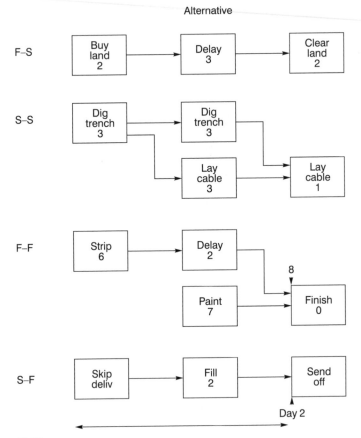

Figure 11.28

12

Precedence or activity on node (AoN) diagrams

Some planners prefer to show the interrelationship of activities by using the node as the activity box and interlinking them by lines. Because the durations are written in the activity box, dummy activities are eliminated. In a sense, each connecting line is, of course, a dummy because it is timeless. The network produced in this manner is called variously a 'precedence diagram', a 'circle and link diagram' or an 'activity on node diagram'.

Precedence diagrams have a number of advantages over arrow diagrams in that

1 No dummies are necessary;
2 They may be easier to understand by people familiar with flow sheets;
3 Activities are identified by one number instead of two so that a new activity can be inserted between two existing activities without changing the identifying node numbers of the existing activities;
4 Overlapping activities can be shown very easily without the need for the extra dummies shown in Figure 11.25.

Analysis and float calculation (see Chapter 15) is identical to the methods employed for arrow diagrams and, if the box is large enough, the earliest and latest start and finishing times can be written in.

A typical precedence network is shown in Figure 12.1, where the letters in the box represent the description or activity numbers. Durations are shown above-centre and the earliest and latest starting and finish times are given in

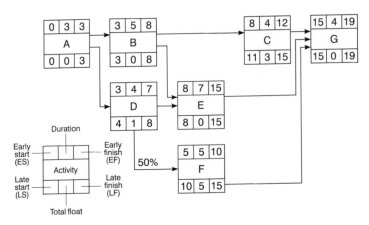

Figure 12.1

the corners of the box, as explained in the key diagram. The top line of the activity box gives the earliest start (ES), duration (D) and earliest finish (EF). Therefore:

$$EF = ES + D$$

The bottom line gives the latest start and the latest finish. Therefore:

$$LS = LF - D$$

The centre box is used to show the total float.

ES is, of course, the *highest* EF of the previous activities leading into it, i.e. the ES of activity E is 8, taken from the EF of activity B.
LF is the *lowest* LS of the previous activity *working backwards*, i.e. the LF of A is 3, taken from the LS of activity B.
The earliest start (ES) of activity F is 5 because it can start after activity D is 50% complete, i.e.

ES of activity D is 3
Duration of activity D is 4
Therefore 50% of duration is 2
Therefore ES of activity F is 3 + 2 = 5

Sometimes it is advantageous to add a percentage line on the bottom of the activity box to show the stage of completion before the next activity can start (Figure 12.2). Each vertical line represents 10% completion. Apart from showing when the next activity starts, the percentage line can also be used to indicate the percentage completion of the activity as a statement of progress once work has started, as in Figure 12.3.

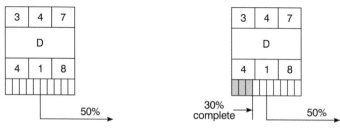

Figure 12.2   **Figure 12.3**

There are two other advantages of the precedence diagram over the arrow diagram.

1 The risk of making the logic errors is virtually eliminated. This is because each activity is separated by a link, so that the unintended dependency from another activity is just not possible.

   This is made clear by referring to Figure 12.4 which is the precedence representation of Figure 11.25.

   As can be seen, there is no way for an activity like 'level bottom' in Stage I to affect activity 'Hand trim' in Stage III, as is the case in Figure 11.24.

2 In a precedence diagram all the important information of an activity is shown in a neat box.

   A close inspection of the precedence diagram (Figure 12.5), shows that in order to calculate the total float, it is necessary to carry out the forward and backward pass. Once this has been done, the total float of any activity is simply the difference between the latest finishing time (LF) obtained from the backward pass and the earliest finishing time (EF) obtained from the forward pass.

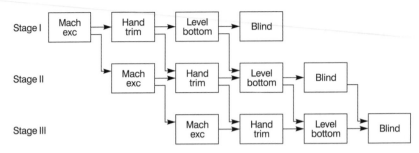

Figure 12.4

On the other hand, the free float can be calculated from the forward pass only, because it is simply the difference of the earliest start (ES) of a subsequent activity and the earliest finishing time (EF) of the activity in question.

This is clearly shown in Figure 12.5.

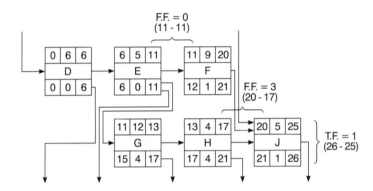

Figure 12.5

Despite the above-mentioned advantages, which are especially appreciated by people familiar with flow diagrams as used in manufacturing industries, many prefer the arrow diagram because it resembles more closely a bar chart. Although the arrows are not drawn to scale, they do represent a forward-moving operation and, by thickening up the actual line in approximately the same proportion as the reported progress, a 'feel' for the state of the job is immediately apparent.

One major disadvantage of precedence diagrams is the practical one of size of box. The box has to be large enough to show the activity title, duration and earliest and latest times, so that the space taken up on a sheet of paper reduces the network size. By contrast, an arrow diagram is very economical, since the arrow is a natural line over which a title can be written and the node need be no larger than a few millimetres in diameter – if the coordinate method is used.

The difference (or similarity) between an arrow diagram and a precedence network is most easily seen by comparing the two methods in the following example. Figure 12.6 shows a project programme and Figure 12.7 the same programme as a precedence diagram. The difference in area of paper required by the two methods is obvious (see also Chapter 27).

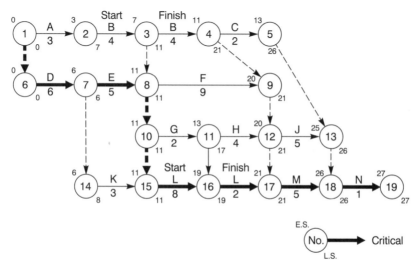

Figure 12.6

Figure 12.7 shows the precedence version of Figure 12.6.

In practice, the only information necessary when drafting the original network is the activity title, the duration and of course the interrelationships of the activities. A precedence diagram can therefore be modified by drawing ellipses just big enough to contain the activity title and duration, leaving the computer (if used) to supply the other information at a later stage. The important thing is to establish an acceptable logic before the end date and the activity floats are computed. In explaining the principles of network diagrams in text books (and in examinations), letters are often used as activity titles, but in practice when building up a network, the real descriptions have to be used.

85

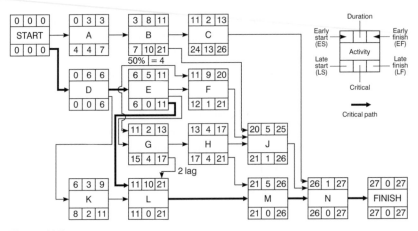

Figure 12.7

An example of such a diagram is shown in Figure 12.8. Care must be taken not to cross the nodes with the links and to insert the arrowheads to ensure the correct relationship.

One problem of a precedence diagram is that when large networks are being developed by a project team, the drafting of the boxes takes up a lot of time and paper space and the insertion of links (or dummy activities) becomes a nightmare, because it is confusing to cross the boxes, which are in effect nodes. It is necessary therefore to restrict the links to run horizontally or vertically between the boxes, which can lead to congestion of the lines, making the tracing of links very difficult.

When a large precedence network is drawn by a computer, the problem becomes even greater, because the link lines can sometimes be so close

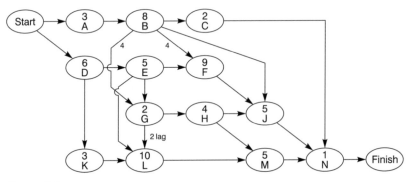

Figure 12.8

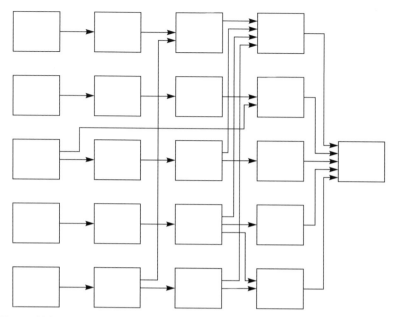

Figure 12.9

together that they will appear as one thick black line. This makes it impossible to determine the beginning or end of a link, thus nullifying the whole purpose of a network, i.e. to show the interrelationship and dependencies of the activities. See Figure 12.9.

For small networks with few dependencies, precedence diagrams are no problem, but for networks with 200–400 activities per page, it is a different matter. The planner must not feel restricted by the drafting limitations to develop an acceptable logic, and the tendency by some irresponsible software companies to advocate eliminating the manual drafting of a network altogether must be condemned. This manual process is after all the key operation for developing the project network and the distillation of the various ideas and inputs of the team. In other words, it is the thinking part of network analysis. The number crunching can then be left to the computer.

13

Lester diagram

With the development of the *network grid*, the drafting of an arrow diagram enables the activities to be easily organized into disciplines or work areas and eliminates the need to enter reference numbers into the nodes. Instead the grid reference numbers (or letters) can be fed into the computer. The grid system also makes it possible to produce acceptable arrow diagrams on a computer which can be used 'in the field' without converting them into the conventional bar chart. An example of such a computerized arrow diagram, which has been developed by Claremont Controls as part of their latest Hornet Windmill program, is given in Figure 13.1. It will be noticed that the link lines never cross a node!

A grid system can, however, pose a problem when it becomes necessary to insert an activity between two existing ones. In practice, resourceful planners can overcome the problem by combining the new activity with one of the existing activities.

If, for example, two adjoining activities were 'Cast Column, 4 days' and 'Cast Beam, 2 days' and it were necessary to insert 'Strike Formwork, 2 days' between the two activities, the planner

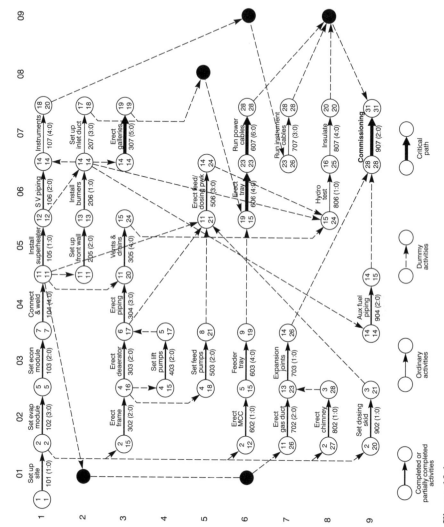

Figure 13.1

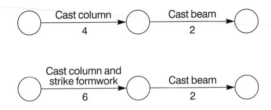

Figure 13.2

would simply restate the first activity as 'Cast Column and Strike Formwork, 6 days' (Figure 13.2).

While this overcomes the drafting problem it may not be acceptable from a cost control point of view, especially if the network is geared to an EVA system (see Chapter 27). Furthermore the fact that the grid numbers were *on* the nodes meant that when it was necessary to move a string along one or more grid spaces, the relationship between the grid number and the activity changed. This could complicate the EVA analysis. To overcome this, the grid number was placed *between* the nodes (Figure 13.3).

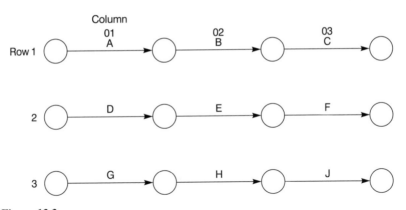

Figure 13.3

It can be argued that a precedence network lends itself admirably to a grid system as the grid number is always and permanently related to the activity and is therefore ideal for EVA. However, the problem of the congested link lines (especially the vertical ones) remains.

Now, however, the perfect solution has been found. It is in effect a combination of the arrow diagram and the precedence diagram and like the marriage of Henry VII which ended the Wars of the Roses, this marriage should end the war of the networks!

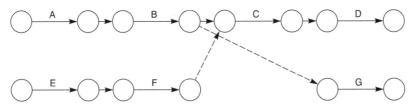

Figure 13.4

The new diagram, which could be called the 'Lester' diagram, is simply an arrow diagram where each activity is separated by a short link in the same way as in a precedence network (Figure 13.4).

In this way it is possible to eliminate or at least reduce logic errors, show total float and free float as easily as on a precedence network, but has the advantages of an arrow diagram in speed of drafting, clarity of link presentation and the ability to insert new activities in a grid system without altering the grid number/ activity relationship. Figure 13.5 shows all these features.

If a line is drawn around any activity, the similarity between the Lester diagram and the precedence diagram becomes immediately apparent. See Figure 13.6.

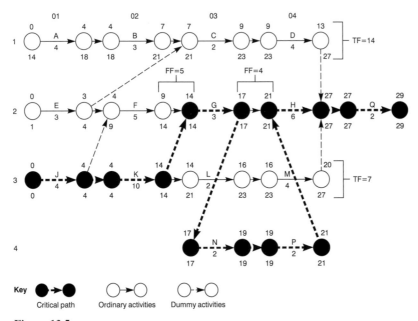

Figure 13.5

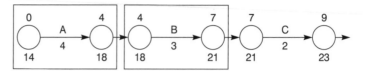

Figure 13.6

Although all the examples in subsequent chapters use arrow diagrams, precedence diagrams or 'Lester' diagrams could be substituted in most cases. The choice of technique is largely one of personal preference and familiarity. Provided the user is satisfied with one system and is able to extract the maximum benefit, there is little point in changing to another.

Time scale networks and linked bar charts

When preparing presentation or tender documents, or when the likelihood of the programme being changed is small, the main features of a network and bar chart can be combined in the form of a time scale network, or a linked bar chart. A time scale network has the length of the arrows drawn to a suitable scale in proportion to the duration of the activities. The whole network can, in fact, be drawn on a gridded background where each square of the grid represents a period of time such as a day, week or month. Free float is easily ascertainable by inspection, but total float must be calculated in the conventional manner.

By drawing the activities to scale and starting each activity at the earliest date, a type of bar chart is produced which differs from the conventional bar chart in that some of the activity bars are on the same horizontal line. The disadvantage of such a presentation is that part of the network has to be redrawn 'downstream' from any activity which changes its duration. It can be seen that if one of the early activities changes in either duration or starting point, the whole network has to be modified.

However, a time scale network (especially if restricted to a few major activities) is a clear and concise communication document for reporting up. It loses its value in communicating down because changes increase with detail and constant revision would be too time consuming.

A linked bar chart is very similar to a normal bar chart, i.e. each activity is on a separate line and the activities are listed vertically at the edge of the paper. However, by drawing interlinking vertical (or inclined) dummy

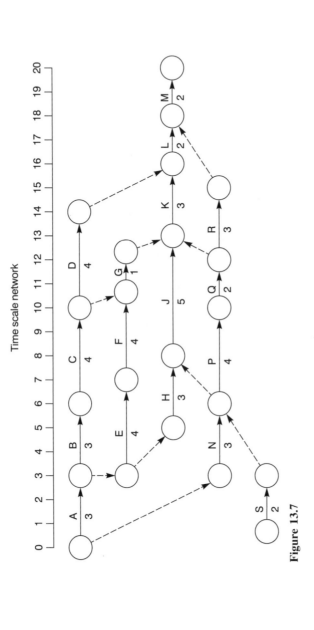

Time scale network

Figure 13.7

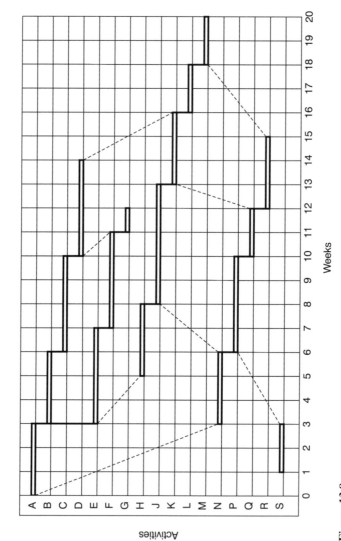

Figure 13.8

activities to join the main bars, a type of programme is produced which clearly shows the interrelationship of the activity bars.

Chapter 16 describes the graphical analysis of networks, and it can be seen that if the ends of the activities were connected by the dummies a linked bar chart would result. Figure 13.7 shows a small time scale network and Figure 13.8 shows the same programme drawn as a linked bar chart.

14

Float

Because float is such an important part of network analysis and because it is frequently quoted – or misquoted – by computer protagonists as another reason why computers *must* be used, a special discussion of the subject may be helpful to those readers not too familiar with its use in practice.

Of the three types of float shown on a printout, i.e. the total float, free float and independent float, only the first – the total float – is in general use. Where resource smoothing is required, a knowledge of free float can be useful, since it is the activities with free float that can be moved backwards or forwards in time without affecting any other activities. Independent float, on the other hand, is really quite a useless piece of information and should be suppressed (when possible) from any computer printout. Of the many managers, site engineers or planners interviewed, none has been able to find a practical application of independent float.

Total float

Total float, in contrast to other types of float, does have a role to play. By definition, it is the time between the anticipated start (or finish) of an activity and the latest permissible start (or finish).

The float can be either positive or negative. A positive float means that the operation or activity will be completed earlier than necessary, and a negative float indicates that the activity will be late. A prediction of the status of any particular activity is, therefore, a very useful and important piece of information for a manager. However, this information is of little use if not transmitted to management as soon as it becomes available, and every day of delay reduces the manager's ability to rectify the slippage or replan the mode of operation.

The reason for calling this type of float 'total float' is because it is the total of all the 'free floats' in a string of activities when working back from where this string meets the critical path to the activity in question.

For example, in Figure 16.2, the activities in the lowest string J to P, have the following free floats: J = 0, K = 10–9 = 1, L = 0, M = 15–14 = 1, N = 21–19 = 2, P = 0. Total float for K is therefore 2 + 1 + 1 + 1 = 4. This is the same as the 4 shown in the lower middle space of the node.

It is very easy to calculate the total floats and free floats in a precedence or Lester diagram. For any activity, the total float is the difference between the *latest finish* and *earliest finish* (or *latest start* and *earliest start*). The free float is the difference between the *earliest finish* of the activity in question and the *earliest start* of the following activity. The diagram in Figure 14.9 makes this clear.

Calculation of float

By far the quickest way to calculate the float of a particular activity is to do it manually. In practice, one does not require to know the float of *all* activities at the same time. A list of floats is, therefore, unnecessary. The important point is that the float of a particular activity which is of immediate interest is obtainable quickly and accurately.

Consider the string of activities in a simple construction process. This is shown in Figure 14.1 in Activity on Arrow (AoA) format and in Figure 14.2 in the simplified Activity on Node (AoN) format.

It can be seen that the total duration of the sequence is 34 days. By drafting the network in the method shown, and by using the day numbers at the end of *each* activity, including dummies, an accurate prediction is obtained immediately and the float of any particular activity can be seen almost by

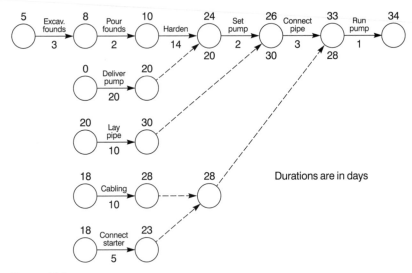

Figure 14.1

inspection. It will be noted that each activity has two dates or day numbers – one at the beginning and one at the end (Figure 14.3). Therefore, where two (or more) activities meet at a node, all the end day numbers are inserted (Figure 14.4). The highest number is now used to calculate the overall project duration, i.e. $30 + 3 = 33$, and the difference between the highest and the other number immediately gives the float of the other activity and *all* the activities

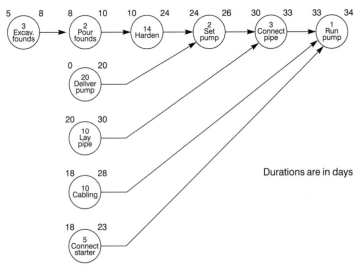

Figure 14.2

node. This is described in detail in Chapter 15 with Figures 15.5 and 15.6. If the network is in the precedence format, the calculation of free float is even easier. All one has to do is to subtract the early finish time in the preceding node from the early start time of the succeeding node. This is clearly shown on Figure 14.9, which is the precedence equivalent to Figure 14.1.

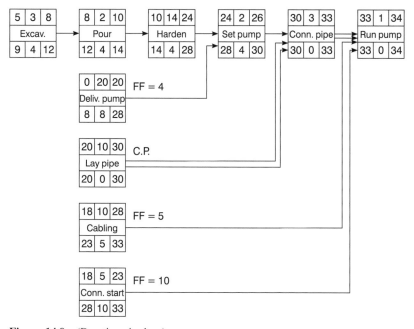

Figure 14.9   (Durations in days)

One of the phenomena of a computer printout is the comparatively large number of activities with free float. Closer examination shows that the majority of these are in fact dummy activities. The reason for this is, of course, obvious, since, by definition, free float can only exist when more than one activity enters a node. As dummies nearly always enter a node with another (real) activity, they all tend to have free float. Unfortunately, no computer program exists which automatically transfers this free float to the preceding real activity, so that the benefit of the free float is not immediately apparent and is consequently not taken advantage of.

15

Arithmetical analysis

This method is the classical technique and can be performed in a number of ways. One of the easiest methods is to add up the various activity durations on the network itself, writing the sum of each stage in a square box at the end of that activity, i.e. next to the end event (Figure 15.1). It is essential that each route is examined separately and where the routes meet, the *largest* sum total must be inserted in the box. When the complete network has been summed in this way, the *earliest* starting will have been written against each event.

Now the reverse process must be carried out. The last event sum is now used as a base from which the activities leading into it are subtracted. The result of these subtractions are entered in triangular boxes against each event (Figure 15.2). As with the addition process for calculating the earliest starting times, a problem arises when a node is reached where two routes or activities meet. Since the *latest* starting times of an activity are required, the *smallest* result is written against the event.

The two diagrams are combined in Figure 15.3. The difference between the earliest and latest times gives the 'float', and if this difference

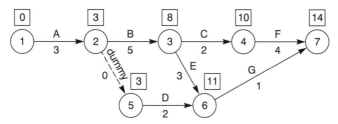

Figure 15.1 Forward pass

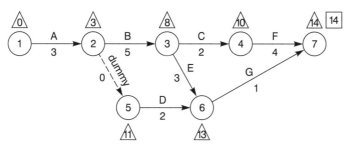

Figure 15.2 Backward pass

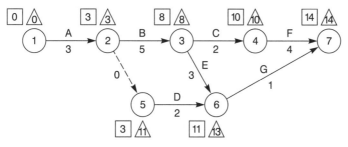

Figure 15.3

is zero (i.e. if the numbers in the squares and triangles are the same) the event is on the critical path.

The equivalent precedence (AoN) diagram is shown in Figure 15.6.

A table can now be prepared setting out the results in a concise manner (Table 15.1).

Slack

The difference between the latest and earliest times of any event is called 'slack'. Since each activity has two events, a beginning event and an end

Table 15.1

a	b	c	d	e	f	g	h
Title	Activity	Duration, D	Latest time end event	Earliest time end event	Earliest time beginning event	Total float (d-f-c)	Free float (e-f-c)
A	1–2	3	3	3	0	0	0
B	2–3	5	8	8	3	0	0
DUMMY	2–5	0	11	3	3	8	0
C	3–4	2	10	10	8	0	0
E	3–6	3	13	11	8	2	0
F	4–7	4	14	14	10	0	0
D	5–6	2	13	11	3	8	6
G	6–7	1	14	14	11	2	2

Column a: activities by the activity titles.
Column b: activities by the event numbers.
Column c: activity durations, D.
Column d: *latest time* of the activities' end event, TL_E.
Column e: *earliest time* of the activities' end event, TE_E.
Column f: *earliest time* of the activities' beginning event, TE_B.
Column g: total float of the activity.
Column h: free float of the activity.

event, it follows that there are two slacks for each activity. Thus the slack of the beginning event can be expressed as $TL_B–TE_B$ and called beginning slack and the slack of the end event, appropriately called end slack, is $TL_E–TE_E$. The concept of slack is useful when discussing the various types of float, since it simplifies the definitions.

Float

This is the name given to the spare time of an activity, and is one of the more important by-products of network analysis. The four types of float possible will now be explained.

Total float

It can be seen that activity 3–6 in Figure 15.3 *must* be completed after 13 time units, but can be started after 8 time units. Clearly, therefore, since the activity itself takes 3 time units, the activity *could* be completed in 8 + 3 = 11 time units. Therefore there is a leeway of $13 - 11 = 2$ time units on the activity. This leeway is called total float, and is defined as latest time of end event minus earliest time of beginning event minus duration, or $TL_E - TE_B - D$.

Figure 15.3 shows that total float is, in fact, the same as beginning slack. Also, free float is the same as total float minus end slack. The proof is given at the end of this chapter.

Free float

Some activities, e.g. 5–6, as well as having total float have an additional leeway. It will be noted that activities 3–6 and 5–6 both affect activity 6–7. However, one of these two activities will delay 6–7 by the same time unit by which it itself may be delayed. The remaining activity, on the other hand, may be delayed for a period without affecting 6–7. This leeway is called free float, and can only occur in one or more activities where several meet at one event, i.e. if x activities meet at a node, it is possible that $x-1$ of these have free float. This free float may be defined as earliest time of end event minus earliest time of beginning event minus duration, or $TE_E - TE_B - D$.

For a more detailed discussion on the use of floats, and a rapid manual method for calculating total float, see Chapter 14.

Interfering float

The difference between the total float and the free float is known as interfering float. Using the previous notation, this can be expressed as

$$(TL_E - TE_B - D) - (TE_E - TE_B - D)$$
$$= TL_E - TE_B - D - TE_E + TE_B + D$$
$$= TL_E - TE_E$$

i.e. as the latest time of the end event minus the earliest time of the end event. It is, therefore, the same as the end slack.

Independent float

The difference between the free float and the beginning slack is known as independent float:

$$\text{since free float} = TE_E - TE_B - D$$
$$\text{and beginning slack} = TL_B - TE_B$$
$$\text{independent float} = TE_E - TE_B - D - (TL_B - TE_B)$$
$$= TE_E - TE_B - D$$

Thus independent float is given by the earliest time of the end event minus the latest time of beginning event minus the duration.

In practice neither the interfering float nor the independent float find much application, and for this reason they will not be referred to in later chapters. The use of computers for network analysis enables these values to be produced without difficulty or extra cost, but they only tend to confuse the user and are therefore best ignored.

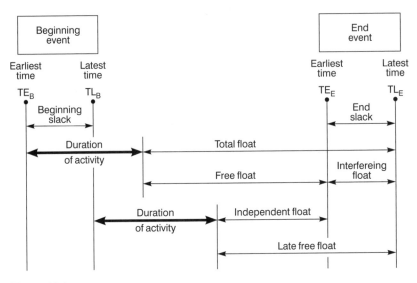

Figure 15.4

Summarizing all the above definitions, Figure 15.4 and the following expressions may be of assistance.

Notation

$$D = \text{duration of activity}$$
$$TE_B = \text{earliest time of beginning event}$$
$$TE_E = \text{earliest time of end event}$$
$$TL_B = \text{latest time of beginning event}$$
$$TL_E = \text{latest time of end event}$$

Definitions

$$\text{beginning slack} = TL_B - TE_B$$
$$\text{end slack} = TL_E - TE_E$$
$$\text{total float} = TL_E - TE_B - D$$

$$\text{free float} = TE_E - TE_B - D$$
$$\text{interfering float} = TL_E - TE_E \ (= \text{end slack})$$
$$\text{independent float} = TE_E - TL_B - D$$
$$\text{late free float} = TL_E - TL_B - D$$

Critical path

Some activities have zero total float, i.e. no leeway is permissible for their execution, hence any delays incurred on the activities will be reflected in the overall project duration. These activities are therefore called critical activities, and every network has a chain of such critical activities running from the beginning event of the first activity to the end event of the last activity, without a break. This chain is called the critical path.

Frequently a project network has more than one critical path, i.e. two or more chains of activities all have to be carried out within the stipulated duration to avoid a delay to the completion date. In addition, a number of activity chains may have only one or two units of float, so that, for all intents and purposes, they are also critical. It can be seen, therefore, that it is important to keep an eye on all activity chains which are either critical or near-critical, since a small change in duration of one chain could quickly alter the priorities of another.

One disadvantage of the arithmetical method of analysis using the table or matrix shown in Table 15.1 is that all the floats must be calculated before the critical path can be ascertained. This drawback is eliminated when the method of analysis described in Chapter 14 is employed.

The concept of free float

Students often find it difficult to understand the concept of free float. The mathematical definitions are unhelpful, and the graphical representation on page 108 can be confusing. The easiest way to understand the difference between total float and free float is to inspect the *end* node of the activity in question. As stated earlier, free float can only occur where two or more activities enter a node. If the *earliest* end times (i.e. the forward pass) for each individual activity are placed against the node, the free float is simply the difference between the highest number of the earliest time on the node and the number of the earliest time of the activity in question.

In the example given in Figure 15.5 the earliest times are placed in squares, so following the same convention it can be seen from the figure (which is a

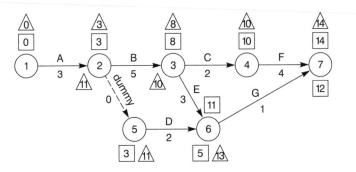

Figure 15.5

redrawing of Figure 15.1 with *all* the earliest and latest node times added)
that

Figure 15.6 shows the equivalent precedence (AoN) diagram from which
the free float can be easily calculated by subtracting the early *finish* time of the
preceding node from the early *start* time of the *succeeding* node.

Free float of activity D = 11 − 5 = 6
Free float of activity G = 14 − 12 = 2

Activity E, because it is not on the critical path has total float of 13 − 11 = 2
but has no free float.

The check of the free float by the formal definition is as follows:

Free float $= TE_E − TE_B − D$
For activity D = 11 − 3 − 2 = 6
For activity G = 14 − 11 − 1 = 2

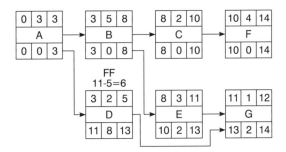

Figure 15.6

The check of the total float by the formal definitions is as follows:

$$\text{Total float} = TL_E - TE_B - D$$

$$\text{For activity } E = 13 - 8 - 3 = 2$$
$$D = 13 - 3 - 2 = 8$$
$$G = 14 - 11 - 2 = 2$$

It was stated earlier that total float is the same as beginning slack. This can be shown by rewriting the definition of total float $= TL_E - TE_B - D$ as total float $= TL_E - D - TE_B$ but $TL_E - D = TL_B$. Therefore

$$\text{Total float} = TL_B - TE_B$$
$$= \text{Beginning slack}$$

To show that free float = total float – end slack, consider the following definitions:

$$\text{Free float} = TE_E - TE_B - D \qquad (15.1)$$

$$\text{Total float} = TL_E - TE_B - D \qquad (15.2)$$

$$\text{End slack} = TL_E - TE_E \qquad (15.3)$$

Subtracting equation (15.3) from equation (15.2)

$$= TL_E - TL_B - D - (TL_E - TE_E)$$
$$= TL_E - TE_B - D - TL_E + TE_E$$
$$= TE_E - TE_B - D \qquad (15.1)$$
$$= \text{Free float}$$

Therefore

equation (15.1) = equation (15.2) – equation (15.3)

or free float = total float – end slack.

16

Graphical analysis, milestones and LoB

It is often desirable to present the programme of a project in the form of a bar chart, and when the critical path and floats have been found by either the arithmetical or computer methods, the bar chart has to be drawn as an additional task. (Most computer programs can actually print a bar chart but these often run to several sheets.)

As explained in Chapter 25, bar charts, while they are not as effective as networks for the actual planning function, are still one of the best methods for allocating and smoothing resources. If resource listing and subsequent smoothing is an essential requirement, graphical analysis can give the best of both worlds. Naturally, any network, however analysed, can be converted very easily into a bar chart, but if the network is analysed graphically the bar chart can be 'had for free', as it were.

Modern computer programs will of course produce bar charts (or Gantt charts) from the inputs almost automatically. Indeed the input screen itself often generates the bar chart as the data are entered. However, when a computer is not available or the planner is not conversant with the particular computer program the graphical method becomes a useful alternative.

The following list gives some of the advantages over other methods, but before the system is used on large jobs planners are strongly advized to test it for themselves on smaller contracts so that they can appreciate the short-cut methods and thus save even more planning time.

1 The analysis is extremely rapid, much quicker than the arithmetical method. This is especially the case when, after some practice, the critical path can be found by inspection.
2 As the network is analysed, the bar chart is generated automatically and no further labour need be expended to do this at a later stage.
3 The critical path is produced *before* the floats are known. (This is in contrast to the other methods, where the floats have to be calculated first before the critical path can be seen.) The advantage of this is that users can see at once whether the project time is within the specified limits, permitting them to make adjustments to the critical activities without bothering about the non-critical ones.
4 Since the results are shown in bar chart form, they are more readily understood by persons familiar with this form of programme. The bar chart will show more vividly than a printout the periods of heavy resource loading, and highlights periods of comparative inactivity. Smoothing is therefore much more easily accomplished.
5 By marking the various trades or operational types in different colours, a rapid approximate resource requirement schedule can be built up. The resources in any one time period can be ascertained by simply adding up vertically, and any smoothing can be done by utilizing the float periods shown on the chart.
6 The method can be employed for single or multi-start projects. For multi-project work, the two or more bar charts can (provided they are drawn to the same time and calendar scale) be superimposed on transparent paper and the amount of resource overlap can be seen very quickly.

Limitations

The limitations of the graphical method are basically the size of the bar chart paper and therefore the number of activities. Most programmes are drawn on either A1 or A0 size paper and the number of different activities must be compressed into the 840 mm width of this sheet. (It may, of course, be possible to divide the network into two, but then the interlinking activities must be carefully transferred.) Normally, the divisions between bars is about 6 mm, which means that a maximum of 120 activities can be analysed. However, bearing in mind that in a normal network 30% of the activities are dummies, a network of 180 to 200 activities could be analysed graphically on one sheet.

Briefly, the mode of operation is as follows:

1 Draw the network in arrow diagram or precedence format and write in the activity titles (Figures 16.1 and 16.2). Although a forward pass has been carried out on both these diagrams, this is not necessary when using the graphical method of analysis.

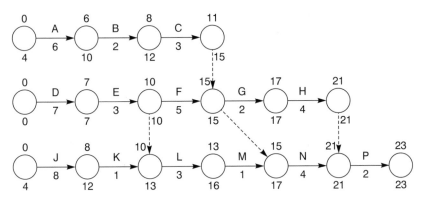

Figure 16.1

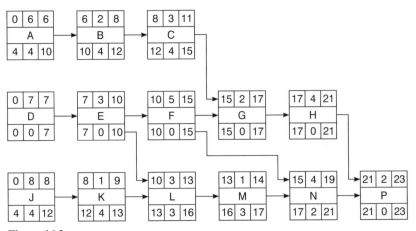

Figure 16.2

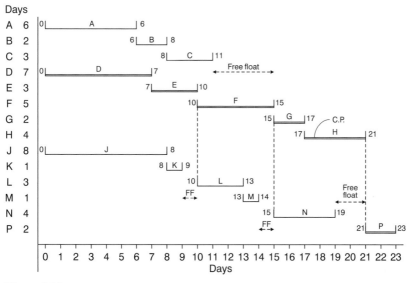

Figure 16.3

2 Insert the durations.
3 List the activities on the left hand vertical edge of a sheet of graph paper (Figure 16.3) showing:

(a) Activity title.
(b) Duration (in days, weeks, etc.).
(c) Node no. (only required when using these for bar chart generation).

4 Draw time scale along the bottom horizontal edge of the graph paper.
5 Draw a horizontal line from day 0 of the first activity which is proportional to the duration (using the time scale selected) e.g. 6 days would mean a line 6 divisions long (Figure 16.3). To ease identification an activity letter or no. can be written above the bar.
6 Repeat this operation with the next activity on the table starting on day 0.
7 When using arrow (AoA) networks, mark dummy activities by writing the end time of the dummy next to the start time of the dummy e.g. 4→7 would be shown as 4,7 (Figure 16.5).
8 All subsequent activities must be drawn with their start time (start day no.) directly below the end time (end day no.) of the previous activity having the same time value (day no.).

9 If more than one activity has the same end time (day no.), draw the new activity line from the activity end time (day no.) furthest to the *right*.

10 Proceed in this manner until the end of the network.

11 The critical path can now be traced back by following the line (or lines) which runs back to the start without a horizontal break.

12 The break between consecutive activities on the bar chart is the *Free Float* of the preceding activity.

13 The summation of the free floats in one string, before that string meets the critical path is the *Total Float* of the activity from which the summation starts, e.g. in Figure 16.3, the total float of activity K is 1 + 1 + 2 = 4 days, the total float of activity M is 1 + 2 + 3 days and the total float of activity N is 2 days.

The advantage of using the start and end times (day nos.) of the activities to generate the bar chart is that there is no need to carry out a forward pass. The correct relationship is given automatically by the disposition of the bars. This method is therefore equally suitable for arrow and precedence diagrams.

An alternative method can however be used by substituting the day numbers by the node numbers. Clearly this method, which is sometimes quicker to draw, can only be used with arrow diagrams as precedence diagrams do not have node numbers. When using this method, the node numbers are listed next to the activity titles (Figure 16.5) and the bars are drawn from the starting node of the first activity with a length equal to the duration. The next bar starts vertically below the end node with the same node number as the starting node of the activity being drawn.

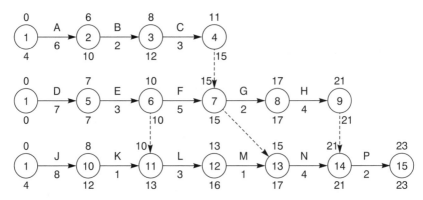

Figure 16.4

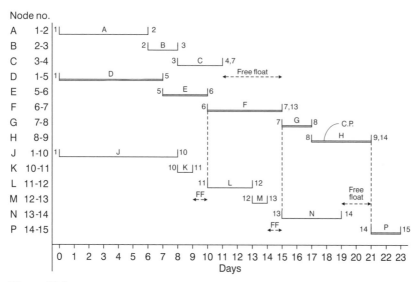

Figure 16.5

As with day no. method, if more than one activity has the same end node number, the one furthest to the right must be used as a starting time. Figure 16.4 shows the same network with the node numbers inserted and Figure 16.5 shows the bar chart generated using the node numbers.

Figure 16.6 shows a typical arrow diagram and Figure 16.7 shows a bar chart generated using the starting and finishing node numbers. Note that these node numbers have been listed on the left hand edge together with the durations to ease plotting.

Time for analysis

Probably the most time-consuming operations in bar chart preparation is the listing of the activity titles, and for this there is no short cut. The same time, in fact, must be expended typing the titles straight into the computer. However, in order to arrive at a quick answer it is only necessary at the initial stage to insert the node numbers, and once this listing has been done (together with the activity times) the analysis is very rapid. It is possible to determine the critical path for a 200-activity network (after the listing has been carried out) in less than an hour. The backward pass for ascertaining floats takes abut the same time.

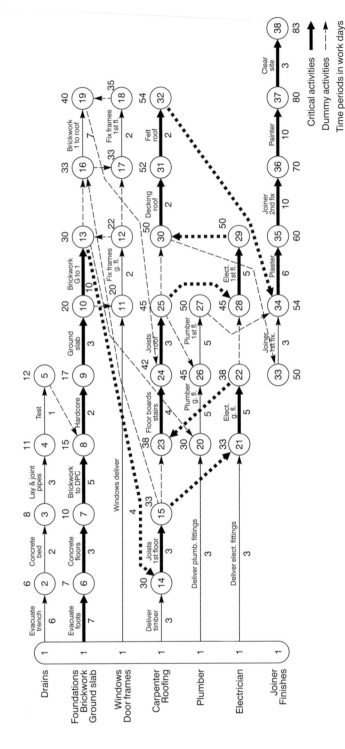

Figure 16.6

Activity	S	F	Time	Dummies	Floats	0 5 10 15 20 25 30 35 40 45 50 55 60 65 70 75 80 85
Excavate trench	1	2	6		3	
Concrete bed	2	3	2		3	
Lay & joint pipes	3	4	3		3	
Test	4	5	1	8,	3	
Excavate foots	4	6	7		0	
Concrete foots	6	7	3		0	
Brickwork to d.p.c	7	8	7		0	
Hardcore	8	9	2		0	
Ground slab	9	10	3	11,	0	
Brickwork g - 1	10	13	10	16, 20, 17, 14,	0	
Windows delivered	1	11	4		24	
Fix frames g. fl.	11	12	2	13, 14, 16, 17, 20,	8	
Deliver timber	1	14	3		27	
Joists 1st fl.	14	15	3	16, 21, 23, 17,	0	
Brickwork 1 - r	16	19	7	24,	0	
Fix frames 1st fl.	17	18	2	19, 24,	7	
Deliver plumb. ftgs	1	20	5		39	
Plumber g. fl.	20	26	5		14	
Deliver elec. ftgs	1	21	3		30	
Electric g. fl.	21	22	5	23, 28	0	
Floor boards stair	23	24	4	26, 28, 30, 33	0	
Joists roof	24	25	3		0	
Plumber 1st fl.	26	27	5	34,	4	
Electr. 1st fl.	28	29	5	30, 33	0	
Decking roof	30	31	2		0	
Felt roof	21	32	2	34,	0	
Joiner 1st fix	33	34	3		1	
Plasterer	34	35	6		0	
Joiner 2nd fix	35	36	10		0	
Painter	36	37	10		0	
Clear site	37	38	3		0	

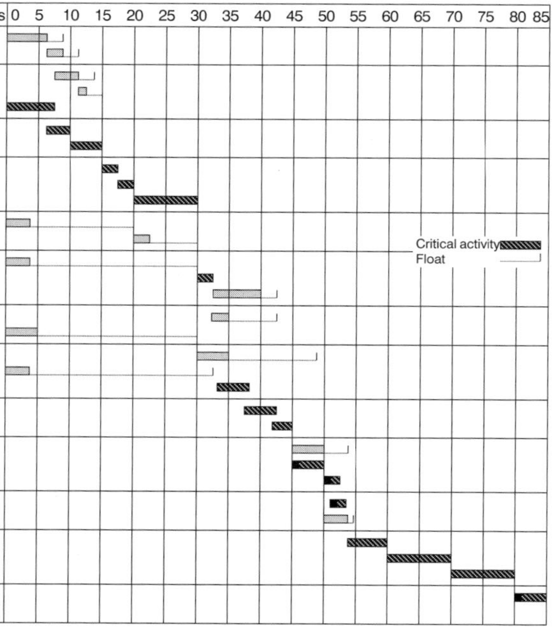

Critical activity
Float

Figure 16.7

Milestones

Important deadlines in a project programme are highlighted by specific points in time called *Milestones*. These are timeless activities usually at the beginning or end of a phase or stage and are used for monitoring purposes throughout the life of the project. Needless to say, they should be SMART, which is an acronym for Specific, Measurable, Achievable, Realistic, Timebound. Often milestones are used to act as trigger points for progress payments or deadlines for receipt of vital information, permits or equipment deliveries.

Milestone reports are a succinct way of advising top management of the status of the project and should act as a spur to the project team to meet these important deadlines. This is especially important if they relate to large tranches of progress payments.

Milestones are marked on bar charts or networks by a triangle or diamond and can be turned into a monitoring system in their own right when used in milestone *slip charts*, sometimes also known as *trend charts*.

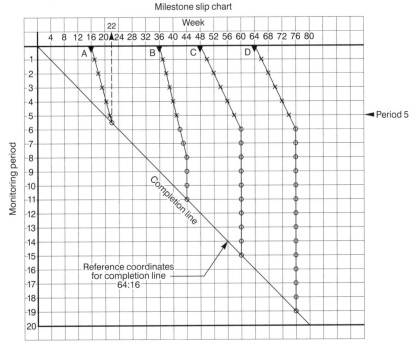

Figure 16.8

Figure 16.8 shows such a slip chart which was produced at reporting period 5 of a project. The top scale represents the project calendar and the vertical scale is the main reporting periods in terms of time. If both calendars are drawn to the same scale, a line drawn from the top left-hand corner to the bottom right-hand corner will be at 45° to the two axes.

The pre-planned milestones at the start of the project are marked on the top line with a black triangle (▼).

As the project progresses, the predicted or anticipated dates of achievement of the milestones are inserted so that the slippage (if any) can be seen graphically. This should then prompt management action to ensure that the subsequent milestones do not slip! At each reporting stage, the anticipated slippages of milestones as given by the programme are re-marked with an X while those that have not been re-programmed are marked with an O. Milestones which *have* been met will be on the diagonal and will be marked with a triangle (▽).

As the programmed slippage of each milestone is marked on the diagram, a pattern emerges which acts not only as a historical record of the slippages but can also be used to give a crude prediction of future milestone movements.

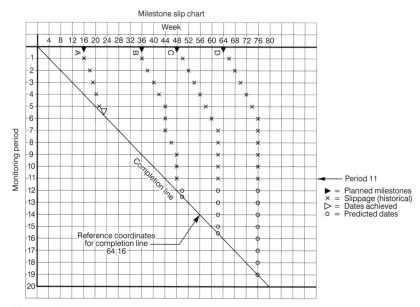

Figure 16.9

A slip chart showing the status at reporting period 11 is shown on Figure 16.9. It can be seen that milestone A was reached in week 22 instead of the original prediction of week 16. Milestones B, C and D have all slipped with the latest prediction for B being week 50, for C being week 62 and D being week 76. It will be noticed that before the reporting period 11, the programmed predictions are marked X and the future predictions, after week 11, are marked O.

If a milestone is not on the critical path, it may well slip on the slip chart without affecting the next milestone. However, if two adjacent milestones on the slip chart *are* on the critical path, any delay on the first one must cause a corresponding slippage on the second. If this is then marked on the slip chart, it will in effect become a prediction, which will then alert the project manager to take action.

Once the milestone symbol meets the diagonal line, the required deadline has been achieved.

Line of balance

Network analysis is essentially a technique for planning one-off projects, whether this is a construction site, a manufacturing operation, a computer software development, or a move to a new premises. When the overall project consists of a number of identical or batch operations, each of which may be a subproject in its own right, it may be of advantage to use a technique called *line of balance*.

The quickest way to explain how this planning method works is to follow a simple example involving the construction of four identical, small, single-storey houses of the type shown in Figure 28.1. For the sake of clarity, only the first five activities will be considered and it will be seen from Figure 28.2, that the last of the five activities, *E – 'floor joists'*, will be complete in week 9.

Assuming one has sufficient resources and space between the actual building plots, it is possible to start work on every house at the same time and therefore finish laying all the floor joists by week 9. However, in real life this is not possible, so the gang laying the foundations to house No. 1 will move to house No. 2 when foundation No. 1 is finished. When foundation No. 2 is finished, the gang will start No. 3 and so on. The same procedure will be carried out by all the following trades, until all the houses are finished.

Another practical device is to allow a time buffer between the trades so as to give a measure of flexibility and introduce a margin of error. Frequently

Table 16.1

Activity letter	Activity description	Adjusted duration (weeks)	Dependency	Total float (weeks)	Buffer (weeks)
A	Clear ground	2.0	Start	0	0.0
B	Lay foundations	2.8	A	0	0.2
C	Build dwarf walls	1.9	B	0	0.1
D	Oversite concrete	0.9	B	1	0.1
E	Floor joists	1.8	C and D	0	0.2

such a buffer will occur naturally for such reasons as hardening time of concrete, setting time of adhesive, drying time of plaster or paint.

Table 28.1, can now be partially redrawn showing in addition the buffer time, which was originally included in the activity duration. The new table is now shown in Table 16.1.

Figure 16.10 shows the relationship between the trades involved. Each trade (or activity) is represented by two lines. The distance between these lines is the duration of the activity. The distance between the activities is the buffer period. As can be seen, all the work of the activities A to E is carried out at the same rate, which means that for every house, enough resources are available for every trade to start as soon as its preceding trade is finished. This is shown to be the case in Figure 16.10.

However, if only one gang is available on the site for each trade, e.g. if only one gang of concretors laying the foundations (activity B) is available, concreting on house 2 cannot start until ground clearance (activity A) has been completed. The figure would then be as shown in Figure 16.11. If the number of concretors could be increased, so that two gangs were available on site, the foundations for house 2 could be started as soon as the ground had been cleared.

Building the dwarf wall (activity C) requires only 1.9 weeks per house, which is a faster rate of work than laying foundations. To keep the bricklaying gang going smoothly from one house to the next, work can only start on house 1 in week 7.2, i.e. after the buffer of about 2.5 weeks following the completion of the foundations of house 1. In this way, by the time the dwarf walls are started on house 4, the foundations (activity B) of house 4 will just have been finished. (In practice of course there would be a further buffer to allow the concrete to harden sufficiently for the bricklaying to start.)

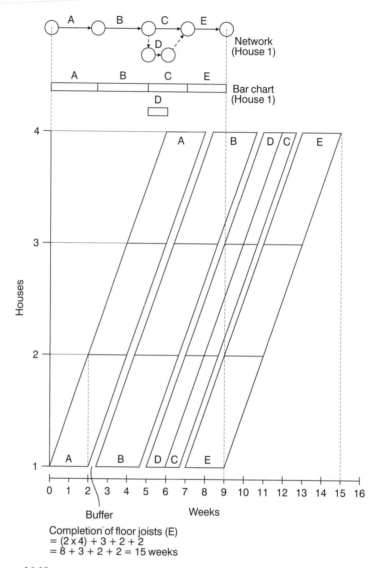

Figure 16.10

As the oversite concreting (activity D) only takes 0.9 weeks, the one gang of labourers doing this work will have every oversite completed well before the next house is ready for them. Their start date could be delayed if necessary by as much as 3.5 weeks, since apart from the buffer, this activity (D) has also 1 week float.

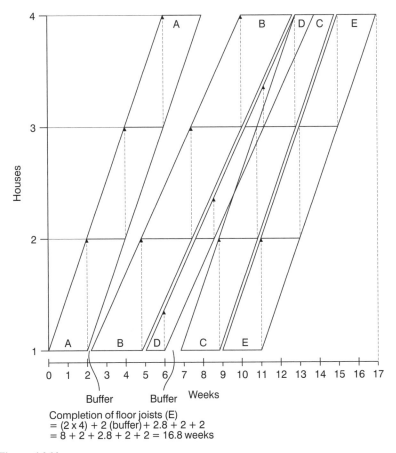

Completion of floor joists (E)
= (2 x 4) + 2 (buffer) + 2.8 + 2 + 2
= 8 + 2 + 2.8 + 2 + 2 = 16.8 weeks

Figure 16.11

It can be seen therefore from Figure 16.11 that by plotting these operations with the time as the horizontal axis and the number of houses as the vertical axis, the following becomes apparent.

If the slope of an operation is less (i.e. flatter) than the slope of the preceding operation, the chosen buffer is shown at the *start* of the operation. If, on the other hand, the slope of a succeeding operation is *steeper*, the buffer must be inserted at the *end* of the previous operation, since otherwize there is a possibility of the trades clashing when they get to the last house.

What becomes very clear from these diagrams is the ability to delay the start of an operation (and use the resources somewhere else) and still meet the overall project programme.

When the work is carried out by trade gangs, the movement of the gangs can be shown on the LoB chart by vertical arrows as indicated in Figure 16.11.

Readers who wish to obtain more information on LoB techniques are advised to obtain the booklet issued by the National Building Agency in 1968.

17

Computer analysis

Most manufacturers of computer hardware, and many suppliers of computer software, have written programs for analysing critical path networks using computers. While the various commercially available programs differ in detail, they all follow a basic pattern, and give, by and large, a similar range of outputs. In certain circumstances a contractor may be obliged by his contractual commitments to provide a computerized output report for his client. Indeed, when a client organization has standardized on a particular project management system for controlling the overall project, the contractor may well be required to use the same proprietary system so that the contractor's reports can be integrated into the overall project control system on a regular basis.

History

The development of network analysis techniques more or less coincided with that of the digital computer. The early network analysis programs were, therefore, limited by the storage and processing capacity of the computer as well as the input and output facilities.

The techniques employed mainly involved producing punched cards (one card for each activity) and feeding them into the machine via a card reader. These procedures were time consuming and tedious, and, because the punching of the cards was carried out by an operator who usually understood little of the program or its purpose, mistakes occurred which only became apparent after the printout was produced.

Even then, the error was not immediately apparent – only the effect. It then often took hours to scan through the reams of printout sheets before the actual mistake could be located and rectified. To add to the frustration of the planner, the new printout may still have given ridiculous answers because a second error was made on another card. In this way it often required several runs before a satisfactory output could be issued.

In an endeavour to eliminate punching errors attempts were made to use two separate operators, who punched their own set of input cards. The cards were then automatically compared and, if not identical, were thrown out, indicating an error. Needless to say, such a practice cost twice as much in manpower.

Because these early computers were large and very expensive, usually requiring their own air-conditioning equipment and a team of operators and maintenance staff, few commercial companies could afford them. Computer bureaux were therefore set up by the computer manufacturers or special processing companies, to whom the input sheets were delivered for punching, processing and printing.

The cost of processing was usually a lump sum fee plus x pence per activity. Since the computer could not differentiate between a real activity and a dummy one, planners tended to go to considerable pains to reduce the number of dummies to save cost. The result was often a logic sequence, which may have been cheap in computing cost but was very expensive in application, since frequently important restraints were overlooked or eliminated. In other words, the tail wagged the dog – a painful phenomenon in every sense. It was not surprising, therefore, that many organizations abandoned computerized network analysis or, even worse, discarded the use of network analysis altogether as being unworkable or unreliable.

There is no doubt that manual network analysis is a perfectly feasible alternative to using computers. Indeed, one of the largest petrochemical complexes in Europe was planned entirely using a series of networks, all of which were analysed manually.

continue. However, the basic outputs produced by the early mainframe machines are still the core of the output reports available. These are:

Total float (including the critical path for which the total float is obviously 0)
Preceding event (or preceding activity)
Activity number
Earliest start
Latest start
Earliest finish
Latest finish.

Of the above, the first four are the most useful. The total float shows the order of criticality, starting with the critical activities. As the float increases, the criticality reduces.

The preceding event report enables a particular activity to be found rapidly, since activities are listed in ascending order of preceding event numbers. When a grid system is used, the order is by ascending number of each horizontal band. For AON methods, preceding activity numbers are given.

The activity number report is useful when the critical path program is related to a cost analysis system, such as SMAC. The time and cost position can therefore be found for any particular activity in which one may be interested. The earliest start report is used primarily to find all the activities which should be started (as early as possible) by a required date. The chronological listing of earliest starts enables this be found very rapidly.

The actual format of the reports is slightly different for every software company, and in most cases can be produced in bar chart format as well as being grouped by report code, i.e. a separate report for each discipline, department, sub-contractor, etc. These report codes can, of course, be edited to contain only such information as is required (or considered to be necessary) by the individual departments.

It is recommended that the decision to produce any but the most basic printouts, as well as any printouts in report code, be delayed until the usefulness of a report has been studied and discussed with department managers. There is always a danger with computer outputs that recipients request more reports than they can digest, merely because they know they are available at the press of a button. Too much paper becomes self-defeating, since the very bulk frightens the reader to the extent of it not being read at all.

With the proliferation of the personal computer (PC) and the expansion of IT, especially the Internet, many of the projects management techniques can now be carried out on-line. The use of e-mail and the Intranet allows information to be distributed to the many stakeholders of a project almost instantaneously. Where time is important – and it nearly always is – such a fast distribution of data or instructions can be of enormous benefit to the project manager. It does, however, require all information to be carefully checked before dissemination precisely because so many people receive it at the same time. It is an unfortunate fact that computer errors are more serious for just this reason as well as the naive belief that computers are infallible.

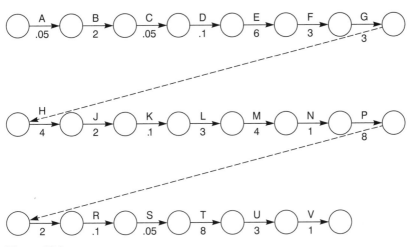

Figure 18.1

margin or float in the journey to the station. This float is, of course, the difference between the time taken to walk and run to the station. In other words, the path is not as critical as it might appear, i.e. we have not in our original sequence – or network – pared each activity down to its minimum duration. We had something up our sleeve.

However, let us suppose that we cannot run to the station because we have a bad knee; how then can we make up lost time? This is where network analysis comes in. Let us look at the activities succeeding the making of toast (L) and see how we can make up the lost time of, say, two minutes. The remaining activities are:

		Times (min)
M	fry eggs	4.0
N	serve breakfast	1.0
P	eat breakfast	8.0
Q	clean shoes	2.0
R	kiss wife goodbye	0.10
S	don coat	0.05
T	walk to station	8.0
U	queue and buy ticket	3.0
V	board train	1.0
		27.15

The total time taken to perform these activities is 27.15 minutes.

The first question therefore is, have we any activity which is unnecessary? Yes. We need not kiss the wife goodbye. But this only saves us 0.1 minute and the saving is of little benefit. Besides, it could have serious repercussions. The second question must therefore be, are there any activities which we can perform simultaneously? Yes. We can clean our shoes while the eggs fry. The network shown in Figure 18.2 can thus be redrawn as demonstrated in Figure 18.3. The total now from M to V adds up to 25.15 minutes. We have, therefore, made up our lost two minutes without apparent extra effort. All we have to do is to move the shoe-cleaning box to a position in the kitchen where we can keep a sharp eye on the eggs while they fry.

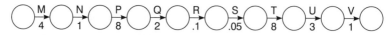

Figure 18.2

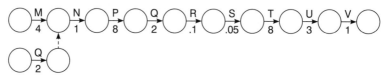

Figure 18.3

Encouraged by this success, let us now re-examine the whole operation to see how else we can save a few minutes, since a few moments extra in bed are well worth saving. Let us therefore see what other activities can be performed simultaneously:

1 We could brush our teeth under the shower;
2 We could put the kettle on before we shaved so that it boils while we shave;
3 We could make the toast while the kettle boils or while we fry the eggs;
4 We could forget about the ticket and pay the ticket collector at the other end;
5 We can clean our shoes while the eggs fry as previously discussed.

Having considered the above list, we eliminate (1) since it is not nice to spit into the bath tub, and (4) is not possible because we have an officious guard on our barrier. Se we are left with (2), (3) and (5). Let us see what our network looks like now (Figure 18.4). The total duration of the operation or

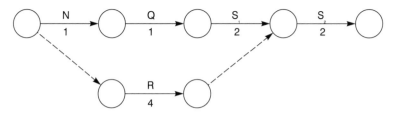

Figure 18.8

S (fit internal lining) and doing two days' work while the shelves and cupboards are being built. The network of this section would, therefore, appear as in Figure 18.8. We have saved two days provided that labour can be made available to start insulating the rafters.

If we adjudicate the bids (F) before waiting for planning permission, we can save another two days. This section of the network will, therefore, appear as in Figure 18.9.

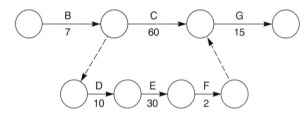

Figure 18.9

Total saving to this stage is 2 + 2 = 4 days. We have to find another eight days, so let us look at the activities which take longest: C (obtaining planning permission) cannot be reduced since it is outside our control. It is very difficult to hurry a local authority. G (builder delivers materials) is difficult to reduce since the builders will require a reasonable mobilization period to buy materials and allocate resources. However, if we select the builder before planning permission has been received, and we do, after all, have 18 days float in loop D-E-F, we may be able to get him to place preliminary orders for the materials required first, and thus enable work to be started a little earlier. We may have to guarantee to pay the cost for this material if planning permission is not granted, but as time is of the essence we are prepared to take the risk. The saving could well be anything from one to 15 days.

Let us assume we can realistically save five days. We have now reduced the programme by 2 + 2 + 5 = 9 days. The remaining days can now only be saved by reducing the actual durations of some of the activities. This means more resources and hence more money. However, the rich uncle cannot be put off, so we offer to increase the contract sum if the builder can manage to reduce V, T, W and X by one day each, thus saving three days altogether. It should be noted that we only save three days although we have reduced the time of four activities by one day each. This is, of course, because V and T are carried out in parallel, but our overall period – for very little extra cost – is now 96 days, a saving of 60 days or 38%.

Example 3

This example from the IT industry, uses the AoN (precedence) method of network drafting. This is now the standard method for this industry, probably because of the influence of MS Project and because networks in IT are relatively small, when compared to the very large networks in construction which can have between two hundred and several thousand activities. The principles are of course identical.

A supermarket requires a new stock control system linked to a new check-out facility. This involves removing the existing check-out, designing and manufacturing new hardware and writing new software for the existing computer, which will be retained.

The main activities and durations (all in days) for this project are as follows:

		Days
A	Obtain brief from client (the supermarket owner)	1
B	Discuss the brief	2
C	Conceptual design	7
D	Feasibility study	3
E	Evaluation	2
F	Authorization	1
G	System design	12
H	Software development	20
J	Hardware design	40
K	Hardware manufacture	90
L	Hardware delivery (transport)	2
M	Removal of existing check-out	7
N	Installation of new equipment	6
P	Testing on site	4
Q	Hand over	1
R	Trial operation	7
S	Close out	1

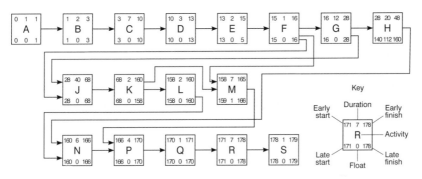

Figure 18.10 (Duration in days)

The network for this project is shown in Figure 18.10, from which it can be seen that there are virtually no parallel activities, so that only two activities, M (Removal of existing check-out) and H (Software development) have any float. However, the float of M is only 1 day, so that for all intents and purposes it is also critical. It may be possible, however, to start J (Hardware design) earlier, after G (System design) is 50% complete. This change is shown on the network in Figure 18.11. As a result of this change, the overall project period has been reduced from 179 days to 173 days. It could be argued that the existing check-out (M) could be removed earlier, but the client quite rightly wants to make sure that the new equipment is ready for dispatch before removing the old one. As the software developed under H is only required in time for the start of the installation (N), there is still plenty of float (106 days), even after the earlier start of hardware design (J) to make sure everything is ready for the installation of the new equipment (N).

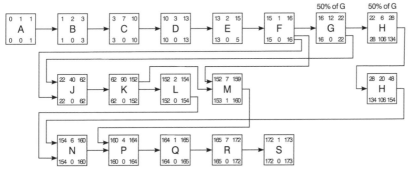

Figure 18.11 (Duration in days)

In practice, this means that the start of software development (H) could be delayed if the resources allocated to H are more urgently required by another project.

Summary of operation

The three examples given are, of course, very small simple programmes, but they do show the steps that have to be taken to get the best out of network analysis. These are:

1 Draw up a list of activities and anticipated durations;
2 Make as many activities as possible run in parallel;
3 Examine new sequences after the initial network has been drawn;
4 Start a string of activities as early as possible and terminate as late as possible;
5 Split activities into two or more steps if necessary;
6 If time is vital, reduce durations by paying more for extra resources;
7 Always look for new techniques in the construction or operation being programmed.

It is really amazing what savings can be found after a few minutes' examination, especially after a good night's sleep.

that logic changes can be discussed and provisionally agreed right away. On a site, where the contract has been divided into a number of operational areas, this method is particularly useful since area managers are notorious for shunning paperwork – especially reports. Even very large projects can be controlled in this manner, and the personal contact again helps to generate the close relationship and involvement so necessary for good morale.

Where an efficient cost reporting system is in operation, and provided that this is geared to the network, the feedback for the programme can be combined with the weekly cost report information issued in the field or shop.

A good example of this is given in Chapter 27, which describes the SMAC Cost Control System. In this system, the cost control and cost reporting procedures are based on the network so that the percentage complete of an operation can be taken from the site returns and entered straight onto the network. The application of SMAC is particularly interesting, since the network can be manually analysed while the cost report is produced by a computer, both using the same database.

One of the greatest problems found by main contractors is the submission of updated programmes from subvendors or subcontractors. Despite clauses in the purchase order or subcontract documents, requiring the vendor to return a programme within a certain number of weeks of order date and update it monthly, many vendors just do not comply. Even if programmes are submitted as requested, they vary in size and format from a reduced computer printout to a crude bar chart, which shows activities possibly useful to the vendor but quite useless to the main contractor or client.

One reason for this production of unsatisfactory information is that the main contractor (or consultant) was not specific enough in the contract documents setting out exactly what information is required and when it is needed. To overcome this difficulty, the simplest way is to give the vendor a pre-printed bar chart form as part of the contract documents, together with a list of suggested activities which *must* appear on the programme.

A pre-printed table, as drawn in Figure 19.5, shows by the letter X which activities are important for monitoring purposes, for typical items of equipment or materials. The list can be modified by the vendor and obviously each main contractor can draw up his own requirements depending on the type of industry he is engaged in, but the basic requirements from setting out drawings to final test certificates are included. The dates by which some of the key documents are required should, of course, be given in the purchase order or contract document, since they may be linked to stage payments and/or penalties.

The advantage of the main contractor requesting the programme to be produced to his own format, a copy of which is shown in Figure 19.6, is that:

1 All the returned programmes are of the same size and type and can be more easily interpreted and filed by the main contractor's staff.
2 Where the vendor is unsophisticated, the main contractor's programme is of educational value to the vendor.
3 Since the format is ready-made, the vendor's work is reduced and will be returned by him earlier.
4 Since all the programmes are on A4 size paper, they can be reproduced and distributed more easily and speedily.

To ensure that the vendor understood the principles and used the correct method for populating the completed bar chart, an instruction sheet as shown in Figure 19.7 was attached to the blank bar chart.

Figure 19.5 Suggested activities for a manufacturer's bar chart

	Pumps	Heat exchanger	Air fins	Compress and turbines	Vessels towers	Valves	Struct. steel	Instr. panels	Large motors	Switchgear MCC invertors	Transformers	Fans	Pipe work
Drawings A – Setting plans	X	X	X	X	X	X	X	X	X	X	X	X	X
Drawings B – As specified	X	X	X	X	X	X	X	X	X	X	X	X	X
Drawings C – (Final)	X	X	X	X	X	X	X	X	X	X	X	X	X
Foster Wheeler Eng. cut-off	X	X	X	X	X	X	X	X	X	X	X		X
Place sub-orders	X	X	X	X	X	X	X	X	X	X	X	X	X
Receive forgings		X		X	X								X
Receive plate		X			X		X						
Receive seals	X			X		X	X		X			X	
Receive couplings	X		X	X									
Receive gauges/instrum.								X		X	X		
Receive tubes/fittings	X	X	X	X	X						X	X	X
Receive bearings	X		X			X			X			X	
Receive motor/actuator	X		X	X		X							
Casting of casing	X			X					X			X	
Casting impeller	X			X								X	
Casting bedplate	X			X								X	
Machine casting	X		X	X					X			X	
Machine impeller	X		X	X					X			X	
Machine flanges	X	X	X	X	X	X						X	
Machine gears	X			X					X			X	
Machine shaft	X		X	X		X			X			X	
Assemble rotor	X		X	X					X			X	
Assemble equipment	X	X	X	X	X	X		X	X	X		X	
Weld frame/supports		X	X	X			X	X	X	X			
Roll and weld shell		X			X	X	X	X	X	X			
Drill tube plate		X											
Form dished ends		X			X								
Weld/roll tubes		X	X										X
Weld nozzles	X	X	X	X	X	X							
Fit internals					X						X		
Access platforms			X	X									
Light presswork/guards	X	X					X	X		X		X	
Heat treatment					X								
Wiring								X	X	X	X		
Windings									X		X		
Lube-oil system	X		X	X					X			X	
Control system				X				X					
Galvanizing/plating	X				X	X	X	X	X	X	X	X	X
Painting/priming	X	X	X	X	X	X	X	X	X	X	X	X	X
Testing pressure/mech.	X	X	X	X	X	X		X	X	X	X	X	X
Testing witness/perform.	X	X	X	X	X		X	X	X	X	X	X	X
Prepare despatch	X	X	X	X	X	X		X	X	X	X	X	X
Data books/oper. instructions	X	X	X	X	X	X	X	X	X	X	X	X	X
Weld procedures	X	X	X	X	X	X		X	X	X	X	X	X
Spares schedules	X	X	X	X	X	X	X	X	X	X	X	X	X
Test certs	X	X	X	X	X	X	X	X	X	X	X	X	X

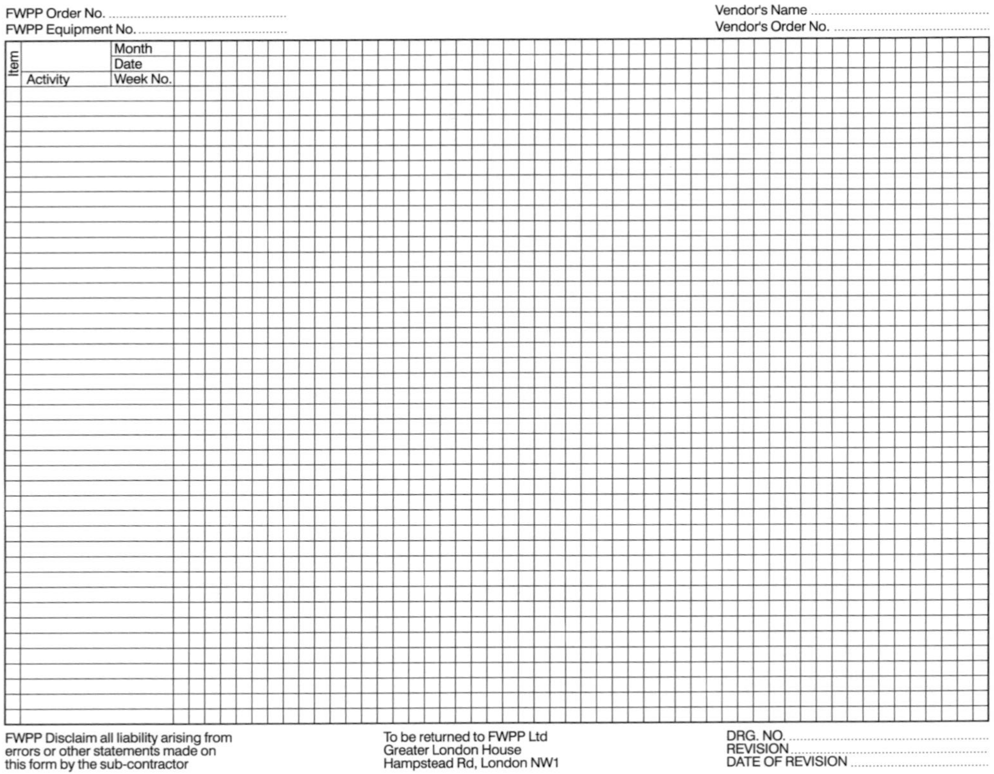

FWPP Order No. ....
FWPP Equipment No. ....

Item	Month																													
	Date																													
Activity	Week No.																													

Vendor's Name ....
Vendor's Order No. ....

To be returned to FWPP Ltd
Greater London House
Hampstead Rd, London NW1

FWPP Disclaim all liability arising from
errors or other statements made on
this form by the sub-contractor

DRG. NO. ....
REVISION ....
DATE OF REVISION ....

Figure 19.6 Manufacturer's bar chart

Foster Wheeler Power Products Ltd

*Instructions to vendors for completing
FWPP's standard programme format*

1 Vendors are required to complete a Manufacturing Programme using the FWPP Standard Bar Chart form enclosed herewith.

2 The block on the top at the page given the FWPP Order Number, FWPP Equipment Number, Vendor's Name and Vendor's Order Number will be filled in by FWPP Purchasing Department at time of order issue.

3 Where a starting date is not known, Vendors must give the programme in week numbers with Week 1 as the date of the order. Subsequently, after order has been placed, the correct FWPP Week Number must be substituted together with the corresponding calendar date.

4 The left-hand column headed 'Activity' must be filled in by the Vendor showing the various stages of the manufacturing process. This should start with production of the necessary drawings requested in the Purchase Order document and continue through various stages of materials arriving at the Vendor's works, manufacuturing stages, assembly stages, testing stages and ending with actual delivery date.

5 For the benefit of vendors the attached Table shows some typical stages which FWPP Expeditors will be monitoring but it must be emphasized that these are for guidance only and must be amended or augmented by the Vendor to suit his method of production.

The Table consists of eleven (11) common items of equipment normally associated with Petrochemical Plants and where an item of equipment does not fall into one of these categories, vendors are required to build up their own detailed lists.

6 Activities with a duration of one (1) week or more should be represented by a thick line

    thus: ████████████████

while shorter activities or specific events such as cut-off dates or despatch dates should be shown by a triangle

          despatch
    thus: ▽

7 This programme must be returned to FWPP within three (3) weeks of receiving the Purchase Order.

Figure 19.7

20

The case for manual analysis

Although network analysis is applicable to almost every type of organization as shown by the examples in Chapter 23, most of the planning functions described in this book have been confined to those related to engineering construction projects. The activities described cover the full spectrum of operations from the initial design stage, through detailing of drawings and manufacture, up to and including construction. In other words, from conception to handover.

In this age of specialization there is a trend to create specialist groups to do the work previously carried out by the members of more conventional disciplines. One example is teaching where teaching methods, previously devized and perfected by practising teachers, are now developed by a new group of people called educationalists.

Another example of specialization is planning. In the days of bar charts, planning was carried out by engineers or production staff using well-known techniques to record their ideas on paper and transmit them to other members of the team. Nowadays, however, the specialist planner or scheduler has come to the fore, leaving the engineer time to get on with his engineering.

The planner

Planning in its own right does not exist. It is always associated with another activity or operation, i.e. design planning, construction planning, production planning, etc. It is logical, therefore, that a design planner should be or should have been a designer, a construction planner should be familiar with construction methods and techniques, and a production planner should be knowledgeable in the process and manufacturing operations of production – whether it be steelwork, motors cars or magazines.

As long as the specialist planner has graduated from one of the accepted engineering disciplines and is familiar with the problems of a particular project, a realistic network will probably be produced. By calling in specialists to advise him in the fields with which he is not completely conversant, he can ensure that the network will be received with confidence by all the interested parties.

The real problem arises when the planner has not the right background, i.e. when he has not spent a period on a drawing board or has not experienced the hold-ups and frustrations of a construction site. Strangely enough, the less familiar a planner is with the job he is planning, the less he is inclined to seek help. This may well be due to his inability to ask the right questions, or he may be reluctant to discuss technical matters for fear or revealing his own lack of knowledge. One thing is certain, a network which is not based on sound technical knowledge is not realistic, and an unrealistic network is dangerous and costly, since decisions may well be made for the wrong reasons.

All that has been said so far is a truism which can be applied not only to planning but to any human activity where experts are necessary in order to achieve acceptable results. However, in most disciplines it does not take long for the effects of an inexperienced assistant to be discovered, mainly because the results of his work can be monitored and assessed within a relatively short time period. In planning, however, the effects of a programme decision may not be felt for months, so that it may be very difficult to ascertain the cause of the subsequent problem or failure.

The role of the computer

Unfortunately, the use of computers – especially the large mainframe machines – has enabled inexperienced planners to produce impressive outputs which are frequently utterly useless. Precisely because the computing industry has created an aura of awe and admiration around itself, anyone who familiarizes himself with the right jargon can give an impression of considerable knowledge – for a time at least.

There is a great danger in shifting the emphasis from the creation of the network to the analysis by machine, so that many people believe that to carry out an analysis of a network one must have a computer. In fact, of course, the very opposite is true. The kernel of network analysis is the drafting, checking, refining and redrafting of the network itself, an operation which must be carried out by a team of experienced participants of the job being planned. To understand this statement, it is necessary to go through the stages of network preparation and subsequent updating.

Preparation of the network

The first function of the planner in conjunction with the project manager is to divide the project into manageable blocks. The name is appropriate since, like building blocks, they can be handled by themselves, shaped to suit the job, but are still only a part of the whole structure to be built.

The number and size of each block is extremely important since, if correctly chosen, a block can be regarded as an entity which suits both the design and the construction phases of a project. Ideally, the complexity of each block should be about the same, but this is rarely possible in practice since other criteria such as systems and geographical location have to be considered. If a block is very complex, it can be broken down further, but a more convenient solution may be to produce more than one network for such a block. The aim should be to keep the number of activities down to 200–300 so that they can be analysed manually if necessary.

As the planner sketches his logic roughly, and in pencil on the back of an old drawing, the construction specialists are asked to comment on the type and sequence of the activities. In practice, these sessions – if properly run – generate an enthusiasm that is a delight to experience. Often consecutive activities can be combined to simplify the network, thus easing the subsequent analysis. Gradually the job is 'built', difficulties are encountered and overcome, and even specialists who have never been involved in network planning before are carried away by this visual unfolding of the programme.

The next stage is to ask each specialist to suggest the duration of the activities in his discipline. These are entered onto the network without question. Now comes the moment of truth. Can the job be built on time? With all the participants present, the planner adds up the durations and produces his

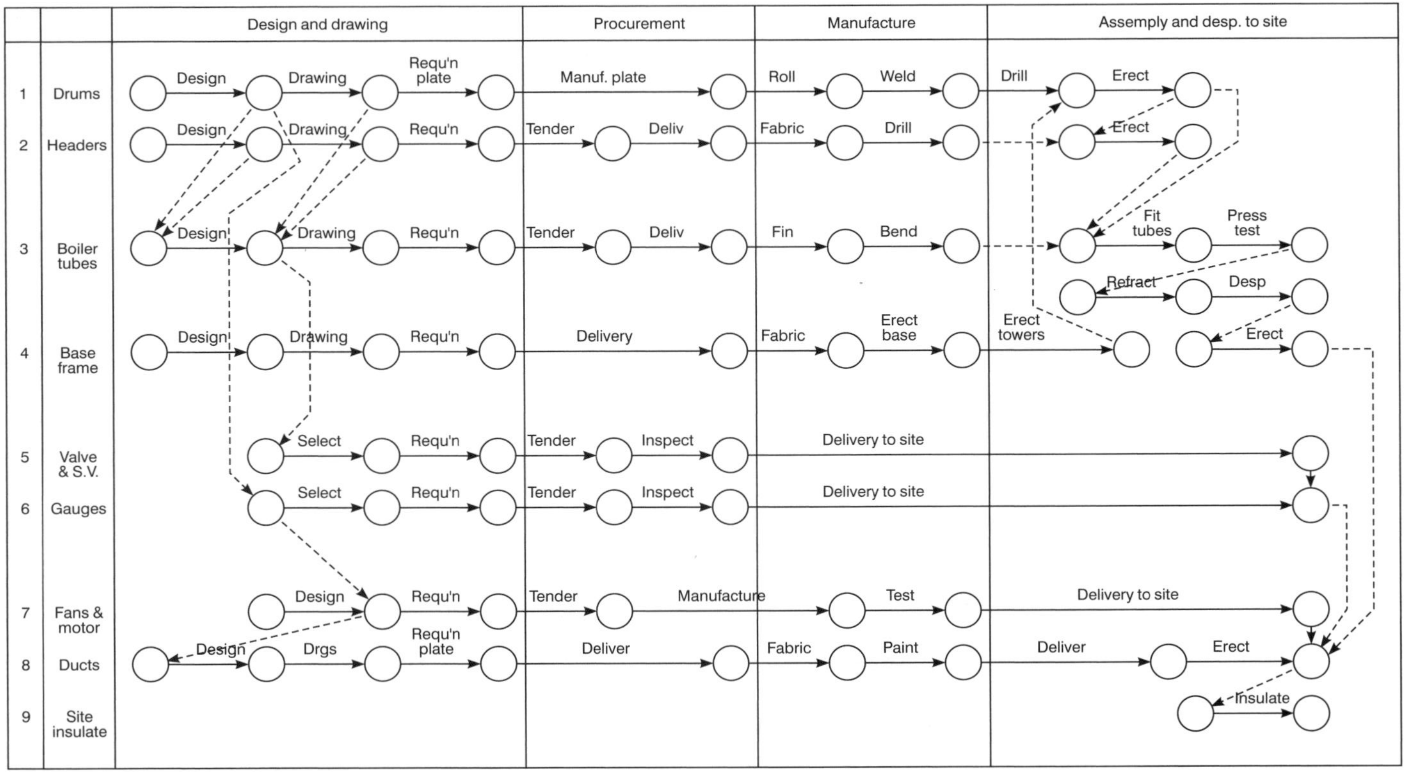

Figure 21.5 Simplified boiler network

required first to service an existing operational unit, it would be prudent to draw a network which is based on (4) (operational systems) but incorporating also (5) (stages of completion). In practice, (3) (geographical proximity) would almost certainly be equally relevant since the water treatment plant and boiler plant would be adjacent.

It must be emphasized that the networks shown in Figures 21.1 to 21.4 are representative only and do not show the necessary inter-relationships or degree of detail normally shown on a practical construction network. The oversimplication on these diagrams may in fact contradict some of the essential requirements discussed in other sections of this book, but it is hoped that the main point, i.e. the differences between the various types of construction network formats, has been highlighted.

Banding

If we study Figure 21.1 we note that it is very easy to find a particular activity on the network. For example, if we wanted to know how long it would take to excavate the foundations of exchanger B, we would look down the column EXCAVATE until we found the line EXCHANGER B, and the intersection of this column and line shows the required excavation activity. This simple identification process was made possible because the diagram in Figure 21.1 was drawn using very crude subdivisions or bands to separate the various operations.

For certain types of work this splitting of the network into sections can be of immense assistance in finding required activities. By listing the various types of equipment or materials vertically on the drawing paper and writing the operations to be performed horizontally, one produces a grid of activities which almost defines the activity. In some instances the line of operations may be replaced by a line of departments involved. For example, the electrical department involvement in the design of a piece of equipment can be found by reading across the equipment line until one comes to the electrical department column.

The principle is shown clearly in Figure 21.5, and it can be seen that the idea can be applied to numerous types of networks. A few examples of banding networks are given below, but these are for guidance only since the actual selection of bands depends on the type of work to be performed and the degree of similarity of operation between the different equipment items.

Vertical listing (Horizontal line)	Horizontal listing (Vertical column)
Equipment	Operations
Equipment	Departments
Material	Operations
Design stages	Departments
Construction stages	Subcontracts
Decision stages	Departments
Approvals	Authorities (clients)
Operations	Department responsibilities
Operations	Broad time periods

It may, of course, be advantageous to reverse the vertical and horizontal bands; when considering, for example, the fifth item on the list, the subcontracts could be listed vertically and the construction stages horizontally. This would most likely be the case when the subcontractors perform similar operations since the actual work stages would then follow logically across the page in the form of normally timed activities. It may indeed be beneficial to draw a small trial network of a few (say, 20–30) activities to establish the best banding configuration.

It can be seen that banding can be combined with the coordinate method of numbering by simply allocating a group of letters of the horizontal coordinates to a particular band.

Banding is particularly beneficial on master networks which cover, by definition, a number of distinct operations or areas, such as design, manufacture, construction and commissioning. Figure 21.5 is an example of such a network.

22

Project management and planning

Responsibilities of the project managers

It is not easy to define the responsibilities of a project manager, mainly because the scope covered by such a position varies not only from industry to industry but also from one company to another. Three areas of responsibility, however, are nearly always part of the project manager's brief:

1 He must build the job to specification and to satisfy the operational requirements.
2 He must complete the project on time.
3 He must build the job within previously established budgetary constraints.

The last two are, of course, connected: generally, it can be stated that if the job is on schedule, either the cost has not exceeded the budget or good grounds exist for claiming any extra costs from the client. It is far more difficult to obtain extra cash if the programme has been exceeded and the client has also suffered loss due to the delay.

Time, therefore, is vitally important, and the control of time, whether at the design stage or the construction stage, should be a matter of top priority with the project manager. It is surprising, therefore, that so few project managers are fully conversant with the mechanics of network analysis and its advantages over other systems. Even if it had no other function but to act as a polarizing communication document, it would justify its use in preference to other methods.

Information from network

A correctly drawn network, regularly updated, can be used to give vital information and has the following beneficial effects on the project.

1 It enables the interaction of the various activities to be shown graphically and clearly.
2 It enables spare time or float to be found where it exists so that advantage can be taken to reduce resources if necessary.
3 It can pinpoint potential bottlenecks and trouble spots.
4 It enables conflicting priorities to be resolved in the most economical manner.
5 It gives an up-to-date picture of progress.
6 It acts as a communication document between all disciplines and parties.
7 It shows all parties the intent of the method of construction.
8 It acts as a focus for discussion at project meetings.
9 It can be expanded into subnets showing greater detail or contracted to show the chief overall milestones.
10 If updated in coloured pencil, it can act as a spur between rival gangs of workers.
11 It is very rapid and cheap to operate and is a base for EVA.
12 It is quickly modified if circumstances warrant it.
13 It can be used when formulating claims, as evidence of disruption due to late decisions or delayed drawings and equipment.
14 Networks of past jobs can be used to draft proposal networks for future jobs.
15 Networks stimulate discussion provided everyone concerned is familiar with them.
16 It can assist in formulating a cash-flow chart to minimize additional funding.

To get the maximum benefit from networks, a project manager should be able to read them as a musician reads music. He should feel the slow movements and the crescendos of activities and combine these into a harmonious flow until the grand finale is reached.

To facilitate the use of networks at discussions, the sheets should be reduced photographically to A3 (approximately 42 cm × 30 cm). In this way, a network can be folded once and kept in a standard A4 file, which tends to increase its usage. Small networks can, of course, be drawn on A3 or A4 size sheets in the first place, thus saving the cost of subsequent reduction in size.

It is often stated that networks are not easily understood by the man in the field, the area manager or the site foreman. This argument is usually supported by statements that the field men were brought up on bar charts and can, therefore, understand them fully, or that they are confused by all the computer printouts, which take too long to digest. Both statements are true. A bar chart is easy to understand and can easily be updated by hatching or colouring in the bars. It is also true that computer output sheets are overwhelming by their sheer bulk and complexity, and the man on the site just cannot afford the time leafing through reams of paper. Even if the output is restricted to a discipline report, only applicable to the person in question, confusion is often caused by the mass of data on earliest and latest starting and finishing times and on the various types of float. As is so often the case, network analysis and computerization are regarded as being synonymous, and the drawbacks of the latter are then invoked (often quite unwittingly) to discredit the former.

The writer's experience, however, contradicts the argument that site people cannot or will not use networks. On the contrary, once the foreman understands and appreciates what a network can do, he will prefer it to a bar chart. This is illustrated by the following example, which describes an actual situation on a contract.

Site-preparation contract

The job described was a civil engineering contract comprising the construction of oversite base slabs, roads, footpaths and foul and stormwater sewers for a large municipal housing scheme consisting of approximately 250 units. The main contractor, who confined his site activities to the actual house building, was anxious to start work as soon as possible to get as much done before the winter months. It was necessary, therefore, to provide him with good roads and a fully drained site.

Contract award was June and the main contractor was programmed to start building operations at the end of November the same year. To enable this quite short civil-engineering stage to be completed on time, it was decided to split the site into four main areas which could be started at about the same time. The size and location of these areas was dictated by such considerations as access points, site clearance (including a considerable area of woodland), natural drainage and house-building sequence.

Once this principle was established by management, the general site foreman was called in to assist in the preparation of the network, although it was known that he had never even heard of, let alone worked to, a critical path programme.

After explaining the basic principles of network techniques, the foreman was asked where he would start work, what machines he would use, which methods of excavation and construction he intended to follow, etc. As he explained his methods, the steps were recorded on the back of an old drawing print by the familiar method of lines and node points (arrow diagram). Gradually a network was evolved which grew before his eyes and his previous fears and scepticism began to melt away.

When the network of one area was complete, the foreman was asked for the anticipated duration of each activity. Each answer was religiously entered on the network without query, but when the forward pass was made, the overall period exceeded the contract period by several weeks. The foreman looked worried, but he was now involved. He asked to be allowed to review some of his durations and reassess some of the construction methods. Without being pressurized, the man, who had never used network analysis before, began the process that makes network analysis so valuable, i.e. he reviewed and refined the plan until it complied with the contractual requirements. The exercize was repeated with the three other areas, and the following day the whole operation was explained to the four chargehands who were to be responsible for those areas.

Four separate networks were then drawn, together with four corresponding bar charts. These were pinned on the wall of the site hut with the instruction that one of the programmes, either networks or bar chart, be updated daily. Great stress was laid on the need to update regularly, since it is the monitoring of the programme that is so often neglected once the plan has been drawn. The decision on which of the programmes was used for recording progress was left to the foreman, and it is interesting to note that the network proved to be the format he preferred.

Since each chargehand could compare the progress in his area with that of the others, a competitive spirit developed quite spontaneously to the delight of management. The result was that the job was completed four weeks ahead of schedule without additional cost. These extra weeks in October were naturally extremely valuable to the main contractor, who could get more units weatherproof before the cold period of January to March. The network was also used to predict cash flow, which proved to be remarkably accurate. (The principles of this are explained in Chapter 26.)

It can be seen, therefore, that in this instance a manual network enabled the project manager to control both the programme (time) and the cost of the job with minimum paperwork. This was primarily because the men who actually carried out the work in the field were involved and were convinced of the usefulness of the network programme.

Confidence in plan

It is vitally important that no one, but no one, associated with a project must lose faith in the programme or the overall plan. It is one of the prime duties of a project manager to ensure that this faith exists. Where small cracks do appear in this vital bridge of understanding between the planning department and the operational departments, the project manager must do everything in his power to close them before they become chasms of suspicion and despondency. It may be necessary to re-examine the plan, or change the planner, or hold a meeting explaining the situation to all parties, but a plan in which the participants have no faith is not worth the paper it is drawn on.

Having convinced all parties that the network is a useful control tool, the project manager must now ensure that it is kept up to date and the new information transmitted to all the interested parties as quickly as possible. This requires exerting a constant pressure on the planning department, or planning engineer, to keep to the 'issue deadlines', and equally leaning on the operational departments to return the feedback documents regularly. To do this, the project manager must use a combination of education, indoctrination, charm and rank pulling, but the feedback *must* be returned as regularly as the issue of the company's pay cheque.

The returned document might only say 'no change', but if this vital link is neglected, the network ceases to be a live document. The problem of feedback for the network is automatically solved when using the SMAC cost control system (explained in Chapter 27), since the manhour returns are directly related to activities, thus giving a very accurate percentage completion of each activity.

It would be an interesting and revealing experience to carry out a survey among project managers of large projects to obtain their unbiased opinion on the effectiveness of networks. Most of the managers with whom this problem was discussed felt that there was some merit in network techniques, but, equally, most of them complained that too much paper was being generated by the planning department.

Network and method statements

More and more clients and consultants require contractors to produce method statements as part of their construction documentation. Indeed, a method statement for certain complex operations may be a requirement of ISO 9000 Part I. A method statement is basically an explanation of the sequence of operations augmented by a description of the resources (i.e. cranes and other tackle) required for the job. It must be immediately apparent that a network can be of great benefit, not only in explaining the sequence of operations to the client but also for concentrating the writer's mind when the sequence is committed to paper. In the same way as the designer produces a freehand sketch of his ideas, so a construction engineer will be able to draw a freehand network to crystallize his thoughts.

The degree of detail will vary with the complexity of the operation and the requirements of the client or consultant, but it will always be a clear graphical representation of the sequences, which can replace pages of narrative. Any number of activities can be 'extracted' from the network for further explanation or in-depth discussion in the accompanying written statement.

The network, which can be produced manually or by computer, will mainly follow conventional lines and can, of course, be in arrow diagram or precedence format. For certain operations, however, such as structural steelwork erection, it may be advantageous to draw the network in the form of a table, where the operations (erect column, erect beam, plumb and level, etc.) are in horizontal rows. In this way, a highly organized, easy-to-read network can be produced. Examples of such a procedure are shown in Figures 22.1 and 22.2. There are doubtless other situations where this system can be adopted, but the prime objective must always be clarity and ease of understanding. Complex networks only confuse clients, and reflect a lack of appreciation of the advantages of method statements.

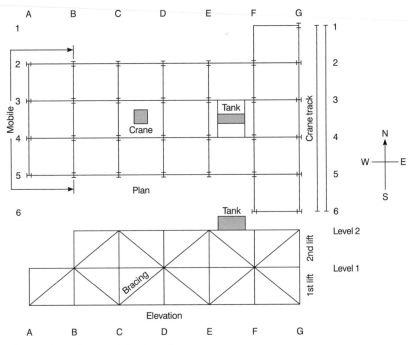

Figure 22.1 Structural framing plan

Integrated systems

The trend is to produce and operate integrated project management systems. By using the various regular inputs generated by the different operating departments, these systems can, on demand, give the project manager an up-to-date status report of the job in terms of time, cost and resources. This facility is particularly valuable once the project has reached the construction stage. The high cost of mainframe machines and the unreliability of regular feedback – even with the use of terminals – has held back the full utilization of computing facilities in the field, especially in remote sites. The PCs, with their low cost, mobility and ease of operation, have changed all this so that effective project control information can be generated on the spot.

The following list shows the type of management functions which can be successfully carried out either in the office, workshop or on a site by a single computer installation:

    cost accounting
    material control
    plant movement

    4 Production schedules
    5 Materials requisitions
    6 Assembly-line installation
    7 Automatic testing
    8 Packing bay
    9 Inspection procedures
   10 Labour recruitment and training
   11 Spares schedules

The purchasing and supply function involves the procurement of all the necessary raw materials and bought-out items and includes the following activities:

   D–1 Material enquiries
     2 Bought-out items enquiries
     3 Tender documents
     4 Evaluation of bids
     5 Long delivery orders
     6 Short delivery orders
     7 Carton and packaging
     8 Instruction leaflets, etc.
     9 Outside inspection

The sales and marketing function will obviously interlink with the management function and consists of the following activities:

   E–1 Sales advice and feedback
     2 Sales literature   – photographs, copying, printing, films, displays, packaging.
     3 Recruitment of sales staff
     4 Sales campaign and public relations
     5 Technical literature   – scope and production.
     6 Market research

Obviously, the above breakdowns are only indicative and the network shown in Figure 23.1 gives only the main items to be programmed. The actual programme for such a product would be far more detailed and would probably contain about 120 activities.

The final presentation could then be in bar chart form covering a time span of approximately 18 months from conception to main production run.

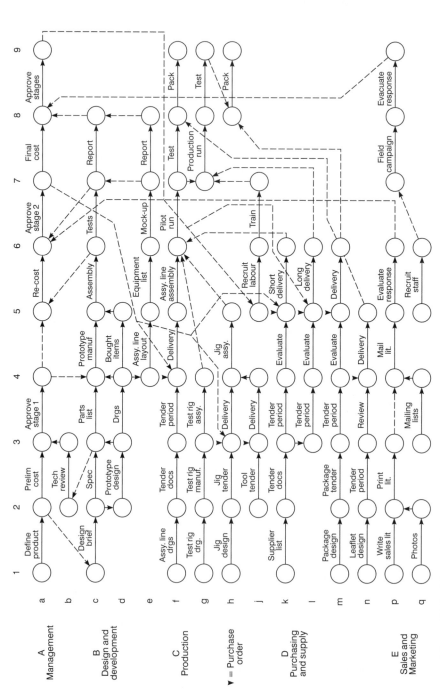

Figure 23.1 New product

2 Moving a factory

One of the main considerations in moving the equipment and machinery of a manufacturing unit from one site to another is to carry out the operation with the minimum loss of production. Obviously, at some stage manufacturing must be halted unless certain key equipment is duplicated, but if the final move is carried out during the annual works' holiday period the loss of output is minimized.

Consideration must therefore be given to the following points:

1 Equipment or machines which can be temporarily dispensed with;
2 Essential equipment and machines;
3 Dismantling problems of each machine;
4 Re-erection;
5 Service connections;
6 Transport problems – weight, size, fragility;
7 Orders in pipeline;
8 Movement of stocks;
9 Holiday periods;
10 Readiness of new premises;
11 Manpower availability;
12 Overall cost;
13 Announcement of move to customers and suppliers;
14 Communication equipment (telephone, e-mail, fax);
15 Staff accommodation during move;
16 Trial runs;
17 Staff training.

By collecting these activities into main functions, a network can be produced which will facilitate the organization and integration of the main requirements. The main functions would therefore be:

A Existing premises and transport;
B New premises – commissioning;
C Services and communications;
D Production and sales;
E Manpower, staffing.

The network for the complete operation is shown in Figure 23.2. It will be noticed that, as with the previous example, horizontal banding (as described in Chapter 21) is of considerable help in keeping the network disciplined.

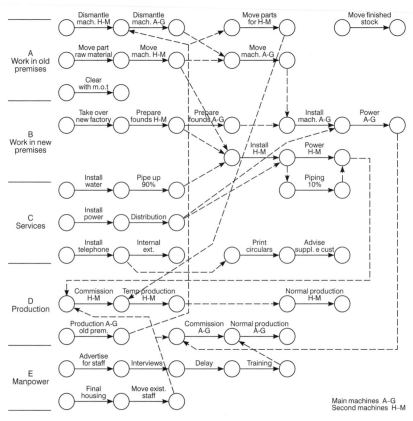

Figure 23.2 Moving a factory

By transferring the network onto a bar chart it will be possible to arrange for certain activities to be carried out at weekends or holidays. This may require a rearrangement of the logic which, though not giving the most economical answer in a physical sense, is still the best overall financial solution when production and marketing considerations are taken into account.

3 Centrifugal pump manufacture

The following network shows the stages required for manufacturing centrifugal pumps for the process industry. The company providing these pumps has no foundry, so the unmachined castings have to be bought in.

Assuming that the drawings for the pump are complete and the assembly line set up, a large order for a certain range of pumps requires the following main operations:

1 Order castings – bodies, impellers;
2 Order raw materials for shafts, seal plates, etc.;
3 Order seals, bearings, keys, bolts;
4 Machine castings, impellers;
5 Assemble;
6 Test;
7 Paint and stamp;
8 Crate and dispatch;
9 Issue maintenance instructions and spares list.

Figure 23.3 shows the network of the various operations complete with coordinate node numbers, durations and earliest start times. The critical path is shown by a double line and total float can be seen by inspection. For example, the float of all the activities on line C is 120–48 = 72 days. Similarly, the float of all activities on line D is 120–48 = 72 days.

Figure 23.4 is the network redrawn in bar-chart form, on which the floats have been indicated by dotted lines. It is apparent that the preparation of documents such as maintenance manuals, spares lists and quotes can be delayed without ill effect for a considerable time, thus releasing these technical resources for more urgent work such as tendering for new enquiries.

4 Planning a mail order campaign

When a mail order house decides to promote a specific product a properly coordinated sequence of steps have to be followed to ensure that the campaign will have the maximum impact and success. The following example shows the activities required for promoting a new set of records and involves both the test campaign and the main sales drive.

The two stages are shown separately on the network (Figure 23.5) since they obviously occur at different times, but in practice intermediate results could affect management decisions on packaging and text on the advertising leaflet. At the end of the test shot management will have to decide on the percentage of records to be ordered to meet the initial demand.

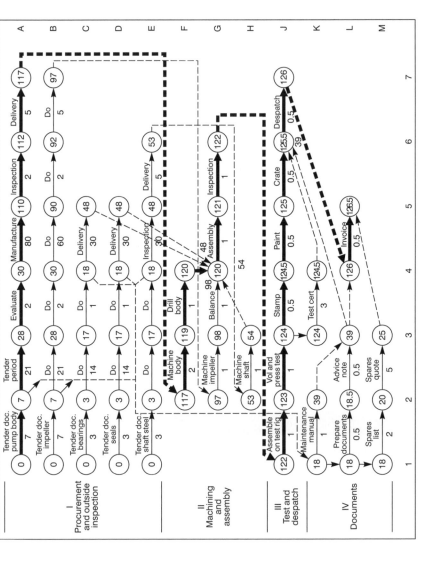

Figure 23.3 Pump manufacture (duration in days)

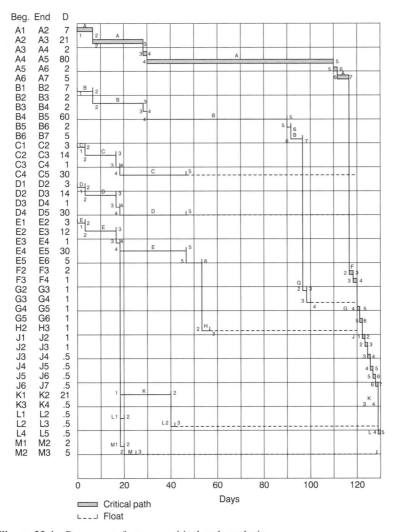

Figure 23.4 Pump manufacture – critical path analysis

In practice, the test shot will consist of three or more types of advertising leaflet and record packaging, and the result of each type will have to be assessed before the final main campaign leaflets are printed.

Depending on the rate of return of orders, two or more record ordering and dispatch stages will have to be allowed for. These are shown on the network as B1 and B2.

189

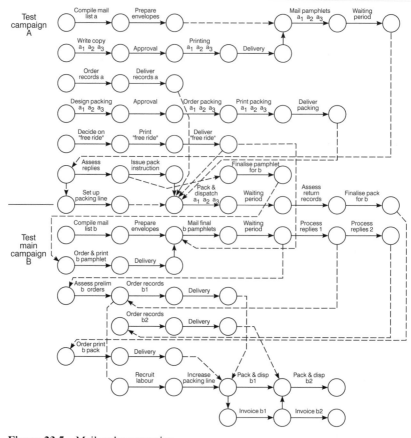

Figure 23.5   Mail order campaign

5   Manufacture of a package boiler

The programme in this example covers the fabrication and assembly of a large package boiler of about 75 000 kg of superheated steam per hour at 30 bar g and a temperature of 300°C. The separate economizer is not included.

The drum shells, drum ends, tubes, headers, doors and nozzles are bought out, leaving the following manufacturing operations:

1 Weld drums (longitudinal and circumferential seams);
2 Weld on drum ends;
3 Weld on nozzles and internal supports;
4 Drill drums for tube;

5 Stress relieve top and bottom drums;
6 Bend convection bank tubes;
7 Fit and expand tubes in drums – set up erection frame;
8 Weld fins to furnace tubes; pressure test;
9 Produce waterwall panels;
10 Gang bend panels;
11 Erect wall panels;
12 Weld and drill headers; stress relieve;
13 Weld panels to headers;
14 Weld on casing plates;
15 Attach peepholes, access doors, etc.;
16 Pressure test;
17 Seal-weld furnace walls;
18 Fit burners and seals;
19 Air test – inspection;
20 Insulate;
21 Prepare for transport;
22 Dispatch.

There are four main bands in the manufacturing programme:

A Drum manufacture;
B Panel and tube manufacture;
C Assembly;
D Insulation and preparation for dispatch.

The programme assumes that all materials have been ordered and will be available at the right time. Furthermore, in practice, subprogrammes would be necessary for panel fabrication, which includes blast cleaning the tubes and fin bar, automatic welding, interstage inspection, radiography, and stress relieving. Figure 23.6 shows the main production stages covering a period of approximately seven months.

6 Manufacture of a cast machined part

The casting, machining and finishing of a steel product can be represented in network form as shown in Figure 23.7. It can be seen that the total duration of the originally planned operation is 38 hours. By incorporating the principle that if the component has to be moved between workstations (efficiency can be increased if some of the operations are performed while the part is on the move) it is obviously possible to reduce the overall manufacturing time. The

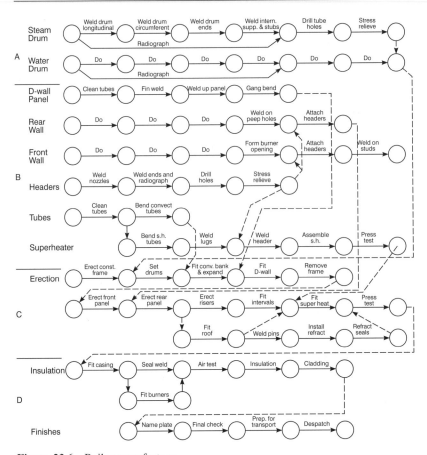

Figure 23.6 Boiler manufacture

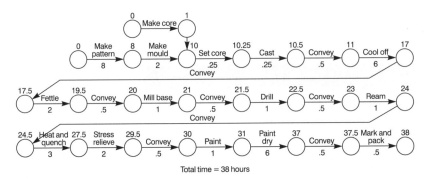

Total time = 38 hours

Figure 23.7 (Original)

sequence of operations, etc. Therefore it is up to the contractor to use his skills and experience to construct the works in the light of circumstances prevailing at the time.

Such vague attempts to forestall genuine claims for disruption carry little weight in a serious discussion among reasonable people, and count even less should the claim be taken to arbitration. The contractor is entitled to receive his access, drawings and free issue equipment in accordance with his stated method of construction, as set out in his tender, and all the excuses or disclaimers by the client or consultant cannot alter this right. Those contractors who have appreciated this facility have undoubtedly profited handsomely by making full use of network techniques, but these must, of course, be prepared accurately.

To obtain the maximum benefit from the network, the contractor must show that:

1 The programme was reasonable and technically feasible;
2 It represented the most economical construction method;
3 Any delays in client's drawings or materials will either lengthen the overall programme or increase costs, or both;
4 Any acceleration carried out by him to reduce the delay caused by others resulted in increased costs;
5 Any absorption of float caused by the delay increased the risk of completion on time and had to be countered by acceleration in other areas or by additional costs.

The last point is an important one, since 'float' belongs to the contractor. It is the contractor who builds it into his programme. It is the contractor who assesses the risks and decides which activities require priority action. The mere fact that a delayed component only reduced the float of an activity, without affecting the overall programme, is not a reason for withholding compensation if the contractor can show increased costs were incurred.

Examples of claims for delays

The following examples show how a contractor could incur (and probably re-claim) costs by late delivery of drawings or materials by the employer.

Example 1

To excavate a foundation the network in Figure 24.1 was prepared by the contractor. The critical path obviously runs through the excavation, giving the

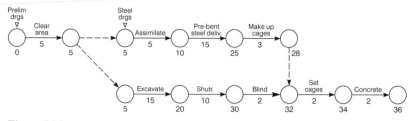

Figure 24.1

path through the reinforcing steel supply and fabrication a float of 4 days. If the drawings are delayed by 4 days, both paths become critical and, in theory, no delays occur. However, in practice, the contractor may now find that the delay in the order for reinforcing steel has lost him his place in the queue of the steel supplier, since he had previously advised the supplier that information would be available by day 10. Now that the information was only given to the supplier on day 14, labour for the cages was diverted to another contract and, to meet the new delivery of day 29, overtime will have to be worked. These overtime costs are claimable.

In any case, the 4-day float which the contractor built in as an insurance period has now disappeared, so that even if the steel had arrived by day 29 and the cage fabrication took longer than 3 days, a claim would have been justified.

Example 2

The network in Figure 24.2 shows a sequence for erecting and connecting a set of pumps. The first pump was promised to be delivered by the client on a 'free issue' basis in Week 0. The second pump was scheduled for delivery in week 4. In the event, both pumps were delivered together in week 4. The client argued that since there was a float of 4 days on pump 1, there was no delay to the programme since handover could still be effected by week 16.

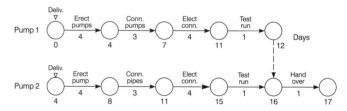

Figure 24.2

25

Resource loading

Most modern computer programs incorporate facilities for resource loading or resource allocation. Indeed, the Hornet program mentioned in Chapter 17 features such a capability, and its method of operation is shown in Chapter 30.

In principle, the computer aggregates a particular resource in any time period and compares this with a previously entered availability level for that resource. If the availability is less than the required level, the program will either.

1 Show the excess requirement in tabular form, often in a different colour to highlight the problem; or
2 Increase the duration of the activity requiring that resource to spread the available resources over a longer period, thus eliminating the unattainable peak loading.

The more preferable action by the computer is (1), the simple report showing the overrun. It is then up to management to make the necessary adjustments by either extending the time period – if the contractual commitments permit – or mobilizing additional resources. In practice, of course, the problem is complicated by such issues as available access or working space as well as financial, contractual or even political restraints. Often it may be possible to make technical changes which alter the resource mix. For example, a shortage of carpenters used for formwork erection may make it necessary to increase the use of pre-cast components with a possible increase in cost but a decrease in time. Project management is more than just writing and monitoring programs. The so-called project management systems are really only there to present to the project manager on a regular basis the position of the project to date and the possible consequences unless some form of remedial action is taken. The type of action and the timing of it rests fairly and squarely on the shoulders of management.

The options by management are usually quite wide, provided sufficient time is taken to think them out. It is in such situations that the 'what if' scenarios are a useful facility on a computer. However, the real implication can only be seen by 'plugging' the various alternatives into the network on paper and examining the down-stream effects in company with the various specialists, who, after all, have to do the actual work. There is no effective substitute for good teamwork!

The alternative approach

Resource smoothing can, of course, be done very effectively without a computer – especially if the program is not very large. Once a network has been prepared it is very easy to convert it into a bar chart, since all the 'thinking' has already been completed. Using the earliest starting and finishing times, the bars can be added to the gridded paper in minutes. Indeed, the longest operation in drawing a bar chart (once a network has been completed) is writing down the activity descriptions on the left-hand side of the paper. By leaving sufficient vertical space between the bars and dividing the grid into week (or day) columns, the resource levels for each activity can be added. Generally, there is no need to examine more than two types of resources per chart, since only the potentially restrictive or quantitatively limited ones are of concern. When all the activity bars have been marked with the resource value, each time period is added up vertically and the total entered in the appropriate space. The next step is to draw a histogram to show the graphical distribution of the resources. This will immediately highlight the peaks and troughs and trigger off the next step – resource smoothing.

Manual resource smoothing is probably the most practical method, since such unprogrammable factors as access, working space, hard-standing for cranes, personality traits of foremen, etc. can only be considered by a human when the smoothing is carried out. Nevertheless, the smoothing operation must still follow the logical pattern given below:

1 Advantage should be taken of float. In theory, activities with free float should be the first to be extended, so that a limited resource can be spread over a longer time period. In practice, however, such opportunities are comparatively rare, and for all normal operations, all activities with total float can be used for the purpose of smoothing. The floats can be indicated on the bars by dotted line extensions, again read straight off the network by subtracting the earliest from the latest times of the beginning node of the activity.

2 When the floats have been absorbed and the resources are distributed over the longer activity durations, another vertical addition is carried out from which a new histogram can be drawn. A typical network, bar chart and histogram is shown in Figure 25.1.

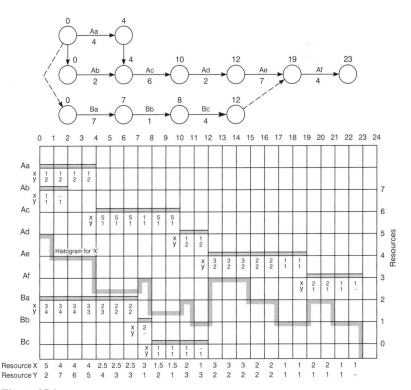

Figure 25.1

3 If the peaks still exceed the available resources for any time period, logic changes will be required. These changes are usually carried out on the network, but it may be possible to make some of them by 'sliding' the bars on the bar chart. For example, a common problem when commissioning a process or steam-raising plant is a shortage of suitably qualified commissioning engineers. If the bars of the bar chart are cut out and pasted onto cardboard with the resources written against each time period on the activity bar, the various operations can be moved on the time-scaled bar chart until an acceptable resource level is obtained. The reason it is not always necessary to use the network is that in a commissioning operation there is often considerable flexibility as to which machine is commissioned first. Whether pump A is commissioned before or after compressor B is often a matter of personal choice rather than logical necessity. When an acceptable solution has been found, the strips of bar can be held on to the backing sheet with an adhesive putty (Blu-Tack) and (provided the format is of the necessary size) photo-copied for distribution to interested parties.

4 If the weekly (or daily) aggregates are totalled cumulatively it is sometimes desirable to draw the cumulative curve (usually known as the S-curve, because it frequently takes the shape of an elongated letter S), which gives a picture of the build-up (and run-down) of the resources over the period of the project. This curve is also useful for showing the cumulative cash flow, which, after all, is only another resource. An example of such a cash flow curve is given in Chapter 28.

The following example shows the above steps in relation to a small construction project where there is a resource limitation. Figure 25.2 shows the AoA configuration and Figure 25.3 shows the same network in AoN

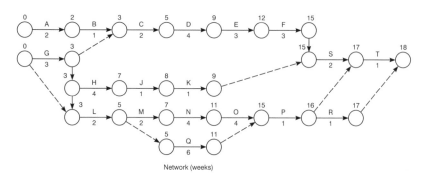

Network (weeks)

Figure 25.2

26

Cash flow forecasting

It has been stated in Chapter 25 that it is very easy to convert a network into a bar chart, especially if the durations and week (or day) numbers have been inserted. Indeed, the graphical method of analysis actually generates the bar chart as it is developed.

If we now divide this bar chart into a number of time periods (say, weeks or months) it is possible to see, by adding up vertically, what work has to be carried out in any time period. For example, if the time period is in months, then in any particular month we can see that one section is being excavated, another is being concreted and another is being scaffolded and shuttered, etc.

From the description we can identify the work and can then find the appropriate rate (or total cost) from the bills of quantities. If the total period of that work takes six weeks and we have used up four weeks in the time period under consideration, then approximately two-thirds of the value of that operation has been performed and could be certificated.

By this process it is possible to build up a fairly accurate picture of anticipated expenditure at the beginning of the job, which in itself might well affect the whole tendering policy. Provided the job is on programme, the cash flow can be calculated, but, naturally, due allowance must be made for the different methods and periods of retentions, billing and reimbursement. The cost of the operation must therefore be broken down into six main constituents:

Labour;
Plant;
Materials and equipment;
Subcontracts;
Site establishment;
Overheads and profit.

By drawing up a table of the main operations as shown on the network, and splitting up the cost of these operations (or activities) into the six constituents, it is possible to calculate the average percentage that each constituent contains in relation to the value. It is very important, however, to deduct the values of the subcontracts from any operation and treat these subcontracts separately. The reason for this is, of course, that a subcontract is self-contained and is often of a specialized nature. To break up a subcontract into labour, plant, materials, etc. would not only be very difficult (since this is the prerogative of the subcontractor) but would also seriously distort the true distribution of the remainder of the project.

Example of cash flow forecasting

The simplest way to explain the method is to work through the example described in Figures 26.1 to 26.6. This is a hypothetical construction project of three identical simple unheated warehouses with a steel framework on independent foundation blocks, profiled steel roof and side cladding, and a reinforced-concrete ground slab. It has been assumed that as an area of site has been cleared, excavation work can start, and the sequences of each warehouse are identical. The layout is shown in Figure 26.1 and the network for the three warehouses is shown in Figure 26.2.

Figure 26.3 shows the graphical analysis of the network separated for each building. The floats can be easily seen by inspection, e.g. there is a two-week float in the first paint activity (58–59) since there is a gap between the

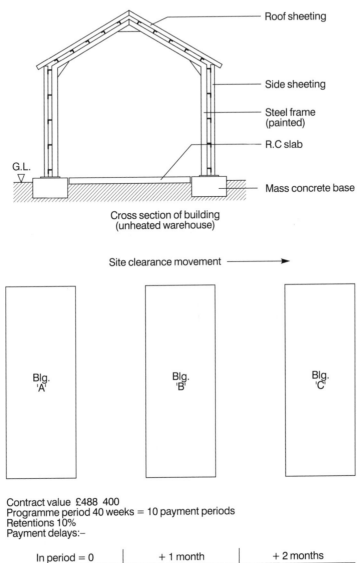

Cross section of building
(unheated warehouse)

Site clearance movement →

Contract value £488 400
Programme period 40 weeks = 10 payment periods
Retentions 10%
Payment delays:–

In period = 0	+ 1 month	+ 2 months
Labour oh & p (direct & s/c)	Sub contract Site establ	Paint Materials

Figure 26.1

Durations in weeks

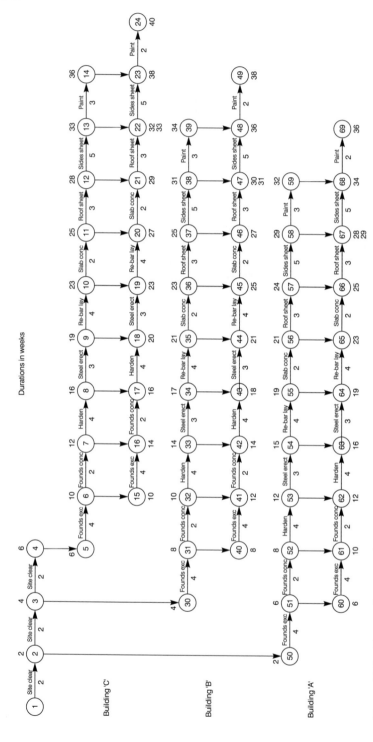

Figure 26.2 Construction network

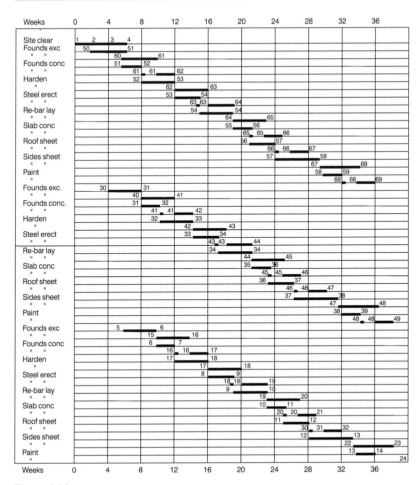

Figure 26.3

following dummy 59–68 and activity 68–69. The speed and ease of this method soon becomes apparent after a little practice.

The bar chart in Figure 26.5 has been drawn straight from the network (Figure 26.2) and the costs in £100 units added from Figure 26.4. For example, in Figure 26.4 the value of foundation excavation for any one building is £9400 per four-week activity. Since there are two four-week activities, the total is £18 800. To enable the activity to be costed in the corresponding measurement period, it is convenient to split this up into

One building Units in £ x 100

Activity	Duration weeks	Total value	Labour Value	Labour %	Plant Value	Plant %	Materials Value	Materials %	Sub Contr Value	Sub Contr %	Site Estb. Value	Site Estb. %	OH & P Value	OH & P %
Clear site	2	62	30	48	20	32	–		3	5	4	7	5	8
Founds exc.	4	94	40	43	40	43	–		–		6	6	8	8
" "	4	94	40	43	40	43	–		–		6	6	8	8
Founds conc.	2	71	20	28	10	14	30	42	–		5	8	6	8
" "	2	71	20	28	10	14	30	42	–		5	8	6	8
Steel erect	3	220	–		–		–		200	91	–		20	9
" "	3	220	–		–		–		200	91	–		20	9
Re-bar lay	4	106	30	28	–		60	56	–		7	7	9	9
" "	4	106	30	28	–		60	56	–		7	7	9	9
Slab conc.	2	71	20	28	10	14	30	42	–		5	8	6	8
" "	2	71	20	28	10	14	30	42	–		5	8	6	8
Roof sheet	3	66	–		–		–		60	91	–		6	9
" "	3	66	–		–		–		60	91	–		6	9
Sides sheet	5	100	–		–		–		90	90	–		10	10
" "	5	100	–		–		–		90	90	–		10	10
Paint	3	66	–		–		–		60	91	–		6	9
" "	2	44	–		–		–		40	91	–		4	9
Total direct		743	250	34	140	19	240	32			50	7	63	8
Total sub-contr.		885							803	91			82	9
Grand total		1628												
For 3 blgs		4884												

Figure 26.4

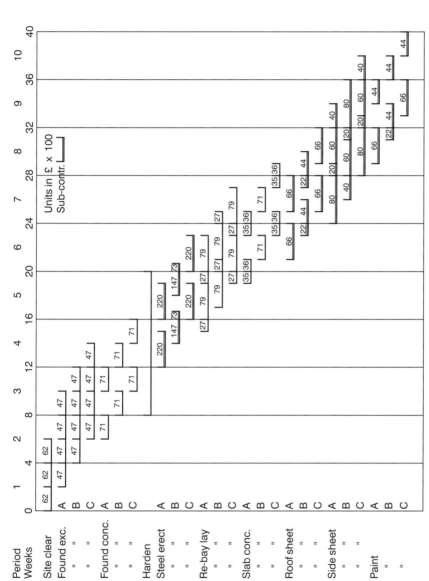

Figure 26.5

Period	0	1	2	3	4	5	6	7	8	9	10	11
Week	0	4	8	12	16	20	24	28	32	36	40	44
Total S/C	%	–	–	–	367	660	381	318	438	354	128	
S/C	91				334	600	347	289	399	322	116	116
OH & P	9				33	60	34	29	39	32	12	12
Direct	%	171	368	448	216	247	468	284	36			
Labour	34	58	125	153	74	84	159	97	12			
Plant	19	33	70	85	41	47	89	54	7			
Material	32	55	118	143	69	79	150	91	11			
Site est.	7	12	26	31	15	17	33	20	3			
OH & P	8	13	29	36	17	20	37	22	3			
Total value		171	368	448	583	907	849	602	474	354	128	116
Outflow	Delay											
Labour	0	58	125	153	74	84	159	97	12			
Plant	2			33	70	85	41	47	89	54	7	
Material	2			55	118	143	69	79	150	91	11	
S/C	1					334	600	347	289	399	322	116
Site est.	1		12	26	31	15	17	33	20	3		
OH & P	0	13	29	36	17	20	37	22	3			
S/C OH&P	0				33	60	34	29	39	32	12	
Out		71	166	303	343	741	957	654	602	579	352	116
In 90%	1		154	331	403	525	816	764	542	427	319	115
Net flow		(71)	(12)	28	60	(216)	(141)	110	(60)	(152)	(33)	(1)

Figure 26.6

two-weekly periods of £4700. Hence in Figure 26.5, foundation excavation for building A is shown as

$$\begin{array}{r} 47 \text{ in period 1} \\ 47 + 47 = 94 \text{ in period 2} \\ 47 \text{ in period 3} \end{array}$$

The summation of all the costs in any period is shown in Figure 26.6.

The table in Figure 26.6 clearly shows the effect of the anticipated delays in payment of certificates and settlement of contractor's accounts. For example, material valued at 118 in period 2 is paid to the contractor after one month in period 3 (part of the 331, which is 90% of 368, the total value of period 2), and is paid to the supplier by the contractor in period 4 after the two-month delay period.

From Figure 26.6 it can be seen that it has been decided to extract overhead and profit monthly as the job proceeds, but this is a policy that is not followed by every company. Similarly, the payment delays may differ in practice, but the principle would be the same.

It will be noted that there is a positive cash flow in only three of the eleven measurement periods, and suitable finance charges must, therefore, be added to the contract value. Another method, of course, would be to ask for a mobilization fee at the beginning of the contract.

27

Cost control and EVA

Apart from ensuring that their project is completed on time, all managers, whether in the office, workshop, factory or on-site, are concerned with cost. There is little consolation in finishing on time, when, from a cost point of view, one wished the job had never started!

Cost control has been a vital function of management since the days of the pyramids, but only too frequently is the term confused with mere cost reporting. The cost report is usually part of every manager's monthly report to his superiors, but an account of the past month's expenditure is only stating historical facts. What the manager needs is a regular and up-to-date monitoring system which enables him to identify the expenditure with specific operations or stages, determine whether the expenditure was cost-effective, plot or calculate the trend, and then take immediate action if the trend is unacceptable.

Network analysis forms an excellent base for any cost-control system, since the activities can each be identified and costed, so that the percentage completion of an activity can also give the proportion of expenditure, if that expenditure is time related. The system is ideal, therefore, for construction sites, drawing offices or factories where the basic unit of control is the man hour.

SMAC – Manhour control

Site Manhour and Cost (SMAC)* is a cost control system developed specifically on a network base for either manual or computerized cost monitoring, which enables performance to be measured and trends to be evaluated, thus providing the manager with an effective instrument for further action. The system can be used for all operations where man hours have to be controlled, and since most functions in an industrial environment are based on manhours and can be planned with networks, the utilization of the system is almost limitless.

The following operations or activities could benefit from the system:

1 Construction-sites
2 Fabrication shops
3 Manufacturing (batch production)
4 Drawing offices
5 Removal services
6 Machinery commissioning
7 Repetitive clerical functions
8 Road maintenance

The criteria laid down when the system was first mooted were:

1 *Minimum site (or workshop) input.* Site staff should spend their time managing the contract and not filling in unnecessary forms.
2 *Speed.* The returns should be monitored and analysed quickly so that action can be taken.
3 *Accuracy.* The manhour expenditure must be identifiable with specific activities which are naturally logged on time sheets.
4 *Value for money.* The useful manhours on an activity must be comparable with the actual hours expended.
5 *Economy.* The system must be inexpensive to operate.
6 *Forward looking.* Trends must be seen quickly so that remedial action can be taken when necessary.

The final system satisfied all these criteria with the additional advantage that the percentage complete returns become a simple but effective feedback for updating the network programme.

*SMAC is the proprietary name given to the cost-control program developed by Foster Wheeler.

One of the most significant differences between SMAC and the conventional progress-reporting systems is the substitution of 'weightings' given to individual activities, by the concept of 'value hours'. If each activity is monitored against its budget hours (or the hours allocated at the beginning of the contract, to that activity) then the 'value hour' is simply the percentage complete of that activity multiplied by its budget hours. In other words, it is the useful hours as against the actual hours recorded on the time sheets.

If all the value hours of a project are added up and the total divided by the total budget hours, the overall per cent complete of the project is immediately seen.

The advantage of this system over the weighting system is that activities can be added or eliminated without having to 're-weight' all the other activities. Furthermore, the value hours are a tangible parameter, which, if plotted on a graph against actual hours, budget hours and predicted final hours, gives the manager a 'feel' of the progress of the job that is second to none. The examples in Tables 27.1 and 27.2 show the difference between the two systems.

Table 27.1   Weighting system

1 Activity no.	2 Activity	3 Budget × 100	4 Weighting	5 % Complete	6 % Weighted	7 Actual hours × 100
1	A	1000	0.232	100	23.2	1,400
2	B	800	0.186	50	9.3	600
3	C	600	0.140	60	8.4	300
4	D	1200	0.279	40	11.2	850
5	E	300	0.070	70	4.9	250
6	F	400	0.093	80	7.4	600
Total		4300	1.000		64.4	4,000

Overall % complete = 64.4%.

Predicted final hours $\dfrac{4000}{0.644} = 6211 \times 100$ hours

Efficiency $= \dfrac{4300 \times 0.644}{4000} = 69.25\%$

As stated earlier, two of the criteria of the system were the absolute minimum amount of form filling for reporting progress, and the accurate assessment of percentage complete of specific activities. The first requirement is met by cutting down the reporting items to three essentials.

1 The activity numbers of the activities worked on in the reporting period (usually one week).
2 The *actual* hours spent on each of these activities, taken from the time cards.
3 The assessment of the percentage complete of each reported activity. This is made by the 'man on the spot.'

The third item is the most likely one to be inaccurate, since any estimate is a mixture of fact and opinion. To reduce this risk (and thus comply with the second criterion, i.e. accuracy) the activities on the network have to be chosen and 'sized' to enable them to be estimated, measured or assessed in the field, shop or office by the foreman or supervisor in charge. This is an absolute prerequisite of success, and its importance cannot be over-emphasized.

Individual activities must not be so complex or long (in time) that further breakdown is necessary in the field, nor should they be so small as to cause unnecessary paperwork. For example, the erection of a length of ducting and supports (Figure 27.1) could be split into the activities shown in Figure 27.2 and 27.3.

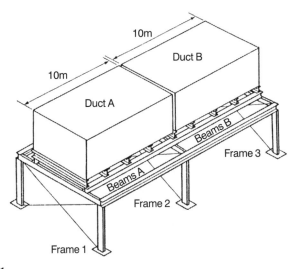

Figure 27.1

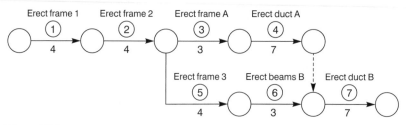

Figure 27.2

Any competent supervisor can see that if the two columns of frame 1 (Activity 1) have been erected and stayed, the activity is about 50% complete. He may be conservative and report 40% or optimistic and report 60%, but this ±20% difference is not important in the light of the total project. When all these individual estimates are summated the discrepancies tend to cancel out. What is important is that the assessment is realistic and checkable. Similarly, if 3 m of the duct between frames 1 and 2 has been erected, it is *about* 30% complete. Again, a margin on each side of this estimate is permissible.

However, if the network were prepared as shown in Figure 27.3 the supervisor may have some difficulty in assessing the percentage complete of activity 1 when he had erected and stayed the columns of frame 1. He now has

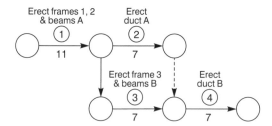

Figure 27.3

to mentally compute the manhours to erect and stay two columns in relation to four columns and four beams. The percentage complete could be between 10% and 30%, with an average of 20%. The ± percentage difference is now 50%, which is more than double the difference in the first network. It can be seen therefore that the possibility of error and the amount of effort to make an assessment or both is greater.

Had the size of each activity been *reduced* to each column, beam or brace, the clerical effort would have been increased and the whole exercize would have been less viable. It is important therefore to consult the men in the field or on the shopfloor before drafting the network and fixing the sequence and duration of each activity.

Control graphs

Apart from the numerical report shown in Figure 27.8, two very useful management control graphs can then be produced.

1 Showing budget hours, actual hours, value hours and predicted final hours, all against a common time base;
2 Showing percentage planned, percentage complete and efficiency, against a similar time base.

The actual shape of the curves on these graphs give the project manager an insight into the running of the job, enabling appropriate action to be taken.

Figure 27.4 shows the site returns of manhours of a small project over a nine-month period, and, for convenience, the table of percentage complete, actual and value hours has been drawn on the same page as the resulting curves. In practice, the greater number of activities would not make such a compressed presentation possible.

A number of interesting points are ascertainable from the curves:

1 There was obviously a large increase in site labour between the fifth and sixth months, as is shown by the steep rise of the actual hours curve.
2 This has resulted in increased efficiency.
3 The learning curve given by the estimated final hours has flattened in month 6 making the prediction both consistent and realistic.
4 Month 7 showed a divergence of actual and value hours (indicated also by a loss of efficiency) which was corrected (probably by management action) by month 8.
5 It is possible to predict the month of actual completion by projecting all the curves forward. The month of completion is then given:
   (a) When the value hours curve intersects the budget line; and
   (b) When the actual hours curve intersects the estimated final hours curve.

In this example, one could safely predict completion of the project in month 10.

It will be appreciated that this system lends itself ideally to computerization, giving the project manager the maximum information with the very minimum of site input. The sensitivity of the system is shown by the immediate change in

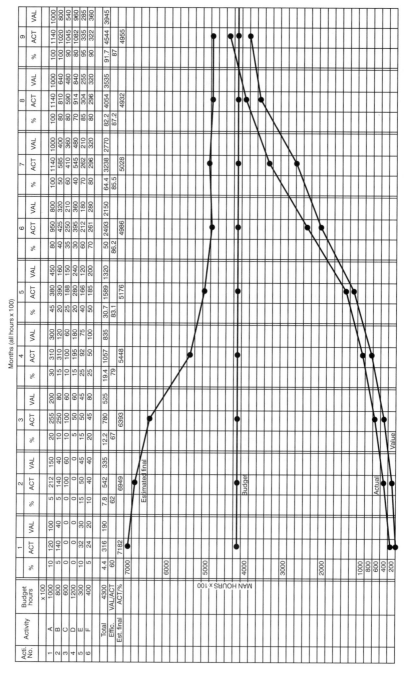

Figure 27.4

the *value* hours are equal or greater than the actual, and the percentage complete is equal or greater than the planned.

The efficiency curve in Figure 27.10 is useful, since any drop is a signal for management action. Curve 'A' is based on the efficiency calculated by dividing the cumulative value hours by the cumulative actual hours for every week. Curve W is the efficiency by dividing the value hours generated in a particular week by the actual hours expended in that week. It can be seen that Curve 'W' (shown only for the periods 5 to 9) is more sensitive to change and is therefore a more dramatic warning device to management.

Finally, by comparing the curves in Figures 27.9 and 27.10 the following conclusions can be drawn:

1 *Value hours exceed actual hours* (Figure 27.9). This indicates that the site is efficiently run.
2 *Final hours are less than budget hours* (Figure 27.9). This implies that the contract will make a profit.
3 *The efficiency is over 100% and rising* (Figure 27.10). This bears out conclusion 1.
4 *The actual percentage complete curve* (Figure 27.10), although less than the planned, has for the last four periods been increasing at a greater rate than the planned (i.e. the line is at a steeper angle). Hence the job may well finish *earlier* than planned (probably in Week 11).
5 By projecting value hour curve forward to meet the budget hour line, it crosses in Week 11 (Figure 27.9).
6 By projecting the actual hour curve to meet the projection of the final hour curve, it intersects in Week 11 (Figure 27.9). Hence Week 11 is the probable completion date.

The computer printout shown in Figure 27.11 is updated weekly by adding the manhours logged against individual activities. However, it is possible to show on the same report the *cost* of both the historical and current manhours. This is achieved by feeding the average manhour rate for the contract into the machine at the beginning of the job and updating it when the rate changes. Hence the new hours will be multiplied by the current rates. A separate report can also be issued to cover the indirect hours such as supervision, inspection, inclement weather, general services etc.

Since the value hour concept is so important in assessing the labour content of a site or works operation, the following summary showing the computation in non-numerical terms may be of help:

A = Actual hours expended (total) F = Final anticipated hours
B = Budget hours (total) L = Manhour loss (or gain)
C = Hours to complete P = Percentage complete
E = Efficiency V = Value hours (total)

Then $V = \Sigma$ of all value hours = Σ (Budget × percentage complete of individual activity)

$$E = \frac{V}{A} \times 100\% \qquad F = \frac{A}{V} \times \frac{B}{100} = \frac{A}{P}$$

$$P = \frac{V}{B} \times 100\% \qquad C = F - A$$

$$L = A - V$$

Overall project completion

Once the manhours have been 'costed' they can be added to other cost reports of plant, equipment, materials, subcontracts, etc., so that an overall percentage completion of a project can be calculated for valuation purposes on the only true common denominator of a project – money.

The total *value* to date divided by the revised budget × 100 is the percentage complete of a job. The value hour concept is entirely compatible with the conventional valuation of costing such as value of concrete poured, value of goods installed, cost of plant utilized – activities which can, by themselves, be represented on networks at the planning stage.

Table 27.3 shows how the two main streams of operations, i.e. those categories measured by cost and those measured by manhours. can be combined to give an overall picture of the percentage completion in terms of cost and overall cost of a project. While the operations shown relate to a construction project, a similar table can be drawn for a manufacturing process, covering such operations as design, tooling, raw material purchase, machinery, assembly, testing, packing, etc.

Cost of overheads, plant amortization, licences, etc. can, of course, be added like any other commodity. An example giving quantities and cost values of a small job involving all the categories shown in Table 27.3 is presented in Tables 27.4–27.6. It can be seen that in order to enable an overall percentage complete to be calculated, all the quantities of the estimate (Table 27.4) have been multiplied by their respective rates – as in fact would be done as part of any budget – to give the estimated costs.

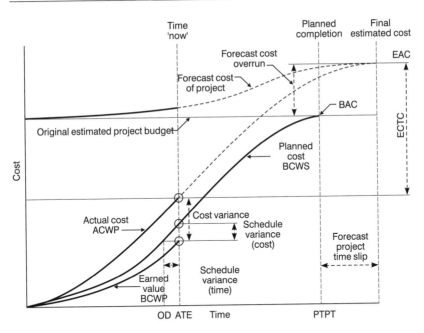

Key

ECTC	is Estimated Cost To Complete
BAC	is Budget At Competition (current) (budget)
BCWS	is Budgeted Cost of Work Scheduled (current) (planned)
BCWP	is Budgeted Cost of Work Performed (earned value)
ACWP	is Actual Cost of Work Performed (actual)
OD	is Original Duration planned for the work to date
ATE	is the Actual Time Expended for the work to date
PTPT	is the Planned Total Project Time
EAC	is Estimated Cost *at* Completion
ETPT	is Estimated Project Time
CPI	is Cost Performance Index = BCWP/ACWP = Efficiency
SPI	is Schedule Performance = BCWP/BCWS (cost based) = OD/ATE = % complete

Figure 27.18

It can be seen that the value hours for erection work are only 3180 against an actual manhours usage of 3500. This represents an efficiency of only

$$\frac{3180}{3500} \times 100 = 91\% \text{ approx.}$$

An adjustment should therefore also be made to the value of plant utilization i.e. $12\,000 \times 91\% = 10\,920$. The adjusted value total would therefore be as shown in column V.

The SMAC system described on the previous pages was developed in 1978 by Foster Wheeler Power Products, primarily to find a quicker and more accurate method for assessing the % complete of multi-discipline, multi-contractor construction projects.

However, about 10 years earlier the Department of Defense in the USA developed an almost identical system called Cost, Schedule, Control System (CSCS) which was generally referred to as Earned Value Analysis (EVA). This was mainly geared to the cost control of defence projects within the USA, and apart from UK subcontractors to the American defence contractors, was not disseminated widely in the UK.

While the principles of SMAC and EVA are identical, there developed inevitably a difference in terminology and methods of calculating the desired parameters. The most important change is the introduction of two parameters.

1 The Cost Performance Index (CPI), which is the Earned Value Cost/Actual Cost or BCWP/ACWP;
2 The Schedule Performance Index (SPI), which is the Earned Value Cost/ Planned Cost or BCWP/BCWS.

The set of curves and key in Figure 27.18, page 251, taken from BS 6079 (Guide to Project Management) show clearly the EVA terms and their SMAC equivalents. The curves also show how the Cost Variance and Schedule Variance are obtained and how the Schedule Performance Index (SPI) based on cost differs from the SPI based on time.

The Estimated Cost of Completion (EAC) is calculated in SMAC by dividing the Actual by the % complete, i.e. Actual/% complete.

In EVA the EAC is calculated by dividing the Budget at completion by the CPI, i.e. BAC/CPI.

The results of these two methods is of course the same as shown below:

EAC = Actual/% complete = Actual × Budget/Value = BAC × ACWP/BCWP
therefore EAC = BAC/CPI, since ACWP/BCWP = 1/CPI.

In 1996 the National Security Industrial Association (NISA) of America published their own Earned Value Management System (EVMS) which dropped the terms such as ACWP, BCWP and BCWS used in CSCS and adopted the simpler terms of Earned Value, Actual and Schedule instead. In all probability the CSCS terminology will be dropped in favour of the more understandable EVMS terminology.

Figure 27.19 clearly shows the earned value terms in both English (in **bold**) and EV jargon (in *italics*).

Integrated computer system

Until 1992, the SMAC system was run as a separate computer program in parallel with a conventional CPM system. Now, however, with the cooperation of Claremont Controls, utilizing their 'Hornet' program and Cogeneration Investments Limited (part of British Gas), a completely integrated computer program is available which, from one set of input data, entered into the computer on *one* input screen, calculates and prints out the CPM and SMAC results on *one* sheet of paper as well as drafting the network (of approx. 400 activities) in arrow diagram format on A1 or A0 paper. The network can also be produced in precedence format but this may require a larger sheet. The only weekly update information required is the time sheet which records the very minimum details required to control site progress, i.e. the activity number, the manhours expended that week and the assessment of the % complete (to the nearest 5%) of only those activities worked on during that week. The computer program does the rest.

Provided that all the subcontractors return their information regularly and on time, the weekly information produced enables the project manager to see:

1 The manhours spent on any activity or group of activities;
2 The % complete of any activity;
3 The overall % complete of the total project;
4 The overall manhours expended;
5 The value (useful) hours expended;
6 The efficiency of each activity;
7 The overall efficiency;
8 The estimated final hours for completion;
9 The approximate completion date;
10 The manhours spent on extra work;
11 The relationship between programme and progress;
12 The relative performance of subcontractors or internal subareas of work.

The system can of course be used for controlling individual work packages, whether carried out by direct labour or by subcontractors, and by multiplying

EARNED VALUE

English	=	% complete	×	Budget
BCWP	=	*% complete*	×	*BAC*

			English
			EV Jargon

Overall % complete	=	$\dfrac{\textbf{Earned Value}}{\textbf{Budget}}$	
	=	$\dfrac{BCWP}{BAC}$	*(Budgeted Cost of Work Performed)* *(Budget at Completion)*

Efficiency	=	$\dfrac{\textbf{Earned Value}}{\textbf{Actual}}$	
CPI	=	$\dfrac{BCWP}{ACWP}$	*(Budgeted Cost of Work Performed)* *(Actual cost of Work Performed)*

SPI (Cost based)	=	$\dfrac{\textbf{Earned Value}}{\textbf{Planned}}$	
	=	$\dfrac{BCWP}{BCWS}$	*(Budgeted Cost of Work Performed)* *(Budgeted cost of Work Scheduled)*

SPI (Time based)	=	$\dfrac{\textbf{Original duration}}{\textbf{Actual Time Expended}}$	
	=	$\dfrac{OD}{ATE}$	*(Original Duration)* *(Actual Time Expended to date)*

Cost Variance	=	**Earned Value – Actual**
	=	*BCWP – ACWP*

Schedule Variance	=	**Earned Value – Planned**
	=	*BCWP – BCWS*

Estimated Final Cost	=	$\dfrac{\textbf{Actual}}{\textbf{Overall \% complete}}$	
	=	$\dfrac{ACWP}{\textit{Overall \% complete}}$	
or	=	$\dfrac{\textbf{Budget}}{\textbf{Efficiency}}$	
	=	$\dfrac{BAC}{CPI}$	*(Budget at Completion)* *(Cost Performance Index)*

Estimated Final Time	=	$\dfrac{\textbf{Planned Total Project Time}}{\textbf{SPI}}$
Estimated Final Time	=	$\dfrac{PTPT}{\textit{SPI (Time based)}}$

CPI	=	Cost Performance Index	**SPI**	=	Schedule Performance Index
BAC	=	Budget At Completion	**OD**	=	Original Duration to date
ATE	=	Actual Time to date	**PTPT**	=	Planned Total Project Time

Figure 27.19

the total *actual* manhours by the average labour rate, the cost to date is immediately available. The final results should be carefully analysed and can form an excellent base for future estimates.

As previously stated, apart from printing the SMAC information and the conventional CPM data, the program also produces a computer drawn network. This is drawn on a grid with the activity numbers being in effect the grid coordinates. This has the advantage of 'banding' the activities into disciplines, trades or subcontracts and greatly facilitates finding any activity when discussing the programme with other parties. Unlike a normal arrow diagram, where the vertical grid lines are *on* the nodes, they are in this case *between* the nodes so that the coordinates are in effect the *activity* number as in a precedence diagram. The early and late start and finish dates are inserted in the event nodes from the input data. When the new % complete figures are inserted during regular updating, the early start and finish dates are automatically adjusted to reflect the progress. Critical activities are shown by a double line on the network.

A more detailed description of the 'Hornet' program is given in Chapter 30.

28

Worked examples

The previous chapters describe the various methods and techniques developed to produce meaningful and practical network programmes. In this chapter most of these techniques are combined in two fully worked examples. One is mainly of a civil engineering and building nature and the other is concerned with mechanical erection – both are practical and could be applied to real situations.

The first example covers the planning, man-hour control and cost control of a construction project of a bungalow. Before any planning work is started, it is advantageous to write down the salient parameters of the design and construction, or what is grandly called the 'design and construction philosophy'. This ensures that everyone who participates in the project knows not only what has to be done but why it is being done in a particular way. Indeed, if the design and construction philosophy is circulated *before* the programme, time- and cost-saving suggestions may well be volunteered by some recipients which, if acceptable, can be incorporated into the final plan.

Example 1 Small bungalow

Design and construction philosophy

1 The bungalow is constructed on strip footings.
2 External walls are in two skins of brick with a cavity. Internal partitions are in plasterboard on timber studding.
3 The floor is suspended on brick piers over an oversite concrete slab. Floorboards are T & G pine.
4 The roof is tiled on timber-trussed rafters with external gutters.
5 Internal finish is plaster on brick finished with emulsion paint.
6 Construction is by direct labour specially hired for the purpose. This includes specialist trades such as electrics and plumbing.
7 The work is financed by a bank loan, which is paid four-weekly on the basis of a regular site measure.
8 Labour is paid weekly. Suppliers and plant hire are paid 4 weeks after delivery. Materials and plant must be ordered 2 weeks before site requirement.
9 The *average* labour rate is £5 per hour or £250 per week for a 50-hour working week. This covers labourers and tradesmen.

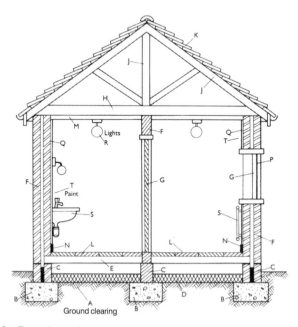

Figure 28.1 Bungalow (six rooms)

10 The cross-section of the bungalow is shown in Figure 28.1 and the sequence of activities is set out in Table 28.1, which shows the dependencies of each activity. All durations are in weeks.

The activity letters refer to the activities shown on the cross-section diagram of Figure 28.1, and on subsequent tables only these activity letters will be used. The total float column can, of course, only be completed when the network shown in Figure 28.2 has been analysed (see Table 28.1).

Table 28.1

Activity letter	Activity – description	Duration (weeks)	Dependency	Total float
A	Clear ground	2	Start	0
B	Lay foundations	3	A	0
C	Build dwarf walls	2	B	0
D	Oversite concrete	1	B	1
E	Floor joists	2	C and D	0
F	Main walls	5	E	0
G	Door and window frames	3	E	2
H	Ceiling joists	2	F and G	4
J	Roof timbers	6	F and G	0
K	Tiles	2	H and J	1
L	Floorboards	3	H and J	0
M	Ceiling boards	2	K and L	0
N	Skirtings	1	K and L	1
P	Glazing	2	M and N	0
Q	Plastering	2	P	2
R	Electrics	3	P	1
S	Plumbing and heating	4	P	0
T	Painting	3	Q, R and S	0

0 = Critical

Table 28.2 shows the complete analysis of the network including TL_e (latest time end event), TE_e (earliest time and event), TE_b (earliest time beginning event), total float and free float. It will be noted that none of the activities have free float. As mentioned in Chapter ??, free float is often confined to the dummy activities, which have been omitted from the table.

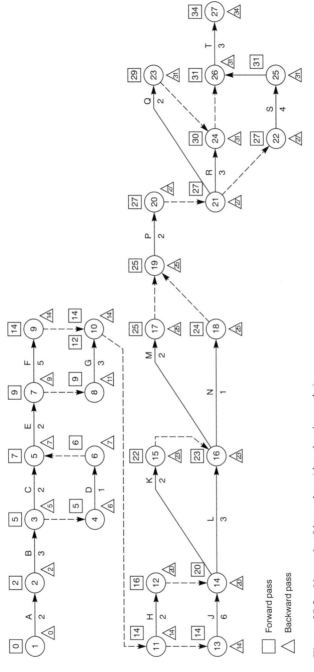

Figure 28.2 Network of bungalow (duration in weeks)

Table 28.2

a Activity letter	b Node no.	c Duration	d TL_e	e TE_e	f TE_b	g d-f-c Total float	h e-f-c Free float
A	1–2	2	2	2	0	0	0
B	2–3	3	5	5	2	0	0
C	3–5	2	7	7	5	0	0
D	4–6	1	7	6	5	1	0
E	5–7	2	9	9	7	0	0
F	7–9	5	14	14	9	0	0
G	8–10	3	14	12	9	2	0
H	11–12	2	20	16	14	4	0
J	13–14	6	20	20	14	0	0
K	14–15	2	23	22	20	1	0
L	14–16	3	23	23	20	0	0
M	16–17	2	25	25	23	0	0
N	16–18	1	25	24	23	1	0
P	19–20	2	27	27	25	0	0
Q	21–23	2	31	29	27	2	0
R	21–24	3	31	30	27	1	0
S	22–25	4	31	31	27	0	0
T	26–27	3	34	34	31	0	0

To enable the resource loading bar chart in Figure 28.3 to be drawn it helps to prepare a table of resources for each activity (Table 28.3). The resources are divided into two categories:

A Labourers
B Tradesmen

This is because tradesmen are more likely to be in short supply and could affect the programme.

The total labour histogram can now be drawn, together with the total labour curve (Figure 28.4). It will be seen that the histogram has been hatched to differentiate between labourers and tradesmen, and shows that the maximum demand for tradesmen is eight men in weeks 27 and 28. Unfortunately, it is only possible to employ six tradesmen due to possible site congestion. What is to be done?

Table 28.3 Labour resources per week

Activity letter	Resource A Labourers	Resource B Tradesman	Total
A	6	–	6
B	4	2	6
C	2	4	6
D	4	–	4
E	–	2	2
F	2	4	6
G	–	2	2
H	–	2	2
J	–	2	2
K	2	3	5
L	–	2	2
M	–	2	2
N	–	2	2
P	–	2	2
Q	1	3	4
R	–	2	2
S	1	3	4
T	–	4	4

The advantage of network analysis with its float calculation is now apparent. Examination of the network shows that in weeks 27 and 28 the following operations (or activities) have to be carried out:

Activity Q	Plastering	3 men for 2 weeks
Activity R	Electrics	2 men for 3 weeks
Activity S	Plumbing and heating	3 men for 4 weeks

The first step is to check which activities have float. Consulting Table 28.2 reveals that Q (Plastering) has 2 weeks float and R (Electrics) has 1 week float. By delaying Q (Plastering) by 2 weeks and accelerating R (Electrics) to be carried out in 2 weeks by 3 men per week, the maximum total in any week is reduced to 6. Alternatively, it may be possible to extend Q (Plumbing) to 4 weeks using 2 men per week for the first two weeks and 1 man per week for the next two weeks. At the same time, R (Electrics) can be extended by one week by employing 1 man per week for the first two weeks and 2 men per

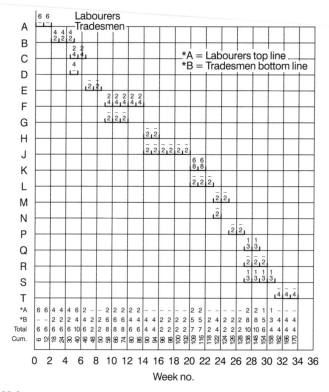

Figure 28.3

week for the next two weeks. Again, the maximum total for weeks 27–31 is 6 tradesmen.

The new partial disposition of resources and revized histograms after the two alternative smoothing operations are shown in Figures 28.5 and 28.6. It will be noted that:

1 The overall programme duration has not been exceeded because the extra durations have been absorbed by the float.
2 The total number of man weeks of any trade has not changed – i.e. Q (Plastering) still has 6 man weeks and R (Electrics) still has 6 man weeks.

If it is not possible to obtain the necessary smoothing by utilizing and absorbing floats the network logic may be amended, but this requires a careful reconsideration of the whole construction process.

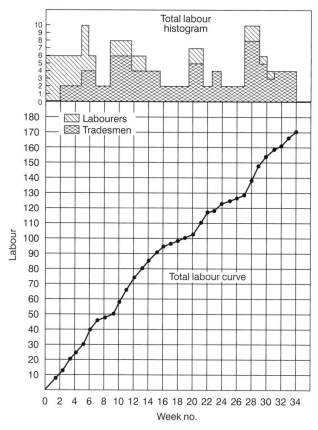

Figure 28.4

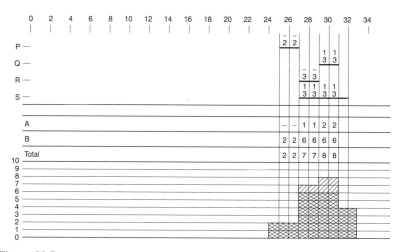

Figure 28.5

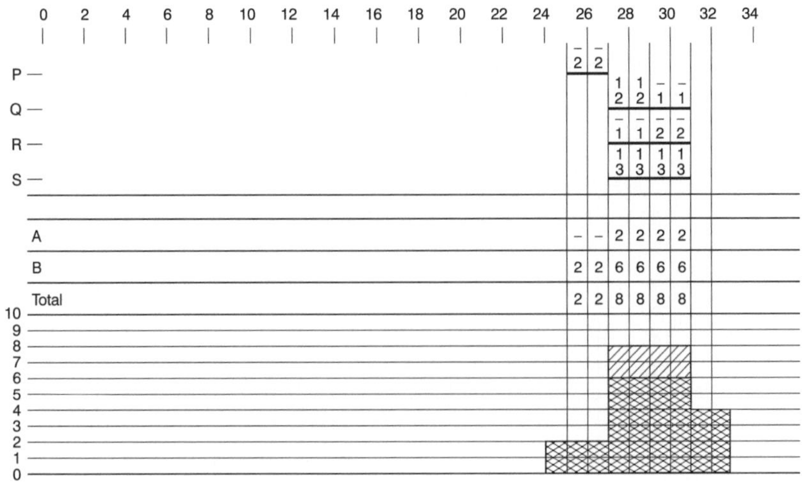

Figure 28.6

Table 28.4

a Activity letter	b Duration (weeks)	c No. of men	d b × c × 50 Budget hours
A	2	6	600
B	3	6	900
C	2	6	600
D	1	4	200
E	2	2	200
F	5	6	1500
G	3	2	300
H	2	2	200
J	6	2	600
K	2	5	500
L	3	2	300
M	2	2	200
N	1	2	100
P	2	2	200
Q	2	4	400
R	3	2	300
S	4	4	800
T	3	4	600
Total			8500

The next operation is to use the SMAC system to control the work on site. Multiplying for each activity the number of weeks required to do the work by the number of men employed on that activity yields the number of man weeks. If this is multiplied by 50 (the average number of working hours in a week), the man hours per activity are obtained. A table can now be drawn up listing the activities, durations, number of men and budget hours (Table 28.4).

As the bank will advance the money to pay for the construction in four-weekly tranches, the measurement and control system will have to be set up to monitor the work every 4 weeks. The anticipated completion date is week 34, so that a measure in weeks 4, 8, 12, 16, 20, 24, 28, 32 and 36 will be required. By recording the *actual* hours worked each week and assessing the percentage complete for each activity each week the value hours for each activity can be quickly calculated. As described in Chapter 27, the overall percentage complete, efficiency and predicted final hours can then be calculated. Table 28.5 shows a manual SMAC analysis for four sample weeks (8, 16, 24 and 32).

In practice, this calculation will have to be carried out every week either manually as shown or by computer using a simple spreadsheet. It must be remembered that only the activities actually worked on during the week in question have to be computed. The remaining activities are entered as shown in the previous week's analysis.

For purposes of progress payments, the *value* hours for every 4-week period must be multiplied by the average labour rate (£5 per hour) and, when added to the material and plant costs, the total value for payment purposes is obtained. This is shown later in this chapter.

At this stage it is more important to control the job, and for this to be done effectively, a set of curves must be drawn on a time base to enable all the various parameters to be compared. The relationship between the actual hours and value hours gives a measure of the efficiency of the work, while that between the value hours and the planned hours gives a measure of progress. The actual and value hours are plotted straight from the SMAC analysis, but the planned hours must be obtained from the labour expenditure curve (Figure 28.4) and multiplying the labour value (in men) by 50 (the number of working hours per week). For example, in week 16 the total labour used to date is 94 man weeks, giving $94 \times 50 = 4700$ man hours.

The complete set of curves (including the efficiency and percentage complete curves) are shown in Figure 28.7. In practice, it may be more

Table 28.5

Period	Budget	Week 8 Actual cum.	Week 8 %	Week 8 V	Week 16 Actual cum.	Week 16 %	Week 16 V	Week 24 Actual cum.	Week 24 %	Week 24 V	Week 32 Actual cum.	Week 32 %	Week 32 V
A	600	600	100	600	600	100	600	600	100	600	600	100	600
B	900	800	100	900	800	100	900	800	100	900	800	100	900
C	600	550	100	600	550	100	600	550	100	600	550	100	600
D	200	220	90	180	240	100	200	240	100	200	240	100	200
E	200	110	40	80	180	100	200	180	100	200	180	100	200
F	1500	–	–	–	1200	80	1200	1550	100	1500	1550	100	1500
G	300	–	–	–	300	100	300	300	100	300	300	100	300
H	200	–	–	–	180	60	120	240	100	200	240	100	200
J	600	–	–	–	400	50	300	750	100	600	750	100	600
K	500	–	–	–	–	–	–	500	100	500	550	100	500
L	300	–	–	–	–	–	–	250	80	240	310	100	300
M	200	–	–	–	–	–	–	100	60	120	180	100	200
N	100	–	–	–	–	–	–	50	40	40	110	100	100
P	200	–	–	–	–	–	–	–	–	–	220	100	200
Q	400	–	–	–	–	–	–	–	–	–	480	100	400
R	300	–	–	–	–	–	–	–	–	–	160	60	180
S	800	–	–	–	–	–	–	–	–	–	600	80	640
T	600	–	–	–	–	–	–	–	–	–	100	10	60
Total	8500	2280	27.8%	2360	4450	52%	4420	6110	70.6%	6000	7920	90.4%	7680
Efficiency			103%			99%			98%			96%	
Estimated final hours			8201			8557			8654			8761	

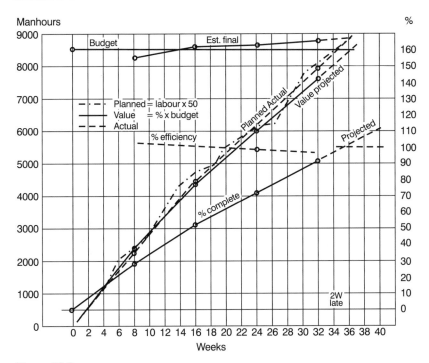

Figure 28.7

convenient to draw the last two curves on a separate sheet, but provided the percentage scale is drawn on the opposite side to the man hour scale no confusion should arise. Again, a computer program can be written to plot these curves on a weekly basis as shown in Chapter 27.

Once the control system has been set up it is essential to draw up the cash flow curve to ascertain what additional funding arrangements are required over the life of the project. In most cases where project financing is required the cash flow curve will give an indication of how much will have to be obtained from the finance house or bank and when. In the case of this example, where the construction is financed by bank advances related to site progress, it is still necessary to check that the payments will, in fact, cover the outgoings. It can be seen from the curve in Figure 28.9 that virtually permanent overdraft arrangements will have to be made to enable the men and suppliers to be paid regularly.

When considering cash flow it is useful to produce a table showing the relationship between the usage of a resource, payment date and the receipt of

Table 28.6

Week intervals	1	2	3	4	5	6	7	8
Order date								
Material delivery			X					
Labour use				X				
Material use				X				
Labour payments				X				
Pay suppliers							O	
Measurement							M	
Receipt from bank								R
Every 4 weeks								
Starting week no. 5								
First week no.	−3	−2	−1	1	2	3	4	5

cash from the bank to pay for it – even retrospectively. It can be seen in Table 28.6 that

1 Materials have to be ordered 4 weeks before use.
2 Materials have to be delivered 1 week before use.
3 Materials are paid for 4 weeks after delivery.
4 Labour is paid in week of use.
5 Measurements are made 3 weeks after use.
6 Payment is made 1 week after measurement.

The next step is to tabulate the labour costs and material and plant costs on a weekly basis (Table 28.7). The last column in the table shows the total material and plant cost for every activity, because all the materials and plant for an activity are being delivered one week before use and have to be paid for in one payment. For simplicity, no retentions are withheld (i.e. 100% payment is made to all suppliers when due).

A bar chart (Figure 28.8) can now be produced which is similar to that shown in Figure 28.3. The main difference is that instead of drawing bars, the length of the activity is represented by the weekly resource. As there are two

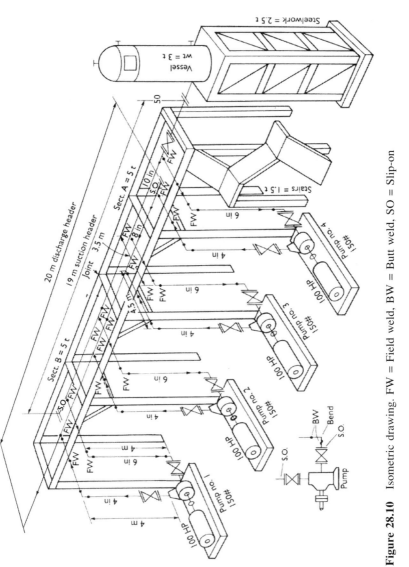

Figure 28.10 Isometric drawing. FW = Field weld, BW = Butt weld, SO = Slip-on

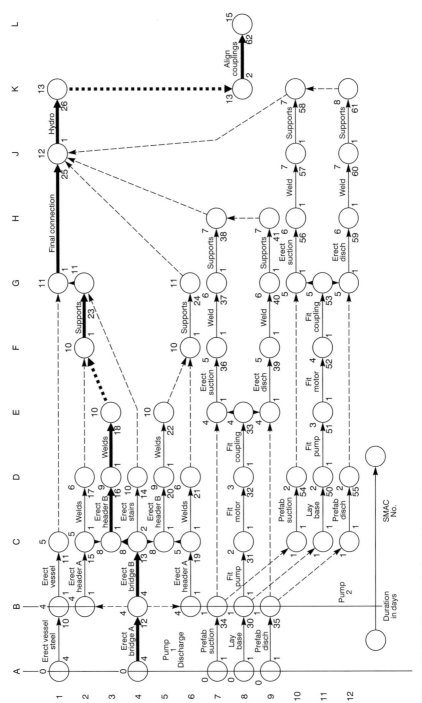

Figure 28.11 Network (using grid system)

ESTIMATE SHEET — SMAC ALLOCATION

A Item	B Unit	C Quant 1 set	D Hours rate	E =C+D man hours 1 set	F Pump man hours 2 sets	SMAC no. 1 set	SMAC man hours 1 set	SMAC no. pump no. 2	SMAC man hours pump no. 2	Duration days 1 set / 2 men/act
Erect vessel steelwork	Tonne	2.5	24.7	61.75		10	62			4
Erect vessel 3 T.	No. + Tonne	1	6.5 + 3.9	10.40		11	11			1
Erect bridge sect A	Tonne	5	12.3	61.50		12	62			4
Erect bridge sect B	Tonne	5	12.3	61.50		13	62			4
Erect stairs	Tonne	1.5	19.7	29.55		14	30			2
10" Suct. head erect sect A	Metre	10	0.90	9.00		15	9			1
10" Suct. head erect sect B	Metre	9	0.90	8.10		16	8			1
10" Suct. head slip-on (valve)	No	2	2.92	5.84		17.1	15			1
10" Suct. head butt joint	No	1	3.25	5.25		17.2	–			–
10" Suct. head fit valve	No	1	3.41	2.41		17.3	–			–
10" Suct. head slip-on (vessel)	No	1	2.92	2.92		17.4	4			–
10" Suct. head slip-on (end)	No	1	2.92	2.92		18.1	–			–
10" Suct. head fit blank	No	1	0.90	0.90		18.2	–			–
10" Suct. head fit supports	No	4	1.44	5.76		23	6			1
10" Suct. head final conn.	No	1	0.90	0.90		25	1			1
8" Disch. head erect sect. A	Metre	8	0.80	6.40		19	6			1
8" Disch. head erect sect. B	Metre	12	0.80	9.60		20	10			1
8" Disch. head butt joint	No	1	2.77	2.77		22	3			1
8" Disch. head slip-on (end)	No	1	2.49	2.49		21.1	3			1
8" Disch. head fit blank	No	1	0.50	0.50		21.2	–			–
8" Disch. head fit supports	No	4	1.44	5.76		24	6			1
Erect base plate	No	1	4.00	4.00	8.00	30	4	50	4	1
Fit pump 100 HP	No	1	14.00	14.00	28.00	31	14	51	14	1
Fit motor	No	1	14.00	14.00	28.00	32	14	52	14	1
Fit coupling	No	1	10.00	10.00	20.00	33	10	53	10	1
Fit 2 valves 6" & 4"	No	2	0.77	1.54	3.08	36.1	7	56.1	7	1
6" Suction erect	Metre	7.5	0.70	5.25	10.50	36.2	–	56.2	–	–
6" Suction make joint	No	1	0.44	0.44	0.88	36.3	–	56.3	–	–
6" Suction butt bend	No	2	2.30	4.60	9.20	37.1	7	57.1	7	1
6" Suction butt header	No	1	2.30	2.30	4.60	37.2	–	57.2	–	–
6" Suction fit supports	No	3	1.44	4.32	8.64	38	4	58	4	1
6" Suction 2 butts bend	* No	2	2.41	4.82	9.64	34.1	6	54.1	6	1
6" Suction slip-on	* No	1	1.44	1.44	2.88	34.2	–	54.2	–	–
4" Disch. erect	Metre	8.5	0.59	5.01	10.03	39	6	59	6	1
4" Disch. make joint	No	1	0.37	0.37	0.74	60.1	4	40.1	4	1
4" Disch. butt joint	No	1	1.82	1.82	3.64	60.2	–	60.2	–	–
4" Disch. butt header	No	1	1.82	1.82	3.64	40.3	–	60.3	4	–
4" Disch. fit supports	No	3	1.44	4.32	8.64	41	4	61	5	1
4" Disch. 2 butts bend	* No	2	1.89	3.78	7.56	35.1	5	55.1	–	1
4" Disch. slip-on	* No	1	1.14	1.14	2.28	35.2	–	55.2	–	–
Hydro-test 54 m	* No	1	12.00	12.00		26	12			1
Align couplings	No	2	25.00	50.00	†	62	50			2
Total							**445**		**85**	**41 12**

* Pre-fabricate on site

† Item 62 is performed in 1 day due to overtime working

No. of man days = (41 + 12)/2 = 53 × 2 = 106

Average hours/man day = 530/106 = 5

Figure 28.12

Table 28.8   Applicable rates from OCPCA norms

Steel erection		Hours
Pipe gantries		12.3/tonne
Stairs		19.7/tonne
Vessel support		24.7/tonne
Vessel (3 tonne)		6.5 + 1.3/tonne
Pump erection (100 hp)		14
Motor erection		14
Bedplate		4
Fit coupling		10
Align coupling		25
Prefab. piping (Sch. 40)		
6-inch suction prep.		0.81/end
4-inch discharge prep.		1.6/butt } 2.41
suction welds		1.44/flange
4-inch discharge prep		0.62/end
discharge welds		1.27/butt } 1.89
discharge slip-on		1.14/flange
Pipe erection	(10-inch)	$0.79 \times 1.15 = 0.90$/m
Pipe erection	(8-inch)	$0.70 \times 1.15 = 0.80$/m
Pipe erection	(6-inch)	$0.61 \times 1.15 = 0.70$/m
Pipe erection	(4-inch)	$0.51 \times 1.15 = 0.59$/m
Site butt welds	(10-inch)	$2.83 \times 1.15 = 3.25$/butt
	(8-inch)	$2.41 \times 1.15 = 2.77$/butt
	(6-inch)	$2.0 \times 1.15 = 2.30$/butt
	(4-inch)	$1.59 \times 1.15 = 1.82$/butt
Slip-ons	(10-inch)	$3.25 \times 0.9 = 2.92$/butt
	(8-inch)	$2.77 \times 0.9 = 2.49$/butt
	(6-inch)	$2.30 \times 0.9 = 2.07$/butt
	(4-inch)	$1.82 \times 0.9 = 1.64$/butt
Fit valves	(10-inch)	$2.1 \times 1.15 = 2.41$/item
	(6-inch)	$0.9 \times 1.15 = 1.04$/item
	(4-inch)	$0.45 \times 1.15 = 0.51$/item
Flanged connection	(10-inch)	$0.78 \times 1.15 = 0.90$/connection
	(8-inch)	$0.43 \times 1.15 = 0.50$/connection
	(6-inch)	$0.38 \times 1.15 = 0.44$/connection
	(4-inch)	$0.32 \times 1.15 = 0.37$/connection
Supports		$1.25 \times 1.15 = 1.44$/support
Hydro test	Set up	$6 \times 1.15 = 6.9$
	Fill and drain	$2 \times 1.15 = 2.3$
	Joint check	$0.2 \times 1.15 = 0.23$/joint
	Blinds	$0.5 \times 1.15 = 0.58$/blind

$$Hydrotest\ Total = 6.9 + 2.3 + (0.23 \times 12)$$
$$= 9.2 + 2.76 = 11.96\ (\text{say } 12)$$

13 Add up vertically per week and draw the labour histogram and S-curve.

14 Carry out a resource-smoothing exercize to ensure that labour demand does not exceed supply for any particular trade. In any case, high peaks or troughs are signs of inefficient working and should be avoided here (Fig 28.14). (Note: This smoothing operation only takes place with activities which have float.)

15 Draw the project control curves using the weekly SMAC analysis results to show graphically the relationship between

> Budget hours
> Planned hours
> Actual hours
> Value hours
> Predicted final hours (Figure 28.15).

16 Draw control curves showing

> Percentage complete (progress)
> Efficiency (Figure 28.15)

The procedures outlined above will give a complete control system for time and cost for the project as far as site work is concerned.

Cash flow

Cash flow charts show the difference between expenditure (cash out flow) and income (cash inflow). Since money is the common unit of measurement, all contract components such as manhours, materials, overheads and consumables have to be stated in terms of money values.

It is convenient to set down the parameters which govern the cash flow calculations before calculating the actual amounts. For the example being considered:

1 There are 1748 productive hours in a year (39 hours/week × 52) – 280 days of annual holidays, statutory holidays, sickness and travelling allowance and induction.

2 Each manhour costs, on average, £5 in actual wages.

3 After adding payments for productivity, holiday credits, statutory holidays, course attendance, radius and travel allowance, the taxable rate becomes £8.40/hour.

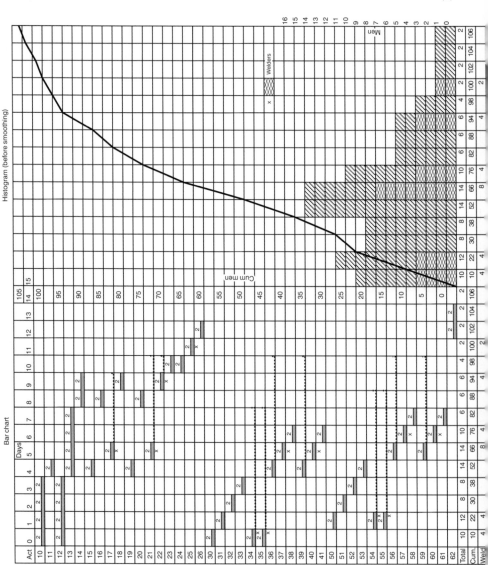

Figure 28.13 Bar chart

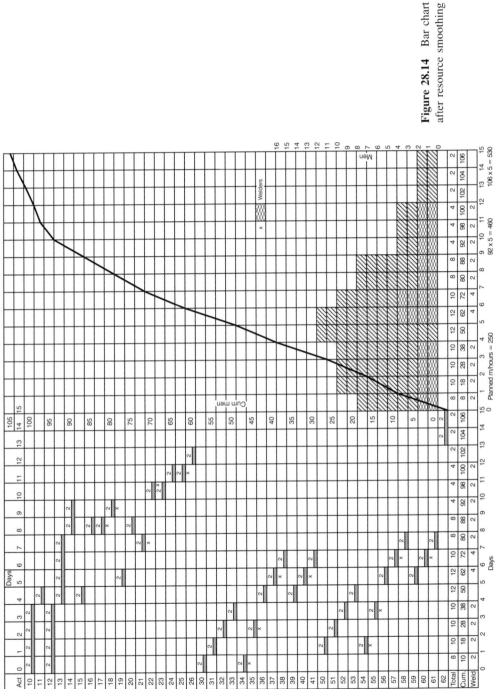

Figure 28.14 Bar chart after resource smoothing

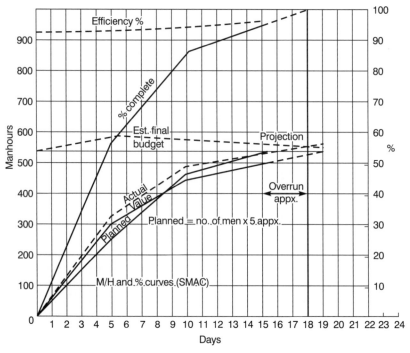

Figure 28.15

4 The addition of other substantive items such as levies, insurance, protective clothing and non-taxable fares and lodging increases the rate by £2.04 to £10.44/hour.

5 The ratio of other substantive items to taxable costs are $\dfrac{2.04}{8.40} = 0.243$

6 An on-cost allowance of 20% is made up of

Consumables	5%
Overheads	10%
Profit	5%
Total	20%

7 The total charge-out rate is, therefore, 10.44 × 1.2 = £12.53 per hour.
8 In this particular example
   (a) The men are paid at the end of each day at a rate of £8.40/hour.
   (b) The other substantive items of £2.04/hour are paid weekly.
   (c) Income is received weekly at the charge-out rate of £12.53/hour.

29

Example of integration of tools and techniques

The example in this chapter shows how all the tools and techniques described so far can be integrated to give a comprehensive project management system. The project chosen is the design, manufacture and distribution of a prototype motor car and while the operations and time scales are only indicative and do not purport to represent a real life situation, the examples show how the techniques follow each other in a logical sequence.

The prototype motor car being produced is illustrated in Figure 29.1 and the main components of the engine are shown in Figure 29.2. It will be seen that the letters given to the engine components are the activity identity letters used in planning networks.

The following gives an oversight of the main techniques and their most important constituents.

As with all projects, the first document to be produced is the *Business Case* which should also include the chosen option investigated for the

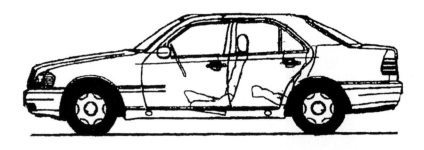

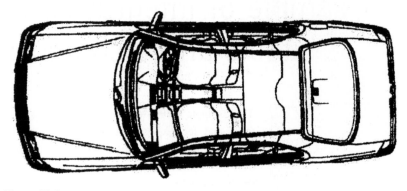

Figure 29.1

Investment Appraisal. In this exercise, the questions to be asked (and answered) are shown in Table 29.1.

It is assumed that the project requires an initial investment of £60 million and that over a 5 year period, 60 000 cars (units) will be produced at a cost of £5000 per unit. The assumptions are that the discount rate is 8% and there are two options for phasing the manufacture:

(a) That the factory performs well for the first two years but suffers some production problems in the next three years (option 1);
(b) That the factory has teething problems in the first three years but goes into full production in the last two (option 2).

The *Discounted Cash Flow* (DCF) calculations can be produced for both options as shown in Tables 29.2 and 29.3.

To obtain the *Internal Rate of Return* (IRR), an additional discount rate (in this case 20%) must be applied to both options. The resulting calculations are

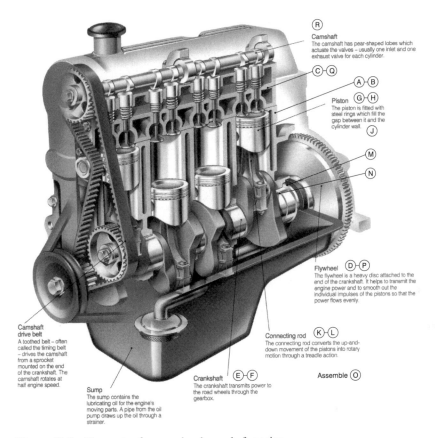

Figure 29.2 The parts of an overhead-camshaft engine

shown in Tables 29.4 and 29.5 and the graph showing both options is shown in Figure 29.3. This gives an IRR of 20.2% and 15.4%, respectively.

It is now necessary to carry out a cash flow calculation for the distribution phase of the cars. To line up with the DCF calculations, two options have to be examined. These are shown in Tables 29.6 and 29.7 and the graphs in Figures 29.4 and 29.5 for option 1 and option 2, respectively. An additional option 2a in which the income in years 2 and 3 is reduced from £65 000K to £55 000K is shown in the cash flow curves of Figure 29.6

All projects carry an element of *Risk* and it is prudent to carry out a risk analysis at this stage. The types of risks that can be encountered, the possible actual risks and the mitigation strategies are shown in Table 29.8. A risk log (or risk register) for five risks is given in Figure 29.7

Table 29.1

Business Case
Why do we need a new model?
What model will it replace?
What is the market?
Will it appeal to the young, the middle aged, families, the elderly, women, trendies, yobos?
How many can we sell per year in the UK, the USA, the EEC and other countries?
What is the competition for this type of car and what is their price?
Will the car rental companies buy it?
What is the max. and min. selling price?
What must be the max. manufacturing cost and in what country will it be built?
What name shall we give it?
Do we have a marketing plan?
Who will handle the publicity and advertising?
Do we have to train the sales force and maintenance mechanics?
What should be the insurance category?
What warranties can be given and for how long?

What are the main specifications regarding
Safety and theft proofing?
Engine size (cc) or a number of sizes?
Fuel consumption?
Emissions (pollution control)?
Catalytic converter?
Max. speed?
Max. acceleration?
Size and weight?
Styling?
Turning circle and ground clearance?

What 'extras' must be fitted as standard?
ABS
Power steering
Air bags
Electric windows and roof
Cruise control
Air conditioning
What % can be recycled

Investment Appraisal (options)
Should it be a Saloon, Coupé, Estate, People Carrier, Convertible, 4 × 4, Mini?
Will it have existing or newly designed engine?
Will it have existing or new platform (chassis)?
Do we need a new manufacturing plant or can we build it in an existing one?
Should the engine be cast iron or aluminium?
Should the body be steel, aluminium or fibreglass?
Do we use an existing brand name or devise a new one?
Will it be fuelled on petrol, diesel, electricity or hybrid power unit?
DCF of investment returns, NPV, cash flow?

Table 29.2

DCF of Investment Returns (Net Present Value)

Initial Investment £60 000K 5 Year period
Total car production 60 000 Units @ £5000/Unit

Option 1

Year	Production Units	Income £K	Cost £K	Net Return £K	Discount Rate	Discount Factor	Present Value £K
1	15 000	100 000	75 000	25 000	8%	0.926	23 150
2	15 000	100 000	75 000	25 000	8%	0.857	21 425
3	10 000	65 000	50 000	15 000	8%	0.794	11 910
4	10 000	65 000	50 000	15 000	8%	0.735	11 025
5	10 000	65 000	50 000	15 000	8%	0.681	10 215
Totals				95 000			77 725

Net Present Value (NPV) = 77 725 − 60 000 = £17 725K
Profit = £95 000K − £60 000K = £35 000K
Average Rate of Return (undiscounted) = £95 000/5 = £19 000K per annum
Return on Investment = £19 000/£60 000 = 31.66%

Table 29.3

DCF of Investment Returns (Net Present Value)

Initial Investment £60 000K 5 Year period
Total car production 60 000 Units @ £5000/Unit

Option 2

Year	Production Units	Income £K	Cost £K	Net Return £K	Discount Rate	Discount Factor	Present Value £K
1	10 000	65 000	50 000	15 000	8%	0.926	13 890
2	10 000	65 000	50 000	15 000	8%	0.857	12 855
3	10 000	65 000	50 000	15 000	8%	0.794	11 910
4	15 000	100 000	75 000	25 000	8%	0.735	18 375
5	15 000	100 000	75 000	25 000	8%	0.681	17 025
Totals				95 000			74 055

Net Present Value (NPV) = 74 055 − 60 000 = £14 055K
Profit = £95 000K − £60 000K = £35 000K
Average Rate of Return (undiscounted) = £95 000/5 = £19 000K per annum
Return on Investment = £19 000/£60 000 = 31.66%

Table 29.4

Internal Rate of Return (IRR)

Option 1

Year	Net Return £K	Disc. Rate	Disc. Factor	Present Value £K	Disc. Rate	Disc. Factor	Present Value £K
1	25 000	15%	0.870	21 750	20%	0.833	20 825
2	25 000	15%	0.756	18 900	20%	0.694	17 350
3	15 000	15%	0.658	9 870	20%	0.579	8 685
4	15 000	15%	0.572	8 580	20%	0.482	7 230
5	15 000	15%	0.497	7 455	20%	0.402	6 030
Totals	60 000			66 555			60 120
Less Investment				−60 000			−60 000
Net Present Value				£6 555K			£120K

Internal Rate of Return (from graph) = 20.2%

Table 29.5

Internal Rate of Return (IRR)

Option 2

Year	Net Return £K	Disc. Rate	Disc. Factor	Present Value £K	Disc. Rate	Disc. Factor	Present Value £K
1	15 000	15%	0.870	13 050	20%	0.833	12 495
2	15 000	15%	0.756	11 340	20%	0.694	10 410
3	15 000	15%	0.658	9 870	20%	0.579	8 685
4	25 000	15%	0.572	14 300	20%	0.482	12 050
5	25 000	15%	0.497	12 425	20%	0.402	10 050
Totals	60 000			60 985			53 690
Less Investment				−60 000			−60 000
Net Present Value				£985K			−£6 310K

Internal Rate of Return (from graph) = 15.4%

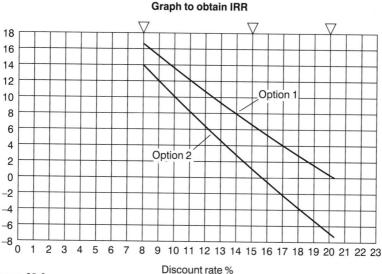

Figure 29.3

Once the decision has been made to proceed with the project, *a Project Life Cycle* diagram can be produced. This is shown on Figure 29.8 together with the constituents of the seven phases envisaged.

The next stage is the *Product Breakdown Structure* (Figure 29.9), followed by a combined *Cost Breakdown Structure* and *Organisation Breakdown Structure* (Figure 29.10). By using these two, the *Responsibility Matrix* can be drawn up (Figure 29.11).

It is now necessary to produce a programme. The first step is to draw an *Activity List* showing the activities and their dependencies and durations.

Table 29.6

Cash Flow

Option 1

Year		1	2	3	4	5	Cumulative
Capital	£K	12 000	12 000	12 000	12 000	12 000	
Costs	£K	75 000	75 000	50 000	50 000	50 000	
Total	£K	87 000	87 000	62 000	62 000	62 000	360 000
Cumulative		87 000	174 000	236 000	298 000	360 000	
Income	£K	100 000	100 000	65 000	65 000	65 000	395 000
Cumulative		100 000	200 000	265 000	330 000	395 000	

Table 29.7

Cash Flow

Option 2

Year	1	2	3	4	5	Cumulative
Capital £K	12 000	12 000	12 000	12 000	12 000	
Costs £K	50 000	50 000	50 000	75 000	75 000	
Total £K	62 000	62 000	62 000	87 000	87 000	360 000
Cumulative	62 000	124 000	186 000	273 000	360 000	
Income £K	65 000	65 000	65 000	100 000	100 000	395 000
Cumulative	65 000	130 000	195 000	295 000	395 000	

These are shown in the first four columns of Table 29.9. It is now possible to draw the *Critical Path Network* in either *AoN* format (Figure 29.12), *AoA* format (Figure 29.13) or as a *Lester diagram* (Figure 29.14).

After analysing the network diagram, the *Total Floats* and *Free Floats* of the activities can be listed (Table 29.10).

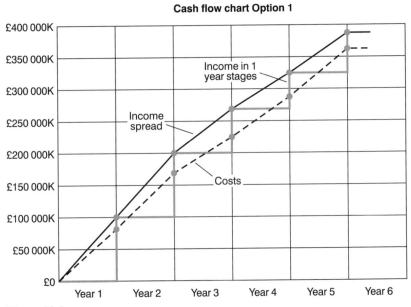

Cash flow chart Option 1

Figure 29.4

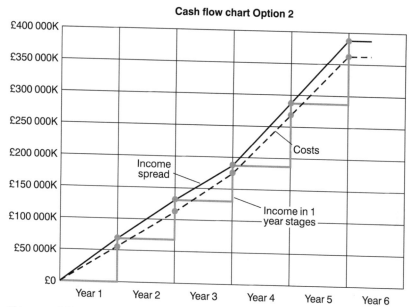

If income falls to £55 000K in years 2 and 3:

Income £K = 65 000   55 000   55 000   100 000   100 000
Cumulative = 65 000   120 000   175 000   275 000   375 000

Figure 29.5

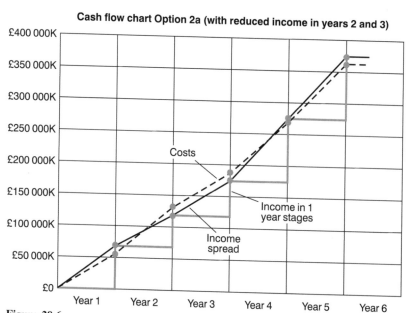

Figure 29.6

Apart from the start and finish, there are four milestones (days 8, 16, 24 and 30). These are described and plotted on the *Milestone Slip Chart* (Figure 29.15).

The network programme can now be converted into a bar chart (Figure 29.16) on which the resources (in men per day) as given in the fifth column

Table 29.8

Risk Analysis

Types of risks
Manufacturing (machinery and facilities) costs
Sales and marketing, exchange rates
Reliability
Mechanical components performance
Electrical components performance
Maintenance
Legislation (emissions, safety, recycling, labour, tax)
Quality

Possible risks
Won't sell in predicted numbers
Quality in design, manufacture, finish
Maintenance costs
Manufacturing costs
New factory costs
Tooling costs
New factory not finished on time
Training problems
Suppliers unreliable
Rust proofing problems
Performance problems
Industrial disputes
Electrical and electronic problems
Competition too great
Not ready for launch date (exhibition)
Safety requirements
Currency fluctuations

Mitigation strategy
Overtime
More tests
More research
More advertising/marketing
Insurance
Re-engineering
Contingency

RISK LOG

| Project: Key: H – High; M – Medium; L – Low | | | | | | | Prepared by: A.L. | Reference: Date: 12.12.2000 |

Type of Risk	Description of Risk	Probability			Impact			Risk Reduction Strategy	Contingency Plans	Risk Owner
		H	M	L	Perf.	Cost	Time			
R1 Manufact.	Factory not finished on time			10%		1M	3 months delay	Work more overtime	Cancel launch of car	PM
R2 Quality	Window mechanism faulty		50%		Not serious	5K	1 week to rectify	Test motor	Use manual winder	Chief Designer
R3 Safety	Air bags may explode			1%	Serious	10K	1 week to rectify	Run more tests	Remove Air bags	Chief Designer
R4 Legislation	Emission levels will be reduced		50%		Serious	3M	1 year to modify CC	Increase research	Buy another proven conv.	Chief Engineer
R5 Sales	Sales forecasts will not be met		30%		Very serious	10M		Increase advertising	Reduce price	PM

Figure 29.7

Product and Project Life Cycle

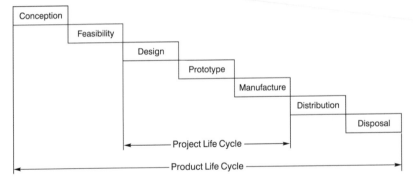

Phases

Conception: Original idea, high level discussions, preliminary market research

Feasibility: Consumer survey, market survey, type and size of car, production run and costs

Design: Vehicle design, tool design, development, component tests

Prototype: Tooling, production line, limited production, arctic and desert testing

Manufacture: Mass production, operator training, spares build up, customizing

Distribution: Deliveries, staff training, sales conferences, marketing, advertising, exhibitions

Disposal: Dismantling production line, selling tools, negotiating licences for spares

The phases could overlap.

The end of each phase could be a decision point to stop or proceed.

Figure 29.8

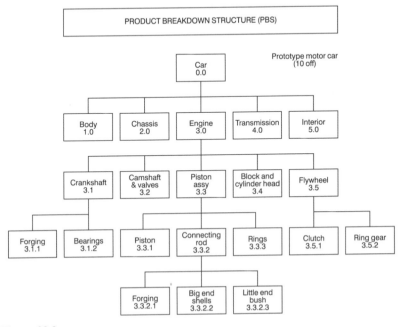

Figure 29.9

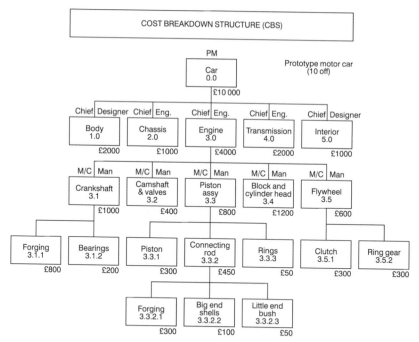

Figure 29.10

of Table 29.9 can be added. After summating the resources for every day, it has been noticed that there is a peak requirement of 12 men in days 11 and 12. As this might be more than the available resources, the bar chart can be adjusted by utilizing the available floats to *smooth* the resources and eliminate the peak demand. This is shown in Figure 29.17 by delaying the start of activities D and F.

Responsibility Matrix

	Sponsor	Project manager	Chief designer	Chief engineer	M/C shop manager	Chassis manager	Styling manager
Body	B	B	A	D	D	D	C
Chassis		B		A	C	C	
Engine	B	B		A	C	D	
Transmission		B		A	C	C	
Interior	B	B	A	D	D	D	C

A Main responsibility
B Must be advised
C Must be consulted
D Requires updates

Figure 29.11

In Figure 29.18, the man days of the unsmoothed bar chart have been multiplied by 8 to convert them into manhours. This was necessary to carry out *Earned Value Analysis*. The daily manhour totals can be shown as a *histogram* and the cumulative totals are shown as an *'S' curve*. In a similar way Figure 29.19 shows the respective histogram and 'S' curve for the smoothed bar chart.

It is now possible to draw up a table of *Actual Manhour* usage and *% complete* assessment for reporting day nos. 8, 16, 24 and 30. These, together with the *Earned Values* for these periods are shown in Table 29.11. Also shown is the efficiency (CPI), SPI, and the predicted final completion costs and times as calculated at each reporting day.

Using the unsmoothed bar chart histogram and 'S' curve as a *Planned manhour* base, the Actual manhours and Earned Value manhours can be

Table 29.9 Activity list of motor car engine manufacture and assembly (10 off), 8 hours/day

Activ. letter	Description	Dependency	Duration days	Men per day	Man hours per day	Total man hours
A	Cast block and cylinder head	Start	10	3	24	240
B	Machine block	A	6	2	16	96
C	Machine cylinder head	B	4	2	16	64
D	Forge and mc. flywheel	E	4	2	16	64
E	Forge crankshaft	Start	8	3	24	192
F	Machine crankshaft	E	5	2	16	80
G	Cast pistons	A	2	3	24	48
H	Machine pistons	G	4	2	16	64
J	Fit piston rings	H	1	2	16	16
K	Forge connecting rod	E	2	3	24	48
L	Machine conn. rod	K	2	2	16	32
M	Fit big end shells	L	1	1	8	8
N	Fit little end bush	M	1	1	8	8
O	Assemble engine	B, F, J, N	5	4	32	160
P	Fit flywheel	D, O	2	4	32	64
Q	Fit cylinder head	C, P	2	2	16	32
R	Fit camshaft and valves	Q	4	3	24	96
Total						1312

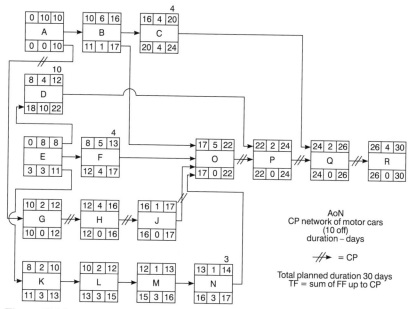

Figure 29.12

plotted on the graph in Figure 29.20. This graph also shows the % *complete* and % *efficiency* at each of the four reporting days.

Finally Table 29.12 shows the actions required for the *Close-Out* procedure.

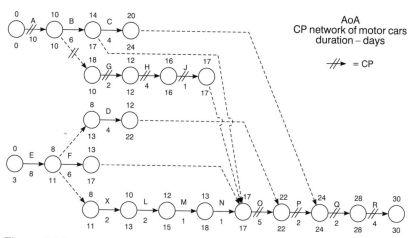

Figure 29.13

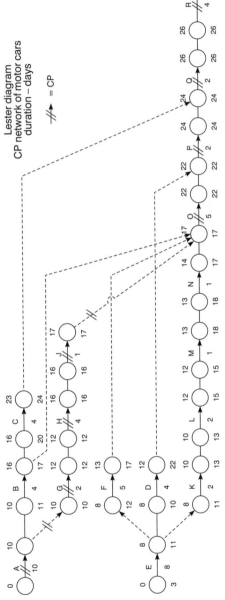

Lester diagram
CP network of motor cars
duration – days

⫽ = CP

Figure 29.14

Table 29.10
Activity Floats

From CP network

Activ. letter	Description	Duration	Total float	Free float
A	Cast block and cylinder head	10	0	0
B	Machine block	6	1	0
C	Machine cylinder head	4	4	4
D	Forge and mc. flywheel	4	10	10
E	Forge crankshaft	8	3	0
F	Machine crankshaft	5	4	4
G	Cast pistons	2	0	0
H	Machine pistons	4	0	0
J	Fit piston rings	1	0	0
K	Forge connecting rod	2	3	0
L	Machine conn. rod	2	3	0
M	Fit big end shells	1	3	0
N	Fit little end bush	1	3	3
O	Assemble engine	5	0	0
P	Fit flywheel	2	0	0
Q	Fit cylinder head	2	0	0
R	Fit camshaft and valves	4	0	0

Milestones

Milestone 1 Forge crankshaft (E)	Day 8
Milestone 2 Machine pistons (H)	Day 16
Milestone 3 Fit flywheel (P)	Day 24
Milestone 4 Completion	Day 30

Milestone slip chart   **Programme**

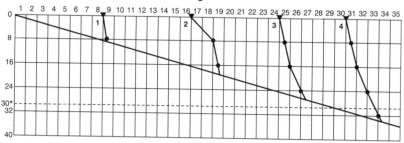

Assume:

* Reporting periods (8, 16, 24 and 30)

Milestone 1 slips ½ day

" 2 " 2 days, then ½ day

" 3 " ½ day, then ½ day, then 1 day

" 4 " ½ day, then ½ day, then 1 day, then 1 day

Figure 29.15

Bar chart of prototype motor cars (10 off)

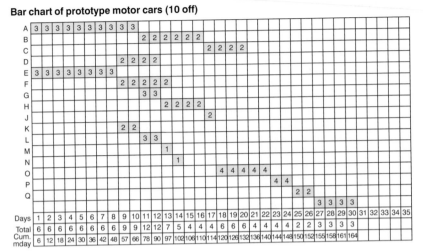

Figure 29.16 Unsmoothed

1 Business case

Need for new model. What type of car. Min./max. price. Manufacturing cost. Units per year Marketing strategy. What market sector is it aimed at. Main specification. What extras should be standard. Name of new model. Country of manufacture.

Bar chart of prototype motor cars (10 off)   After moving D to start at day 18
and moving F to start at day 12

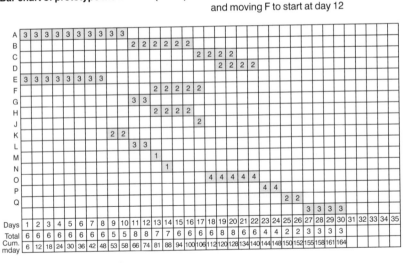

Figure 29.17 Smoothed

2 Investment appraisal

Options: Saloon, Coupé, Estate, Convertible, People carrier, 4 × 4. Existing or new engine. Existing or new platform. Materials of construction for engine, body. Type of fuel. New or existing plant. DCF of returns, NPV, Cash flow.

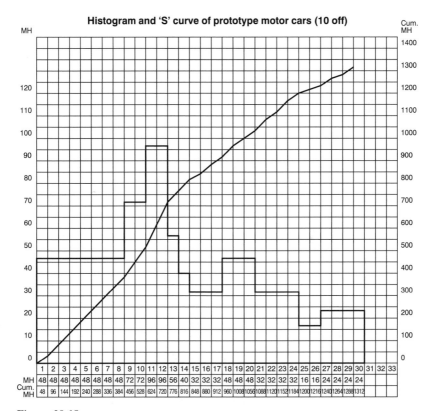

Figure 29.18

3 Project and product life cycle

Conception: Original idea, submission to top management
Feasibility: Feasibility study, preliminary costs, market survey
Design: Vehicle and tool design, component tests
Prototype: Tooling, production line, environmental tests
Manufacture: Mass production, training
Distribution: Deliveries, staff training, marketing
Disposal: Dismantling of plant, selling tools

4 Work and product breakdown structure

Design, Prototype, Manufacture, Testing, Marketing, Distribution, Training.
Body, Chassis, Engine, Transmission, Interior, Electronics.
Cost Breakdown Structure, Organization Breakdown Structure, Responsibility Matrix.

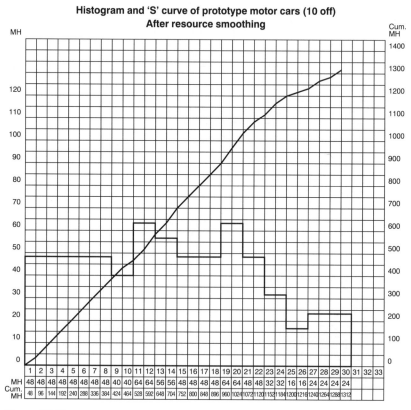

Figure 29.19

5 AoN network

Network diagram, forward and backward pass, floats, critical path, examination for overall time reduction, conversion to bar chart with resource loading, histogram, reduction of resource peaks, cumulative 'S' curve. Milestone slip chart.

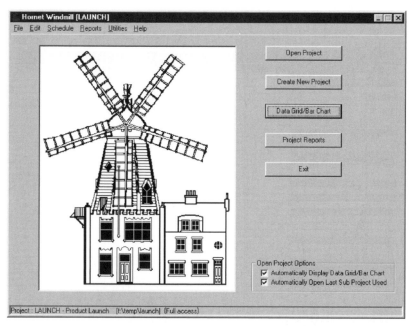

Figure 30.1 Hornet Windmill title screen

shows. Additionally the Hornet range of software is unique in directly supporting the management methods described by the author in earlier chapters of this book – specifically the drafting and numbering of network diagrams, and the SMAC Cost Control methodology. The following review does not detail the product's features and functions – space does not permit this – but describes the range of facilities and the types of reporting that this system offers. By way of example the manner in which the SMAC Cost Control calculations are supported by Hornet Windmill is described.

The main display

The main display in Hornet Windmill is a combined data grid and interactive bar chart display. The data values for the project tasks are displayed on the grid section with task bars shown on the bar chart area.

Both sections of the display scroll vertically through the entire task list, whilst the bar chart section can also be scrolled horizontally through time, and the timescale contracted or expanded to show a larger or smaller slice of the project duration.

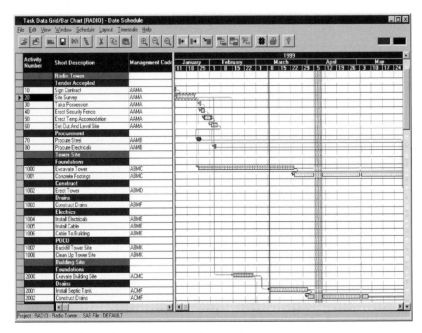

Figure 30.2   Main data grid and bar chart display

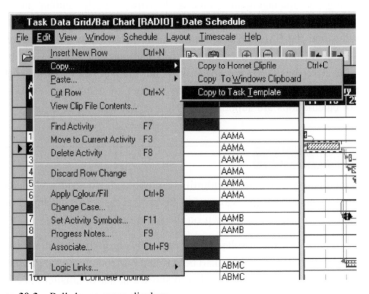

Figure 30.3   Pull-down menu displays

Also on the display are a series of drop-down menus that give access to the wide range of control options, settings and other project functions offered by Hornet Windmill. Under the menus is a toolbar holding a series of buttons that gives direct access to primary functions – like reschedule, link tasks or print a report.

Figure 30.4   Toolbar display

The display is controlled and driven by use of the menus, the toolbar buttons, specific function keys (or key combinations known as 'hot-keys'), the mouse and the normal keyboard. As familiarity is gained with the system increased use is made of the toolbar buttons and special key combinations to access the required functions.

Task numbering

In Hornet Windmill the user can enter task data on the data grid side, or directly on the bar chart display – usually using a combination of both. Each task that is entered must be allocated a unique number or code – this may be a straight number like 10, 100, or an alphanumeric code like BAW34. Generally a normal numeric sequence is recommended as this is easy to trace and sort into sequence. Numbering tasks in a stepped sequence, for example in 10s, allows for any subsequent insertions although this is not essential as Hornet Windmill includes a powerful 'renumber' facility.

Task numbering can be used to great effect in formatting and controlling final reports. Task numbers can be defined down to intervals of 0.1 and 0.01 and the numbering related to the automatic 'grouping' or summarizing of tasks on displays and reports. By changing the selection options you can show a range of tasks split across successive lines – or produce a summary or roll-up report that covers different work sections. The level of summary obtained can be determined by specifying the range of numbers under which summaries are made – for instance, using number intervals of tenths, integers (whole numbers), tens, hundreds and thousands. An example of this is shown in Figure 30.5.

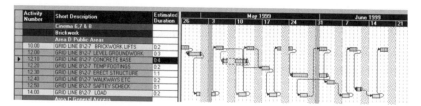

Figure 30.5 Using task numbering to define task groups and summaries

If the original project has been drafted by hand on a large sheet (see Chapter 13) then the task numbers can be related to the row and column numbers on the original sketch. These numbers will then be carried through the system by Hornet Windmill to draw the network diagram for the project in *exactly* the same style as drawn by hand (but neater!).

Task data values

Initially the two data values required for each task are a text title or description (not essential but it does help) and task duration. The latter can be specified in days, or weeks and days, or, if the project is related to smaller time periods, in half-days or hours. Interconnecting logic between the tasks is also required but this is described shortly. One major advantage of a software product over a manual approach is that one can readily associate extra data values with each task, and increase the level of detail or complexity given to each task.

The use of different *calendars* within a project is one of the most commonly used facilities. One can define a whole range of different working calendars – for instance, a five-day working week, a full seven-day working week, and a calendar for just two days' working each weekend.

Each calendar can have a range of holidays added, Christmas, New Year, Easter etc., to give an accurate representation of a working pattern. If appropriate one can define a separate calendar for each member of staff. Calendars can also relate to different types of work or task; for instance, embankment settlement and concrete curing would be associated to a full working calendar as these tasks do not stop over weekends and holidays. Many users also associate tasks that are subcontracted to other companies to a global calendar as they have no interest in showing weekends and holidays for these items. Some tasks may be restricted to weekend or holiday periods only, for example road and rail closures. All these permutations can be reflected by applying project calendars.

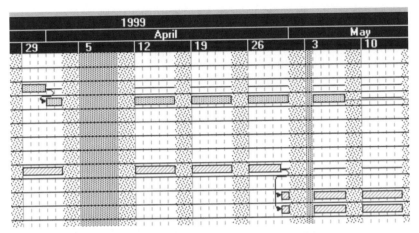

Figure 30.6   The use of calendars to show weekends and holidays

When a project is first planned then all tasks relate to 'future' work and the project schedule will run from the first work on site through to project completion. However, once work is underway the actual progress made in the field will need to be reflected in the project plan. This data is added to the project by recording the dates when each task commenced and, when completed, when it was finished. This information is vital as it allows Hornet Windmill to reschedule the uncompleted sections of the project based on the actual work done in the field. The results from this will show a revized future schedule based on the actual work done. To add this information data columns relating to actual start and finish dates, and a column for progress for tasks underway, are used.

Making the most of the task data

The task data entered into the Hornet Windmill system is already beyond the level of detail that can be managed in a manual calculation method, and with a computerized system much more can be achieved. Different text data fields can be used to hold alternative or extended task titles or notes; possibly task descriptions in an alternative language.

Tasks of different types can be colour coded, or a shading pattern applied, and legends included on reports to offer readers an easily identified coding system.

It is not necessary to restrict oneself to a single coding strategy as one can code tasks by both, say, responsibility *and* work type. One can then offer a

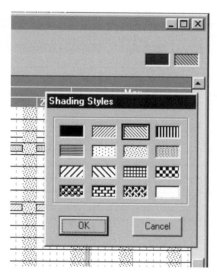

Figure 30.7 Selecting a shading style for task bars

report in two different styles – list tasks by responsibility and colour coding the display by work type, *and* list tasks by work type and colour coding by responsibility.

Additional data values can be included on the task data grid. Text notes and symbol designs can be added to the bar chart display to annotate the final report, for example to mark key stages or *milestones* in the project duration. Hornet Windmill offers a special panel to add and record a series of notes against each task, see Figure 30.8. This can be used as a record or *aide*

Activity Progress Notes - 1002 : Erect Tower		
Date	**Time**	**Notes Text**
06/01/99	10:18	Access to site confirmed for 11th Jan - FPS
12/01/99	14:36	Drilling rig delayed. Replacement now due 8:00am on 15th Jan - FPS
22/01/99	13:15	Confirm final report to be delivered Monday, 25th Feb. - GFP
26/01/99	09:38	Detailed soil results omitted from report - To be ready by 29th. - GFP
05/02/99	11:56	Confirmed report details accepted and no special requirements need be applied for - FPS

Figure 30.8 Panel recording task notes and comments

318

mémoire by the project manager to note pertinent details about the progress of each project task. These notes are automatically timed and dated and can be recalled and printed at any stage, possibly much later, to remind participants of precisely what contributed to the actual events in the field. If necessary file links or references can be created to other letters, designs and drawings held within the project archives – again facilitating any future need to collate information on a key event in the project's development and execution. With a bit of thought the project manager can use the software to build a very powerful planning and reporting capability that encompasses just about every aspect of the project he or she is responsible for.

Coding tasks

As the project gets larger, more and more tasks will be added and any full report will run to many pages. Clearly some method of classifying the tasks into different sections, or different responsibilities, is required and this takes users into the task coding aspects of Hornet Windmill. This is one of the most powerful features of the product and a bit of forethought and care on setting up an appropriate coding strategy initially will ensure maximum focus of reporting later in the project. The simplest – and most versatile – coding method is to select key classifications that are relevant to your project. Examples include site location, work type, subcontractor code, person responsible, location within building etc. Each of these classifications is then

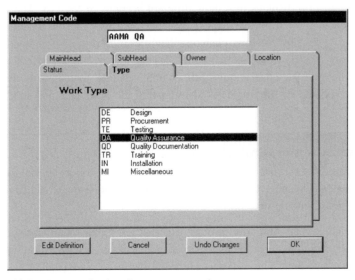

Figure 30.9 A customized coding prompt panel

broken down into a list of possible entries. Set up the coding letters for each entry in the prompt definition panel – each tab on the screen display covers a different coding classification – and you are then ready to code the project tasks.

Each task is coded under each classification using the prompt panel – global editing is possible to set a particular coding entry across a range of selected tasks. Once done these codes can be used to extract and list specific sections of the project, and sort the tasks into an appropriate order. All Hornet Windmill displays and reports support three levels of *Section Headings* and these are linked directly to the coding centres. It is an easy step to list tasks titled by *Site Section* (basement, ground, first, second and roof) and subtitled by Work Type (steel, concrete, flooring, walls, electrical, finishes). It is just as easy to reverse the titling to produce a second version of the report that lists by Work Type as the main heading, then Site Section as the subheading. If the coding classifications include Responsibility then one can list tasks under this heading with a separate report for each person giving them only the tasks they are responsible for. All this can be achieved without needing to recode or reclassify the tasks at any stage.

The task data display also shows the scheduled start and finish dates (both early and late dates), the different float values and other status information. If all potential data values were displayed at the same time then the grid display would be extremely wide and the user would need to scroll the display constantly left and right searching for specific values. Hornet Windmill offers a range of grid displays that show different sections of the task data giving complete control over the display contents. The user is free to adjust the display by resizing columns, changing the order of the columns and adding or removing specific values – the final layouts can be saved and recalled for later use. The grid includes a 'lock left column' facility that ensures the task number is held on the display whilst allowing the other columns to scroll.

The bar chart display

This section of the display is also interactive and allows direct control over the task bars. Bars can be dragged to required time locations and stretched to give the required duration period.

Stretching and dragging actions use the left mouse button to control selection and movement, whilst the right mouse button is used to add intertask logical constraints. The user can add a link between two tasks by using the mouse to draw a line between the end of the preceding task and the start of the

2005	Concrete Footings	7:4
2006	Interior Basement Walls	2:1
2007	Exterior Basement Walls	9:1
2008	Pour Concrete Floor	3:3
2009	Install Fuel Tank	0:3
2010	Install Floor Beams	3:0

Activity 2006
Start Date : 30-Apr-99
Finish Date : 19-May-99
Not Progressed

Figure 30.10   Stretching task bar 2006

2000	Exavate Building Site	2:0
2001	Install Septic Tank	3:2
2002	Construct Drains	4:1
2003	Backfill Building Site	2:1
2004	Clean Up Building Site	0:3

Activity 2001
Start Date : 21-Mar-99
Finish Date : 12-Apr-99
Not Progressed

Figure 30.11   Dragging task bar 2001

succeeding task – the addition of a standard 'finish to start' logic constraint. Similar links in the styles 'start to start' and 'finish to finish' can also be added in this manner. Hornet Windmill supports the use of 'logic delays' on links and these can be added by using the 'Ctrl' key as the new link is drawn.

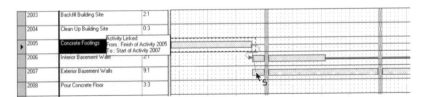

2003	Backfill Building Site	2:1
2004	Clean Up Building Site	0:3
2005	Concrete Footings	2:1
2006	Interior Basement Walls	2:1
2007	Exterior Basement Walls	9:1
2008	Pour Concrete Floor	3:3

Activity Linked
From : Finish of Activity 2005
To : Start of Activity 2007

Figure 30.12   Adding a sequential FS link between tasks 2005 and 2007

In most projects the scheduling of the tasks relies on the entered logic links to determine where the tasks will be positioned in time. Thus as the bars on the display are dragged to a new position the next time the project is rescheduled Hornet Windmill will restore the bar to its correct position. If required this can be overridden by using the 'drag-and-lock' facility where tasks are left in the position given by the user permanently. This approach can be extended to build up an entire programme without the need to add *any* logic links between tasks. In any text on project management theory this approach is classified as the ultimate sin – however, it is a facility that is provided through user request.

Adding logic links on the screen display is a suitable method for relatively small projects as tasks are relatively close together on the display. However, in large projects adding links using a mouse can be tedious and prone to error – and cross-checking the entered logic can be virtually impossible. Hornet Windmill offers two solutions to overcome this problem: using the toolbar buttons to add links between previously selected tasks, or showing the logic links in a grid display that can be used to check, add and edit logic links.

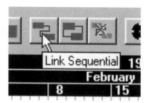

Figure 30.13 The three toolbar buttons for adding and removing logic links

The alternative data displays can be focused on either Precedent links (links running backwards) or Successor links (links running forward), and used alongside the direct entry on the bar chart display. Many users find this a more positive means of establishing the correct logic links on a project.

	Precedent Activity	Precedent Description	Link Type	Precedent Delay	Precedent Calendar
1	1005	Install Cable	FS		Week
▶ 2	2006	Interior Basement Walls	FS		Week
3	2007	Exterior Basement Walls	FS		Week
✳					

Activity Precedents - 1006 : Cable To Building

Figure 30.14 Precedent logic links for task 1006 in a data grid display

Tracing of logic through a project is also supported by two tabular reports – a listing of all precedents *and* successors on a task-by-task basis – and a logic trace report that lists precedents to a given task, then lists the precedents to the precedents, and so on (the report can also work through successors). This form of 'thread' analysis can be invaluable on a large project as it identifies relationships between key tasks even when there is no direct link between them. A sample report is shown in Figure 30.15.

Successor Logic Trace

Starting Task: 10 - Sign Contract

Activity	Description	Critical Status	Predecessor/Successor	
Level 1				
20	Site Survey	Critical	10	Sign Contract
Level 2				
1000	Excavate Tower	Float	20	Site Survey
2000	Exavate Building Site	Critical	20	Site Survey
3000	Lay Road Base	Float	20	Site Survey
30	Take Possession	Critical	20	Site Survey
Level 3				
1001	Concrete Footings	Float	1000	Excavate Tower
2001	Install Septic Tank	Float	2000	Exavate Building Site
2005	Concrete Footings	Float	2000	Exavate Building Site
3001	Surface Road	Float	3000	Lay Road Base
3001	Surface Road	Float	3000	Lay Road Base
40	Erect Security Fence	Critical	30	Take Possession
Level 4				
1002	Erect Tower	Critical	1001	Concrete Footings
2002	Construct Drains	Float	2001	Install Septic Tank
2006	Interior Basement Walls	Float	2005	Concrete Footings
2007	Exterior Basement Walls	Float	2005	Concrete Footings
4000	Obtain Job Acceptance	Critical	3001	Surface Road
50	Erect Temp Accomodation	Critical	40	Erect Security Fence
Level 5				
1003	Construct Drains	Float	1002	Erect Tower
1004	Install Electricals	Critical	1002	Erect Tower
2003	Backfill Building Site	Float	2002	Construct Drains
2008	Pour Concrete Floor	Float	2006	Interior Basement Walls
1006	Cable To Building	Critical	2006	Interior Basement Walls
2008	Pour Concrete Floor	Float	2007	Exterior Basement Walls
1006	Cable To Building	Float	2007	Exterior Basement Walls
60	Set Out And Level Site	Critical	50	Erect Temp Accomodation
Level 6				
1007	Backfill Tower Site	Critical	1003	Construct Drains
1005	Install Cable	Critical	1004	Install Electricals
2004	Clean Up Building Site	Float	2003	Backfill Building Site
2009	Install Fuel Tank	Float	2008	Pour Concrete Floor
2010	Install Floor Beams	Float	2008	Pour Concrete Floor
1007	Backfill Tower Site	Critical	1006	Cable To Building
2003	Backfill Building Site	Critical	1006	Cable To Building
70	Procure Steel	Critical	60	Set Out And Level Site
80	Procure Electricals	Critical	60	Set Out And Level Site
Level 7				
1008	Clean Up Tower Site	Critical	1007	Backfill Tower Site
1006	Cable To Building	Critical	1005	Install Cable
4000	Obtain Job Acceptance	Float	2004	Clean Up Building Site
4000	Obtain Job Acceptance	Float	2009	Install Fuel Tank
2011	Concrete Main Floor /Walls	Float	2010	Install Floor Beams
1002	Erect Tower	Critical	70	Procure Steel
1004	Install Electricals	Critical	80	Procure Electricals
Level 8				
4000	Obtain Job Acceptance	Critical	1008	Clean Up Tower Site
2012	Concrete Roof	Float	2011	Concrete Main Floor /Walls
Level 9				
2013	Lay Roof	Float	2012	Concrete Roof
2014	Complete Interior	Float	2012	Concrete Roof
Level 10				
4000	Obtain Job Acceptance	Float	2013	Lay Roof
2015	Paint & Clean	Float	2014	Complete Interior
Level 11				
4000	Obtain Job Acceptance	Float	2015	Paint & Clean

Date 18/02/99 Project Radio Tower
Time 15:18

Figure 30.15   Successor logic trace report

Scheduling the project

Once the project data has been completed the results can be calculated by using the scheduling facilities of Hornet Windmill. The most common analysis method is to perform a standard Time Schedule or Time Analysis for the entered tasks and logic links. Under this calculation the task start and finish dates – both early and late dates – are calculated based on the task durations and logic links or constraints between them. This is a very quick calculation and the displays are promptly updated to show the new values. The calculation in Hornet Windmill also takes into consideration the relevant working calendar patterns (weekends and holidays) for all tasks and logic links, and builds the future dates on any progress details already entered for the project. The calculation uses a 'time now' or 'project date' as the equivalent to today's date which marks the point between the past and the future in the project schedule.

The scheduling calculation is so quick on modern computers that it is possible to set the system to rerun the scheduling calculation after each addition or revision of the data values. Use of this type of facility is a matter of preference and the majority of users choose to complete a series of revisions before making the calculation – this prevents a constantly changing view of the project being given and on larger projects is quicker to operate.

The scheduling calculations in Hornet Windmill can also take into account the availability of resources – manpower, equipment etc. – and give a future project schedule that takes into account all logical relationships *and* ensures that there will be sufficient resources available to complete the tasks. These calculations are known as Resource Scheduling and offer a range of different calculation facilities – before these calculations can be made the user must define the resource requirements and availabilities for the project.

Adding resources to the project

Project resources can cover a wide range of different commodities and these are often applied quite differently by users. Hornet Windmill is very flexible in what it terms as a resource – a resource is any commodity that has a *quantity* associated to it and that can be linked to the completion of an individual task within the project. This definition covers most things – work content in manhours (or mandays), monetary value, material quantities, equipment needs etc. The user is free to define as many distinct resource types, or *resource centres*, as needed by the project. The user must ensure that the units used on each resource are consistent through the project, although

Resource Allocations - 2015 : Paint & Clean

	Resource	Type	Value	Complete	Remaining	Offset	Duration
1	Labour	Sum	920	0	0		
2	Payment	Sum	15000	0	0		0:1
3	Subcon	Sum	5000	0	0	3:0	
*							

Figure 30.16 Resource allocations for task 2015 in a data grid display

any unit of measure may be applied in each case. One or more of the defined resources may be used to measure progress within the project – this is usually manhours but may be any easily identified unit of measure that runs throughout the project.

Hornet Windmill allows each defined resource to be given 'availability' limits over the duration of the project. These limits will on histogram reports highlight periods when insufficient resource is available in the planned project schedule – ideally these will be picked up well in advance so that the project manager has enough time to take steps to avoid the potential shortfall. The automatic scheduling facilities in Hornet Windmill will automatically reschedule project tasks to ensure future resource availabilities are not exceeded. This form of Resource Scheduling is a useful tool for projects that are heavily resource constrained – although many construction-type projects are constrained more by the logical sequence of tasks rather than simple resource availability. However, the ability to predict accurately future requirements of a wide range of resources over the duration of the project is extremely valuable.

Each task may have any number of different resources associated to it and these are entered on a mini task data grid. In addition to resource name and value, Hornet Windmill allows the user to enter current progress values against each of them – for example, a record of hours already expended and estimated hours to completion; these can then be compared to the original budgeted hours for the task. Once resource values have been allocated to tasks a histogram report showing future resource usage over the project duration can be produced and displayed.

Project reports

Producing the final project reports and distributing them to the relevant parties is a key task of the project manager and any project management system must be able to produce required reports quickly and consistently. These reports will usually take the form of standard reporting styles, e.g. bar charts (Gantt charts), tabular listings, resource histograms and network diagrams, but there is invariably a requirement to produce a slightly customized report that gives a specific style of report to meet particular requests – or to match an existing report that has been developed and used for some time.

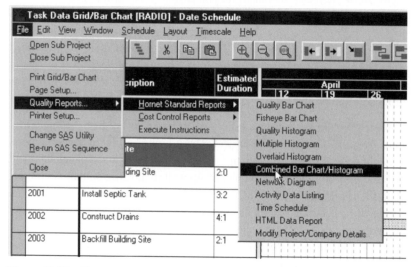

Figure 30.17 The standard reports menu

Hornet Windmill supports a wide range of standard reporting formats that satisfy the most common requirements. It also offers a Report Wizard which is used to build customized reports that include selected project values across the page. All reports in Hornet Windmill are created using a form of macros or program language, report layouts and variable screen prompt panels and these can be applied by the user to build virtually any type of project report that could be envisaged.

All standard reports use a form of tabbed prompt panel into which the user enters required titles, selects the range of tasks to be included and sets required layout options and styles. All task reports allow for the inclusion of headings and subheadings, and the grouping or summary of tasks to provide a roll-up or summary report. Each report saves the settings and selections made by the user – these can be recalled to rerun any defined style at a later date. Reports produced by Hornet Windmill do not have to be distributed in paper form –

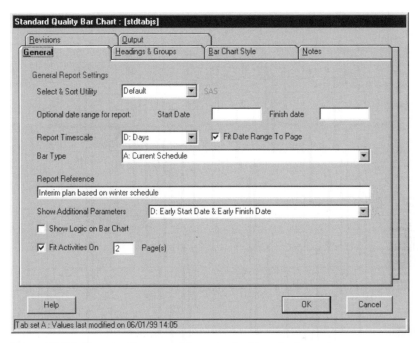

Figure 30.18   Report settings panel for a standard bar chart report

they can be effectively e-mailed or posted on the Internet for all users to view and print.

The range of options and facilities provided in the standard reports is very wide and only the main facilities for each report type are summarized below:

Bar chart reports may be produced on all paper sizes from A4 to A0 and support full colour printing and shading styles, see Figure 30.19. The horizontal timescale supports a 'scale to fit' facility which ensures the full project duration (or a specified date range) fits neatly across the page. The timescale can be shown in a non-linear style – a sort of 'fisheye' – where work already completed is compressed – say the past nine months over the first 30% of the page, the current three-month period occupying the next 50% of the page, and the remaining two years to project completion shown in the final 20% of the page. These page proportions can be adjusted to meet the specific requirements of the user and allow even long projects to be drawn on a single sheet. Bar chart styles may be set to show future task dates as currently scheduled, or show the original or *baseline* schedule alongside current dates,

Widget Design and Production
Overall Long Term Schedule

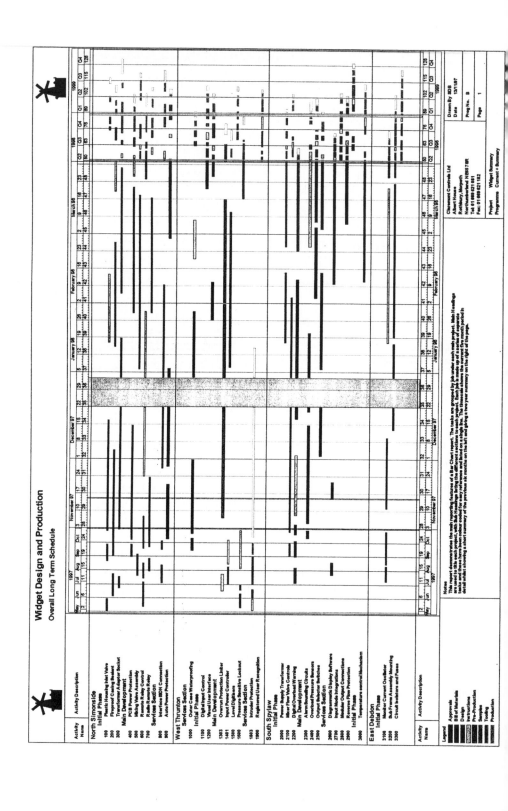

Clearmont Controls Ltd
Albert House
Rothbury, Morpeth
Northumberland NE65 7SR
Tel: 01 669 621 681
Fax: 01 669 621 182

Project   Widget Summary
Programme Current 4 Summary

Drawn By SDS
Date   13/1/97
Prog No. B
Page   1

Notes
This report demonstrates the main reporting features of a Bar Chart report. The tasks are grouped by job under each main project. The tasks are split into the different sections to each project. Each job is made up of a series of separate tasks and these have been coded for the page listing the different sections along the top. The timescales alters with time being a longer or shorter bar. The first column shows the start whilst giving a two year summary of the previous six months on the left and giving a two year summary on the right of the page.

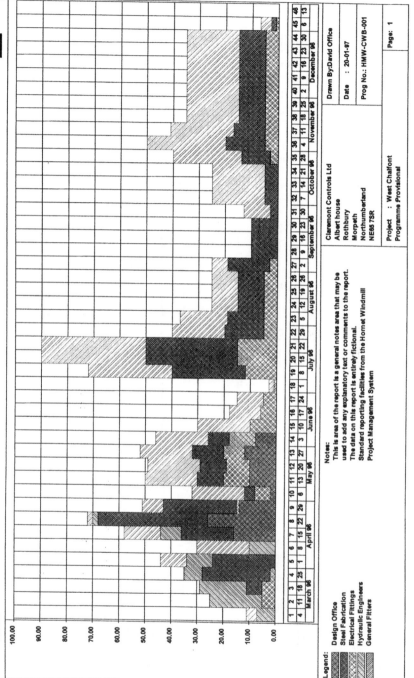

Figure 30.20 Histogram report showing four stacked resource profiles

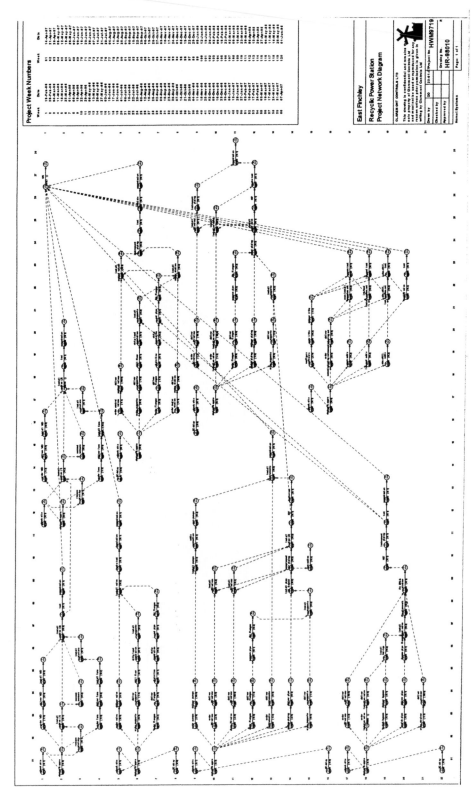

Figure 30.21 Network diagram drawn in the Activity on Arrow style. (Note: All link lines miss the nodes)

or show the current recorded progress marked up on the baseline schedule (giving the characteristic zig-zag progressed bar chart). Other style options to show float, colour-coded task bars, add the logic links and customize the page legend and titles are all supported.

Histogram reports show the planned resource requirements over the duration of the project and are the second most widely graphical project report. All histogram reports in Hornet Windmill allow up to eight different resource profiles to be drawn on each set of axes – either stacked on top of each other or drawn 'side by side', see Figure 30.20. S–curve calculations (cumulative profiles) are supported and the traditional *envelope* between early and late planned dates can be drawn. If required several graph axes can be shown on a single page, or the histogram drawn under a bar chart to give a powerful combined format report.

Network diagram reports may be drawn in either precedence style (activity on node) or arrow style (activity on arrow, see Figure 30.21) and also support various facilities to 'fit diagram to page'. The design and data content shown for each task on the report can be varied and the report will mark the progress recorded against each task, highlight critical tasks and links, and colour code tasks to the users legend scheme. If the project network diagram is to be related to a hand-drafted original using a grid of rows and columns, the task numbering can be used to place the nodes in their appropriate locations on the page. The link lines all miss the nodes.

Tabular reports still provide a valuable format for the issuing of project data – particularly where a report is specifically targeted at those responsible for the attached content. Tabular reports can be combined with 'fill me in' boxes or columns for weekly update and return on project progress. This style of reporting can also be given in a format compatible with the Internet or the company Intranet – allowing direct access to information over a computer network without having to run or print full project management reports. Tabular reports also include the task logic listings – both the precedence and successor report or the logic thread report – referred to earlier.

Project cost control

Entering the man-hours figures for the SMAC Project Cost Control as described in Chapter 27 is extremely straightforward and takes the minimum of input. The user can select the appropriate data grid display to show all the

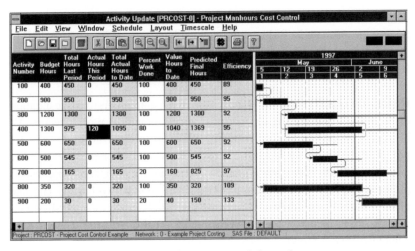

Figure 30.22 Task data grid showing cost control data columns

key cost control parameters on the main task data grid and bar chart display. On the display shown in Figure 30.22 the columns have been sized to display all required values simultaneously.

At this stage it is assumed that all project tasks have been entered, task durations set and the logic links added. A schedule of the project calculates the task start and finish dates, and shows the bar chart as the planned duration of the project. On the display the cursor is taken to the column headed **Budget Hours** and moved down this column adding the appropriate total manhours for each task on the grid in turn. Once completed Hornet Windmill can produce the Cost Control graphs showing the planned progress of the project over time – actual progress has yet to be added.

To add the progress details to the system, values have to be entered into the two columns **Actual Hours This Period** and **Percent Work Done**. Values are required for all tasks that have been progressed in the past week (or whatever the project reporting period is) giving the actual manhours expended, and the manager's assessment of % complete at the end of the period. As values are entered, Hornet Windmill will calculate the other values on the row (these values are shown with grey backgrounds).

If the record of the manhours is already compiled in a different computer system it should be possible to take this data and feed it directly into the Hornet Windmill system; utilities to do this are included with the Hornet software. This can greatly ease the running of the system as time-consuming double entry of data values can be avoided. Similarly, one can use reports and/ or other database systems to collate and import the weekly progress values on the project tasks.

Once the progress values for the period have been entered Hornet Windmill will complete the calculations to show the overall progress of the project to date. This can be viewed as a summary table showing the derived progress values for all reporting periods to date, see Figure 30.23.

SMAC Manhours Summary							
Last Period Date	Last Period Number	Total Budget Manhours	Total Value Hours	Total Actual Hours	Overall % Complete	Predicted Final Manhours	Efficiency %
11 May 97	1	6250	1005	1105	16	6871	90
18 May 97	2	6250	2105	2275	34	6754	92
25 May 97	3	6250	4005	4225	64	6593	94
01 Jun 97	4	6250	5125	5385	82	6567	95

Close

Project : PRCOST - Project Cost Control Example [c:\hornetw\prcost]

Figure 30.23 Summary table from the SMAC Cost Control

The SMAC control system is not an isolated management report as it is linked to a project network. Other management reports can be produced including a bar chart (or Gantt chart) that records the current progress of activities based against the original or planned completion schedule. The sample report shown in Figure 30.24 shows the planned position of activities as hollow bars against the project timescale. The bars are shaded to indicate the current percentage progress of each activity. A double vertical line marks the current date or date of the last progress update and the position of the shading on the bars in relation to this line shows whether activities are ahead or behind their original planned dates.

This report gives a very useful and easily understood snap shot of the current progress for project activities. The same data may be printed in a tabular form listing task dates and progress data in a series of columns, as

Cost Control Example
Quality Bar Chart Report

Activity Name	Activity Description
	Hkijpuos Cectmppapi Bvs Oinslca
	Nmfrstdtn Gc Iesddinswo
100	Ddwwmecya Tn Qf Emrshiruv
200	Rbszblr Irhdmil Hthwepov
	Selacrjxev Bihjnsgo Emros
300	Owslwtemo Kenrfe Blerideg
400	Elsyoc Moo Bnrbmplo Nalen
	Sagxogae Gv Ellnlfnays Ezxhczslp
	Nmfrstdtn Gc Iesddinswo
500	Etfonrrwn Xpntrgc Tlsdsec
600	Drdjkiqmbe Cpcoiqootd Xcs
	Selacrjxev Bihjnsgo Emros
700	Omisorfn Os Yv Cg Iesrtlo
	Toepbxdaiw Nvloaqsvoi Idpaias
800	Oorokop Oneyen Oeujlden G
900	DrdozaeaI Tar Eooltnrnle

Notes:
This bar chart shows the original planned schedule with actual progress to the current week marked on the tasks. The report includes the same main and sub headings as shown on the tabular reports.

Claremont Controls Ltd
Albert House
Rothbury
Morpeth
Northumberland
NE65 7SR

Project : Cost Control Example
Programme Baseline Program

Drawn By:SDB
Date : 03/06/97
Prog No.: 54

Page: 1

Hornet Project Management Systems

Reference: Progress After Weekly Update 4

Cost Control Example

Cost Control Data Listing

Project Manhour and Cost Report
Period Update Summary

Network : 0
Description : Standard Project Network

Period Update No : 4
Date of Update : 01-Jun-97

Activity	Description	Dura-tion	Budget Hours	SCHEDULED DATES Early Start	Early Finish	Late Start	Late Finish	Float	% Comp	MAN-HOURS Actuals This Period	Actuals Total	% Comp	Value	Estimated Final	% Eff.
	Hkijpuos Cectmppapi Bvs Oinsica Nmfrstdtn Gc lesddinswo														
100	Ddwwmecya Tn Qf Emrahiruv	0:2	400	05-May-97	06-May-97	05-May-97	06-May-97		100	0	450	100	400	450	89
200	Rbszblr Irhdmil Hthwspov	1:0	900	07-May-97	13-May-97	21-May-97	27-May-97	2:0	100	0	950	100	900	950	95
	Sub-Heading Totals:		1300							0	1400	100%	1300	1400	93%
	Selacrpxev Bihjnsgo Emros														
300	Owsiwtsmo Kanrfe Blerideg	2:0	1200	14-May-97	27-May-97	04-Jun-97	17-Jun-97	3:0	100	250	1300	100	1200	1300	92
400	Eisyoc Moo Bnrbmpio Nalen	3:0	1300	14-May-97	03-Jun-97	28-May-97	17-Jun-97	2:0	75	350	976	75	976	1300	100
	Sub-Heading Totals:		2600							600	2275	87%	2176	2616	96%
	Main-Heading Totals:		3800							600	3675	91%	3475	4019	95%
	Sagxogae Gv Ellnlfhays Ezdhczslp Nmfrstdtn Gc lesddinswo														
500	Etfonrrwn Xpntrgc Tlsdssc	2:0	600	07-May-97	20-May-97	14-May-97	27-May-97	1:0	100	0	660	100	600	660	92
600	Drdjkiqmbe Cpcolqootd Xcs	1:0	500	21-May-97	27-May-97	28-May-97	03-Jun-97	1:0	100	270	545	100	500	545	92
	Sub-Heading Totals:		1100							270	1196	100%	1100	1196	92%
	Selacrpxev Bihjnsgo Emros														
700	Omlsorfh Os Yv Cg lesrilo	2:0	800	28-May-97	10-Jun-97	04-Jun-97	17-Jun-97	1:0	20	165	165	20	160	825	97
	Sub-Heading Totals:		800							165	165	20%	160	825	97%
	Toepbxdaiw Nmoaqsvoi Idpalas														
800	Oorokop Oneyen Oeujiden G	4:0	360	07-May-97	03-Jun-97	07-May-97	03-Jun-97		100	95	320	100	350	320	109
900	Drdozaeal Tar Eooltnrrie	2:0	200	04-Jun-97	17-Jun-97	04-Jun-97	17-Jun-97		20	30	30	20	40	160	133
	Sub-Heading Totals:		550							125	350	71%	390	494	111%
	Main-Heading Totals:		2460							560	1710	67%	1660	2639	96%
	Report Totals:		6260							1160	5385	82%	6125	6667	95%

Notes: This report lists the planned start and finish dates for all tasks and includes cost control progress values to the current week. The tasks are divided into a series of main and sub headings and the report includes sub-totals for each section.

Claremont Controls Ltd
Albert House
Rothbury
Morpeth
Northumberland

Tel: 01 669 621 081
Fax: 01 669 621 182

Report Printed : 03/06/97   Page : 1
11:28

Hornet Project Management Systems

Reference: Progress After Weekly Update 4

Figure 30.25 Tabular report giving Cost Control summary across project sections

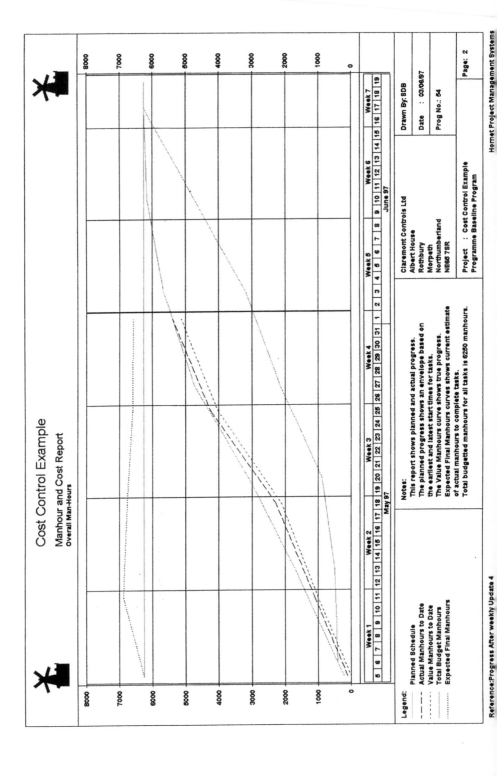

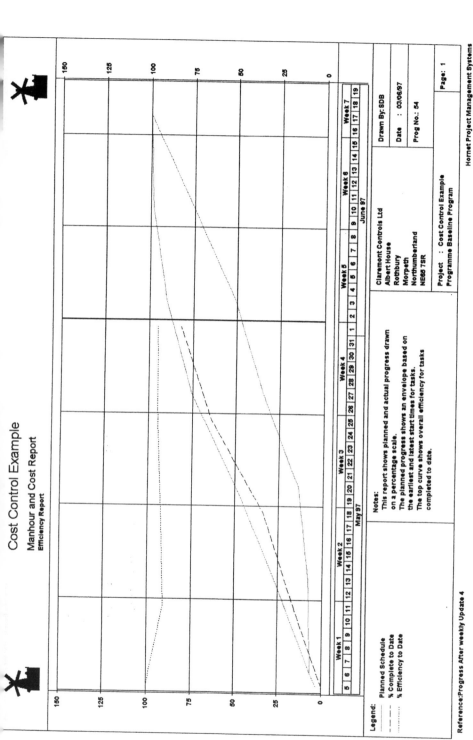

Cost Control Example

Manhour and Cost Report
Efficiency Report

Legend:
Planned Schedule
% Complete to Date
% Efficiency to Date

Notes:
This report shows planned and actual progress drawn on a percentage scale.
The planned progress shows an envelope based on the earliest and latest start times for tasks.
The top curve shows overall efficiency for tasks completed to date.

Claremont Controls Ltd
Albert House
Rothbury
Morpeth
Northumberland
NE65 7SR

Drawn By: SDB
Date : 03/06/97
Prog No.: 54

Project : Cost Control Example
Programme Baseline Program

Page: 1

Reference: Progress After weekly Update 4

Hornet Project Management Systems

Figure 30.27 Cost Control report showing Percentage Planned Manhours and Efficiency for the project

shown in Figure 30.25. This report shows how main and subheadings may be applied to give progress summaries within different sections, in addition to the overall result for the entire project. This can be extremely useful in identifying any sections of the project that are falling behind that would otherwise be masked in a single overall figure.

If required these results can be copied to a spreadsheet application using the Windows Clipboard facility and included in management reports or carried forward into further analysis.

A much clearer picture of project progress is given by printing the two standard Cost Control graphs. The first report, Figure 30.26, shows lines for Planned Manhours, Actual and Value Manhours to Date, and Expected Final Manhours plotted against the project timescale. The second report, Figure 30.27, uses a percentage scale to show Planned, Completed and Efficiency values for each of the reporting periods currently completed. Both these reports will highlight variations from the planned schedule of work at a very early stage and thus give the project manager every opportunity to take any necessary corrective action.

All Hornet reports, including the Cost Control reports shown here, can be modified and extended. This may be needed to change column headings on reports to conform to existing methods, or to extend the report to add further details or breakdowns.

31

MS Project 98

Probably the most popular project management program in use today is MS Project. Since its first introduction, it was updated a number of times and its latest version, MS Project 98 has been further enhanced to enable communications to be made to the Internet as well as improving the existing capabilities relating to resource management, Earned Value Analysis and Intranet support.

The list below shows some of the additional facilities provided by the latest version of MS Project:

Task Usage and Resource Usage
Custom time-period tracking
Cross project linking
Resource contouring
Multiple critical paths
Task splitting
Status date
Customizable Gantt charts
Workgroup features
Web publishing
Personal Web Server for Windows 95
Office Assistant
MS Office compatibility
Database file format
Full ODBC (Open Database Connectivity) support

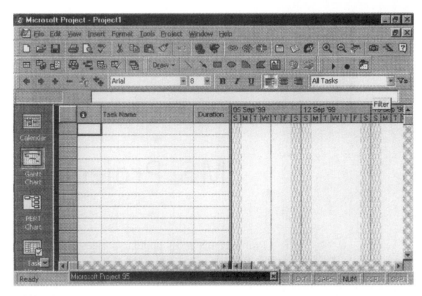

Figure 31.1

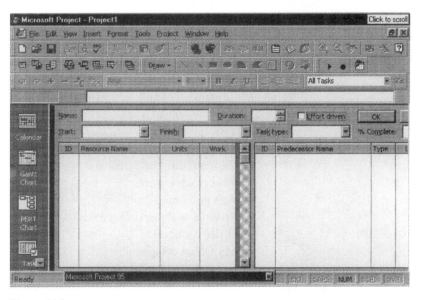

Figure 31.2

The basic principles, which are common to most commercial project management software packages, are described below.

When MS Project is opened, the Application window which contains the Project window appears as shown in Figure 31.1 (**View – Table – Entry**). The Project window shown is the Gantt chart view or Task Entry Table and is the default view of MS Project. The Project window can be split using a special 'split' feature (**Window – Split**) so that the lower section becomes the Task Form, used to enter additional information for each task. This is shown in Figure 31.2.

The first job is to set up the project using the Project Information box as shown in Figure 31.3. This, when completed, will show the Project Start date,

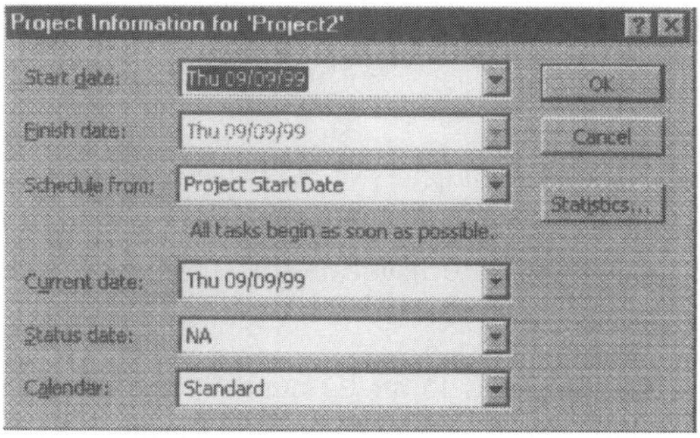

Figure 31.3

Finish date, a selection box which will show which of the two (Start date or Finish date) will be used as a basis for scheduling, the Current date, Status date and the type of calendar selected. The calendar can be Standard, 24 hours or Night Shift. If the Start date has been selected for scheduling, the Finish date will be adjusted automatically, depending on the actual programme.

The default calender of MS Project is set up for an 8-hour day and a 5-day week. If this is not acceptable for the project in question, it can be changed in the 'Change Working Time' dialog box (**Tools – Change Working Time**). This box also allows the new working and non-working times, hours per day and hours per week to be entered and set as the default calender using the 'Create New Base Calender' dialog box (see Figure 31.4).

Resource calendars, based on the 'Base Calender', can be created to suit the working times of any one of the resources employed on the project and are created automatically as soon as resources are added to the tasks.

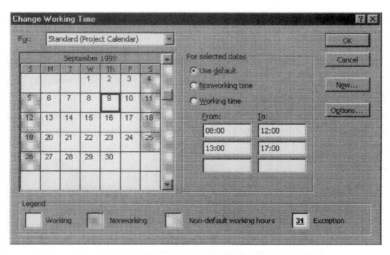

Figure 31.4

After entering the main parameters of the project, such as name, start date, time units, milestone dates etc., the activities or tasks (as they are called in MS Project) and their durations are listed on the 'task entry table' (see Figure 31.2).

This table assigns the tasks to an ID number and has columns for Task Name, Duration, Start, Finish, Predecessors, and Resource Names. The Finish date is calculated automatically by adding the Duration to the Start date.

A Resource Task Form showing any delays to the Start or Finish dates can be called up from **View – More Views – Resource Form** (see Figure 31.5).

As soon as a task has been entered, it is immediately displayed as a bar on a calendar scale to the right of the task entry table (see Figure 31.6).

When all the tasks have been entered, the interrelationship or linking of the tasks can be done by either:

(a) linking the bars in the generated bar (or Gantt) chart (this is done automatically if the predecessors have been entered), or
(b) giving the ID or name of the predecessor activity in the Task Form, which can be viewed on the same screen using the 'split' feature.

While this linking on the screen is relatively easy when all, or nearly all, the activities are visible on the screen, it becomes much more difficult to ensure

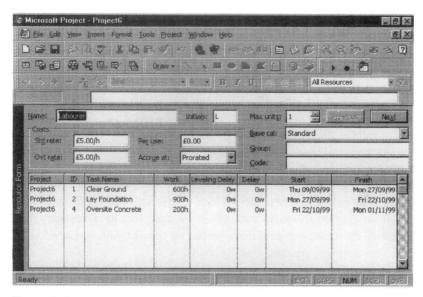

Figure 31.5

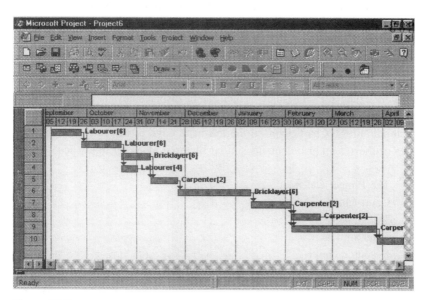

Figure 31.6

that no relationships are missed, when the network is bigger than, say, 30 activities. For this reason the network should always be draughted manually and the interrelationships checked and double checked before they are entered into the computer using the Task Form. The purpose of the computer program is to do the number crunching, not to take the place of the planner or project manager, who should know which activity is dependent on which.

Once all the tasks and their links have been entered, the cursor is placed on the 'Link Tasks' icon, which enables the computer to display the now modified bar chart, giving the completion date and listing the floats. The critical path is highlighted on the bar chart in either a different colour or a different pattern in the bars. Tasks which follow each other without a break are, if so chosen, shown in addition to the task bar, by a summary line stretching the total duration of the unbroken set of tasks. Milestones, i.e. tasks with zero duration, are shown as diamonds.

If the calculated completion date is not acceptable, it is very easy to change either the durations or the interrelationship of the links to give the desired result, assuming of course that the necessary resources are available to meet this date.

Task predecessors can also be changed easily by bringing up the Task Form and changing the name of the task predecessor in the Predecessor Name cell, in the right-hand part of this form. At the same time it is possible to change the ID number and (if required) the type of task relationship such as 'Finish to Start' 'Start to Start', 'Finish to Finish' or 'Start to Finish'. (It should be pointed out that 99% of all task relationships are 'Finish to Start'.) Lead and lag times specified in minutes, hours, days or weeks can also be entered in this screen.

MS Project automatically converts the Gantt chart into a precedence network called a 'PERT Chart', which can be displayed by choosing the PERT Chart command from the **VIEW – PERT Chart** menu or simply clicking the pictorial 'PERT Chart' icon on the left-hand edge of the entry screen. This area of the screen also contains similar pictorial icons for quick access to:

> The Project Calender
> Gantt Chart
> Task Usage
> Tracking Gantt
> Resource Graph
> Resource Sheet
> Resource Usage and
> More views

The nodes displayed in the PERT chart are by default quite large, so that in order to view a larger section of the network, one has to zoom out by pressing the appropriate zoom icon shown as a magnifying glass on the tool bar. The type of border around the task box indicates whether it is an ordinary activity, a critical activity, a summary activity or a milestone.

In practice it is still only possible to see quite a small network on this display due to the inevitable restriction of the screen size (see Figure 31.7). When the network is reduced to its smallest size, it becomes difficult to read the information in the nodes which consist of the task name, ID number, duration, early start date and late start date. If the network consists of a large number of activities, it is essential that it is printed out on a plotter, since if a line printer is used, one ends up with a large number of pieces of paper which have to be taped together. This restriction should be of little concern, since as stated previously, it is far more important to produce the network manually *before* using the computer to calculate the critical path, total floats, free floats and other information.

The position of the task boxes can be changed on the PERT chart by dragging and dropping the task boxes and by moving the link lines with the mouse. The link lines can be chosen to connect the boxes by straight lines (at any angle) or by lines running only at right angles.

Progress (or tracking) can be plotted on the Gantt chart by imputting the actual data for each task. The progress is now indicated by a solid black (or coloured) line within the original task bar. The length of this solid line is proportionate to the actual time expended.

Facilities exist for printing out a number of reports such as all the critical tasks, non-started tasks, the floats (total and free) for all tasks, the project statistics, project overview and resources. In MS Project, the float is called slack, i.e. total slack and free slack.

A filter facility enables the planner to prepare reports containing only selected groups of tasks such as only critical activities.

The latest version of MS Project enables the activities or tasks to be split. This is useful when the second half of an activity has to be interrupted for a while before it can be completed. This can be done by dragging and dropping task bars on the Gantt chart.

Many of these facilities may of course never be used, but at least they are available as part of the latest application for the more sophisticated planner.

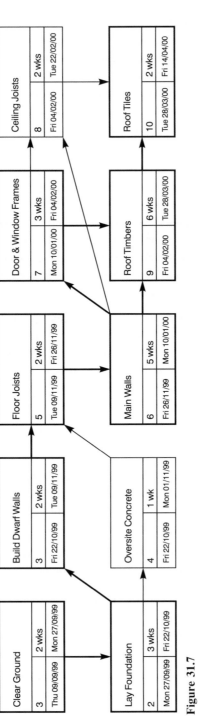

Figure 31.7

Resources

Resources can be entered in a number of ways, but the simplest method is to enter them directly in the left-hand part of the Task Form or in more detail on the Resource Information dialog box, which shows the name of the resource, e.g. foreman, his initials (or abbreviation), the dept or group he belongs to, the number (of foremen) available, the standard rate of pay (per hour), the overtime rate, and the cost per use, e.g. when an agreed rate for a consultant is used (see Figure 31.8).

The resources can also be allocated to tasks by clicking on the 'Resource Assignment' button, which brings up the Resource Assignment dialog box

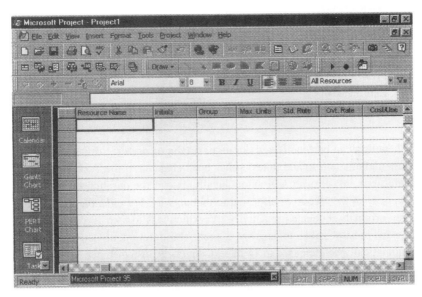

Figure 31.8

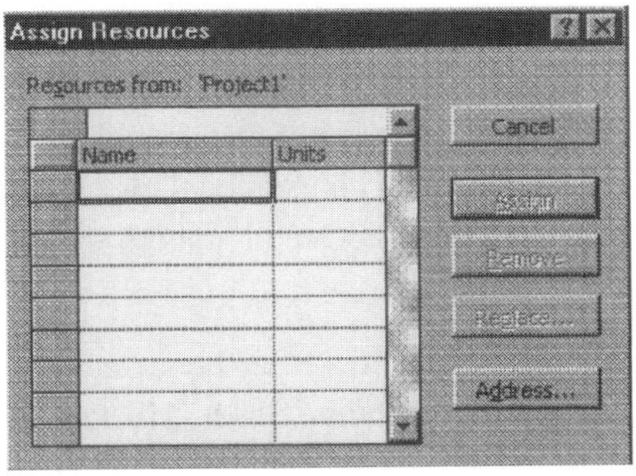

Figure 31.9

that displays all the previously entered resources (see Figure 31.9). By entering the name of the resource in an available cell together with the number of resource units available, the resource can be assigned to the selected task by clicking on the 'Assign' button. A facility exists for assigning a resource to several tasks simultaneously and showing the name of the resource next to the task bar on the Gantt chart.

MS Project now allows work to be assigned using predefined resource contours, which tell the program how the resource's work should be spread over the duration of the assignment. Thus the contours can be:

> Flat
> Back Loaded
> Bell
> Double Peak
> Early Peak
> Front Loaded
> Late Peak or
> Turtle

Scheduling can be time (fixed duration) driven or resource driven. The latter is the default setting and unless it has been changed in the Task Information dialog box, Ms Project will automatically extend the duration of an activity inversely to the resources allocated to that activity. For example, 4 men have been originally allocated to activity 'A', which was to take 12 days, and as it is now only possible to employ 3 men, the duration of activity 'A' will automatically be increased to 16 days. Conversely, if 6 men can be employed, the duration will be reduced to 8 days. Clearly if activity 'A' was on the critical path, the total project time will be changed accordingly.

The resource names can be added to the Gantt chart display next to the activity bars and displayed on the Resource Usage chart which will also indicate any under-or overusage of resources.

The distribution of a particular type of resource or all the resources can be shown graphically in the form of a conventional histogram or resource graph. This view can then be used to reallocate or smooth the resources to meet the availability criteria of the project.

By entering the monetary rates (rate per hour, rate per man, rate per day etc.) for each resource in the Resource Sheet, MS Project will calculate the cost of the resource for every activity. This is shown in the Task Cost table, Figure 31.10, accessed from **View – Table – Cost**. A Task Summary table

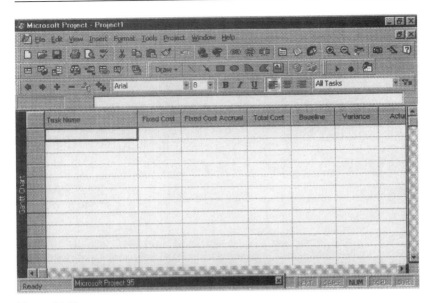

Figure 31.10

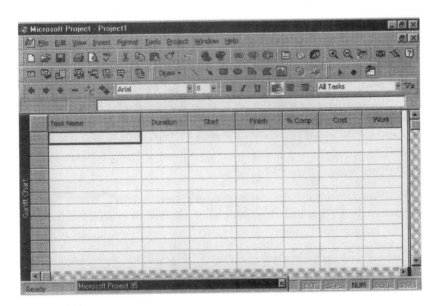

Figure 31.11

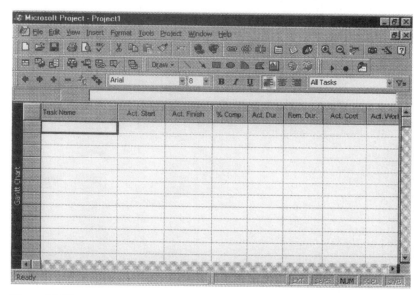

Figure 31.12

which shows the status of the project can be obtained from **View – Table – Summary** and is shown in Figure 31.11.

The Actual Start & Finish, % Complete, Actual & Remaining Duration, Actual Cost and Actual Work performed can be seen on the Task Tracking table, Figure 31.12, accessed from **View – Table – Tracking**. When scrolled, the information will also appear in bar chart form.

The latest version of MS Project can carry out Earned Value calculations, but unfortunately to view the all-important control curves showing the relationship between Actual, Planned and Earned Value, the data must be exported to Microsoft Excel with the aid of a Wizard. It is also possible to model cross-project dependencies by dragging and dropping between the two sets of bars in the different Gantt charts.

MS Project contains the usual comprehensive 'Help' system, and an interactive Office Assistant to provide guidance, and to explain the facilities of MS Project better, some of the views and reports are taken from the example of the bungalow described in Chapter 28.

32

Project close-out

Project close-out

Towards the end of the project, the project manager must make arrangements for a controlled close-out of the project. There is always a risk of time and money being expended on additional work not originally envisaged or where envisaged work is dragged out because no firm cut-off date has been imposed. However, before a project can be handed over, a large number of documents have to be checked and updated to reflect the latest version and as-built condition.

In addition, certain documents obtained and collated during the various phases of the project have to be bound and handed over to the client to enable the plant or systems to be operated and maintained. The following list gives some of the documents that fall into this category:

Stage acceptance certificates
Final handover certificate
Operating instructions or manuals
Maintenance instructions or manuals

Spares lists (usually priced) divided into operating and strategic spares
Lubrication schedules
Quality control records and audit trails
Material test certificates
Equipment test and performance certificates
Equipment, material and system guarantees

All contracts (and subcontracts) must be properly closed out and (if possible) all claims and back charges (including liquidated damages) agreed and settled.

The site must be cleared, all temporary buildings, structures and fences have to be removed, access roads made good and surplus material disposed of. This material can either be sold to the client or operator for spares or, provided the relevant certificates are attached, returned to the supplier or stock. Any uncertificated or unusable material has to be sold for scrap.

Close-out report

Using the information recorded in the project diary and the various project status reports, the project manager must now prepare his project close-out report. This should discuss the degree of compliance with the original project brief (or business case) and acceptance criteria and highlight any important problems encountered together with the solutions adopted.

Apart from giving a short history and post-implementation review of the project, the purpose of this document is to enable future project managers on similar projects to learn from the experience and issues encountered. For this reason the close-out report has to be properly indexed and archived in hard copy or electronic format for easy retrieval.

The report will be sent to the relevant stakeholders and discussed at a formal close-out meeting at which the stakeholders will be able to express their views on the success (or otherwise) of the project. At the end of this meeting the project can be considered to be formally closed.

33

Stages and sequence

Summary of project stages and sequence

The following pages show the stages and sequences in diagrammatic and tabular format.

Figure 32.1 shows the normal sequence of controls of a project from business case to close-out;

Figure 32.2 gives a diagrammatic version of the control techniques for the different project stages;

Figure 32.3 is a heirarchical version of the project sequence which also shows the chapter numbers in the book where the relevant stage or technique is discussed;

Table 32.1 is a detailed tabular breakdown of the sequence for a project control system, again from business case to project close-out.

While the diagrams given will cover most types of projects, it must be understood that projects vary enormously in scope, size and complexity.

The sequences and techniques given may therefore have to be changed to suit any particular project. Indeed certain techniques may not be applicable in their entirety or may have to be modified to suit different requirements. The principles are, however, fundamentally the same.

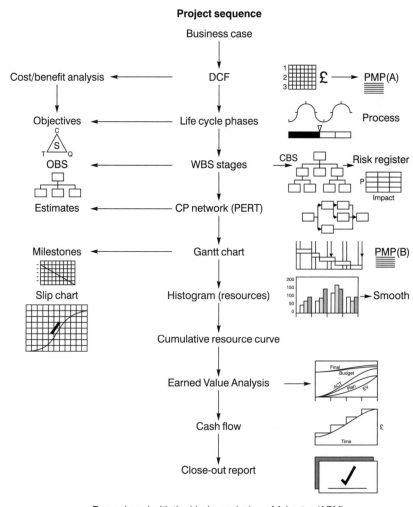

Reproduced with the kind permission of A.Lester (APM)

Figure 32.1

Project stage control techniques

Project

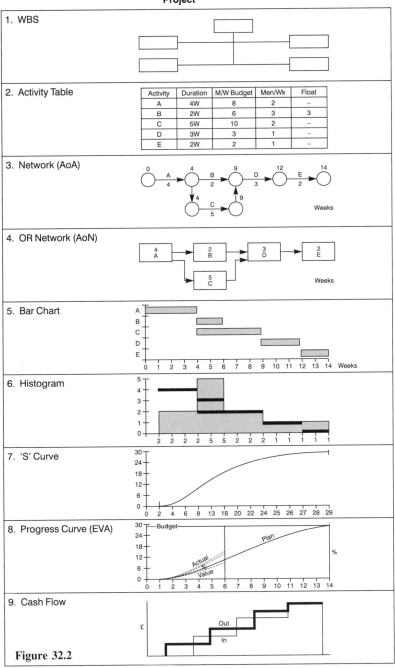

1. WBS	
2. Activity Table	
3. Network (AoA)	
4. OR Network (AoN)	
5. Bar Chart	
6. Histogram	
7. 'S' Curve	
8. Progress Curve (EVA)	
9. Cash Flow	

2. Activity Table

Activity	Duration	M/W Budget	Men/Wk	Float
A	4W	8	2	–
B	2W	6	3	3
C	5W	10	2	–
D	3W	3	1	–
E	2W	2	1	–

Figure 32.2

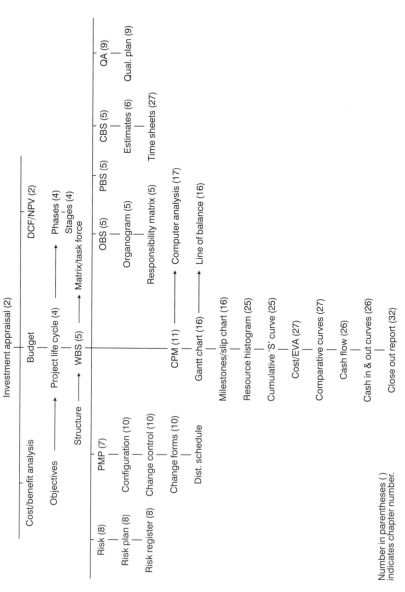

Project sequence

Business case

Investment appraisal (2)

Cost/benefit analysis

Objectives ——→ Project life cycle (4) ——→ Phases (4)

Budget

DCF/NPV (2)

Stages (4)

Structure ——→ WBS (5) ——→ Matrix/task force

OBS (5)   PBS (5)   CBS (5)   QA (9)

Organogram (5)   Estimates (6)   Qual. plan (9)

Responsibility matrix (5)   Time sheets (27)

Computer analysis (17)

Line of balance (16)

Risk (8)

Risk plan (8)   PMP (7)

Risk register (8)   Configuration (10)

Change control (10)

Change forms (10)

Dist. schedule

CPM (11)

Gantt chart (16)

Milestones/slip chart (16)

Resource histogram (25)

Cumulative 'S' curve (25)

Cost/EVA (27)

Comparative curves (27)

Cash flow (26)

Cash in & out curves (26)

Close out report (32)

Number in parentheses ( )
indicates chapter number.

Figure 32.3

Table 32.1   Sequence for project control system

Business case
Cost/benefit analysis
Set objectives
DCF calculations
Establish project life cycle
Establish project phases
Produce project management plan (PMP)
Produce budget (labour, plant, materials, overheads etc.)
Draw work breakdown structure (WBS)
Draw product breakdown structure
Draw Organization Breakdown Structure
Draw Responsibility Matrix
List all possible risks
Carry out risk analysis
Draw up risk management plan
Produce risk register
Draw up activity list
Draw network logic (CPM) (free hand)
Add activity durations
Calculate forward pass
Revise logic (maximize parallel activities)
Calculate 2nd forward pass
Revise activity durations
Calculate 3rd forward pass
Calculate backward pass
Mark critical path (zero float)
Draw final network on grid system
Add activity numbers
Draw bar chart (Gantt chart)
Draw milestone slip chart
Produce resource table
Add resources to bar chart
Aggregate resources
Draw histogram
Smooth resources (utilize float)
Draw cumulative 'S' curve (to be used for EVA)
List activities in numerical order
Add budget values (person hours)
Record weekly actual hours (direct and indirect)
Record weekly % complete (in 5% steps)
Calculate value hours weekly
Calculate overall % complete weekly
Calculate overall efficiency weekly
Calculate anticipated final hours weekly
Draw time/person hour curves (budget, planned, actual, value, anticipated final)

Table 32.1   Continued

Draw time/% curves (% planned, % complete, % efficiency)
Analyse curves
Take appropriate management action
Calculate cost per activity (labour, plant, materials)
Add costs to bar chart activities
Aggregate costs
Draw curve for plant and material costs (outflow)
Draw curve for total cash OUT (this includes labour costs)
Draw curve for total cash IN
Analyse curves
Calculate overdraft requirements
Set up information distribution system
Set up weekly monitoring and recording system
Set up system for recording and assessing changes and extra work
Set up reporting system
Manage risks
Set up regular progress meetings
Write Close-out Report

34

Abbreviations and acronyms used in project management

Abbreviation	Meaning	Usage
ACC	Annual Capital Charge	Finance
ACWP	Actual Cost of Work Performed	EVA
AOA	Activity on Arrow	CPA
AON	Activity on Node	CPA
APM	Association for Project Management	PM
ARM	Availability, Reliability, Maintainability	MOD
BC	Business Case	PM
BCWP	Budgeted Cost of Work Performed	EVA
BCWS	Budgeted Cost of Work Scheduled	EVA
BOK	Body of Knowledge	PM
BS	British Standard	General
BSI	British Standards Institution	General
CAR	Contractor's All Risk	Construct
CBS	Cost Breakdown Structure	PM
CDM	Construction, Design and Management	Construction

Abbreviation	Meaning	Usage
CEN	Comité Europeen de Normalization	General
CIF	Carriage, Insurance, Freight	Procurement
CM	Configuration Management	PM
CPA	Critical Path Analysis	PM
CPA	Contract Price Adjustment	Procurement
CPI	Cost Performance Index	EVA
CPM	Critical Path Methods	CPA
CSCS	Cost & Schedule Control System	EVA
DCF	Discounted Cash Flow	Finance
DDP	Delivery Duty Paid	Procurement
DIN	Deutsche Industrie Normen	General
EVA	Earned Value Analysis	PM
EVMS	Earned Value Management System	EVA
FF	Free Float	CPA
FLAC	Four Letter Acronym	General
FMEA	Failure Mode & Effect Analysis	MOD
FOB	Free on Board	Procurement
FOR	Free on Rail	Procurement
HR	Human Resources	General
H&S	Health & Safety	General
IA	Investment Appraisal	Finance
IPMA	International Project Management Association	PM
IPMT	Integrated Project Management Team	PM
IPR	Intellectual Property Rights	General
IRR	Internal Rate of Return	Finance
IS	Information Systems	General
ISEB	Information Systems Examination Board	General
ISO	International Organization for Standardization	General
IT	Information Technology	General
LCC	Life Cycle Costing	PM
LOB	Line of Balance	Construct
LRM	Linear Responsibility Matrix	PM
MOD	Ministry of Defence	General
NOSCOS	Needs, Objectives, Strategy & Organizations Control System	MOD
NDT	Non Destructive Testing	Construct
NPV	Net Present Value	Finance
OBS	Organization Breakdown Structure	PM
ORC	Optimal Replacement Chart	Finance
ORM	Optimal Replacement Method	Finance

Abbreviation	Meaning	Usage
PBS	Product Breakdown Structure	PM
PDM	Precedence Diagram Method	CPA
PERT	Program Evaluation & Review Technique	CPA
PFI	Private Finance Initiative	Finance
PM	Project Management	PM
PM	Project Manager	PM
PMP	Project Management Plan	PM
PPE	Post Project Evaluation	PM
PPP	Public–Private Partnership	Finance
PRD	Project Definition	PM
QA	Quality Assurance	General
QC	Quality Control	General
QMS	Quality Management System	General
QP	Quality Plan	General
R&D	Research and Development	General
RR	Rate of Return	Finance
SFR	Sinking Fund Return	Finance
SMART	Specific, Measurable, Achievable, Realistic, Timebound	MOD
SOW	Statement of Work	PM
SPI	Schedule Performance Index	EVA
SRD	Sponsor's Requirement Definition	PM
SWOT	Strength, Weakness, Opportunity, Threat	PM
TCP	Time, Cost & Performance	PM
TF	Total Float	CPA
TQM	Total Quality Management	General
TOR	Terms of Reference	General
VA	Value Analysis	General
VE	Value Engineering	General
VM	Value Management	General
WBS	Work Breakdown Structure	PM

See also list of acronyms.

Acronyms used in project management

ARM	Availability, Reliability, Maintainability
CADMID	Concept, Assessment, Demonstration, Monitoring, In-Service, Disposal
CFIOT	Concept, Feasibility, In-Service, Operation, Termination
CS^2 (CSCS)	Cost & Schedule Control System

EMAC	Engineering Manhours And Cost
FLAC	Four Letter Acronym
HASAWA	Health And Safety At Work Act
NAPNOC	No Agreed Price, No Contract
NIMBY	Not In My Back Yard
NOSCOS	Needs, Objectives, Strategy & Organization Control System
NOSOCS&R	Needs, Objectives, Strategy, Organization Control, System & Risk
PAYE	Pay As You Earn
PERT	Program, Evaluation & Review Technique
PESTEL	Political, Economic, Sociological, Technological, Environmental, Legal
PRAM	Project Risk Analysis & Management
PRINCE	Projects in a Controlled Environment
RIDDOR	Reporting of Injuries, Diseases & Dangerous Occurrences Regulations
RIRO	Rubbish In–Rubbish Out
SMAC	Site Manhours And Cost
SMART	Specific, Measurable, Achievable, Realistic & Time bound
SOW	Statement Of Work
SWOT	Strengths, Weaknesses, Opportunities & Threats

Glossary

Activity An operation on a network which takes time (or other resources) and is indicated by an arrow.

Actual cost of work performed (ACWP) Cumulative actual cost (in money or manhours) of work booked in a specific period.

Actual hours The manhours actually expended on an activity or contract over a defined period.

AoN Activity on Node.

AoA Activity on Arrow.

Arithmetical analysis A method for calculating floats arithmetically.

Arrow A symbol on a network to represent an activity or dummy.

Arrow diagram A diagram showing the interrelationships of activities.

Back end The fabrication, construction and commissioning stage of a project.

Backward pass A process for subtracting durations from previous events, working backwards from the last event.

Banding The subdivision of a network into horizontal and vertical sections or bands to aid identification of activities and responsibilities.

Bar chart *See* **Gantt chart**.

Beta (*b*) distribution Standard distribution giving the expected time te = (a + 4m + b)/6.

Budget Quantified resources to achieve an objective, task or project by a set time.

Budgeted cost of work performed (BCWP)   See Earned Value.

Budgeted cost of work scheduled (BCWS)   Quantified cost (in money or manhours) of work scheduled (planned) in a set time.

Budget hours   The hours allocated to an activity or contract at the estimate or proposal stage.

Business case   The document setting out the information and financial plan to enable decision makers to approve and authorize the project.

Calendar   Time scale of programme using dates.

Capital cost   The project cost as shown in the balance sheet.

Cash flow   Inward and outward movement of money of a contract or company.

Change control   The process of recording, evaluating and authorizing project changes.

Change management   The management of project variations (changes) in time, cost and scope.

Circle and link method   *See* **Precedence diagram**.

Close out procedure   The actions implemented and documents produced at the end of a project.

Computer analysis   The method for calculating floats, etc. using a computer.

Configuration management   The management of the creation, maintenance and distribution of documents and standards.

Contingency plan   Alternative action plan to be implemented when a perceived risk materializes.

Cost/benefit analysis   Analysis of the relationship between the cost and anticipated benefit of a task or project.

Cost breakdown structure (CBS)   The hierarchical breakdown of costs when allocated to the work packages of a WBS.

Cost code   Identity code given to a work element for cost control purposes.

Cost control   The ability to monitor, compare and adjust expenditures and costs at regular and sufficiently frequent intervals to keep the costs within budget.

Cost performance index   The ratio of the earned value (useful) cost and the actual cost.

Cost reporting   The act of recording and reporting commitments and costs on a regular basis.

Cost variance   The arithmetical difference between the earned value cost and the actual cost. This could be positive or negative.

CPA   Critical path analysis. The technique for finding the critical path and hence the minimum project duration.

CPM   Critical path method. *See* **CPA**

CPS   Critical path scheduling. *See* **CPA**.

Critical activity   An activity on the critical path which has zero float.

Critical path   A chain of critical activities, i.e. the longest path of a project.

Dangle   An activity which has a beginning node but is not connected at its end to a node which is part of the network.

Deliverable   The end product of a project or defined stage.

Dependency   The restriction on an activity by one or more preceding activities.

Direct cost   The measurable cost directly attributed to the project.

Discounted Cash Flow (DCF)   Technique for comparing future cash flows by discounting by a specific rate.

Distribution schedule   A tabular record showing by whom and to whom the documents of a project are distributed.

Dummy activity   A timeless activity used as a logical link or restraint between real activities in a network.

Duration   The time taken by an activity.

Earliest finish   The earliest time at which an activity can be finished.

Earliest start   The earliest time at which an activity can be started.

Earned value hours   *See* **Value hours**.

End event   The last event of a project.

EVA   Earned Value Analysis.

Event   The beginning and end node of an activity, forming the intersection point with other activities.

Feasibility study   Analysis of one or more courses of action to establish their feasibility or viability.

Feedback   The flow of information to a planner for updating the network.

Float   The period by which a non-critical activity can be delayed.

Free float   The time by which an activity can be delayed without affecting a following activity.

Forward pass   A process for adding durations to previous event times starting at the beginning of a project.

Front end   The design and procurement stage of a project. This may or may not include the manufacturing period of equipment.

Functional organization   Management structure of specialist groups carrying out specific functions or services.

Gantt chart   A programming technique in which activities are represented by bars drawn to a time scale and against a time base.

Graphics   Computer generated diagrams.

Graphical analysis   A method for calculating the critical path and floats using a linked bar chart technique.

Grid   Lines drawn on a network sheet to act as coordinates of the nodes.

Hammock   An activity covering a number of activities between its starting and end node.

Hardware   The name given to a computer and its accessories.

Histogram   A series of vertical columns whose height is proportional to a particular resource or number of resources in any time period.

Independent float   The difference between free float and the slack of a beginning event.

Indirect cost   Cost attributable to a project, but not directly related to an activity or group within the project.

Input   The information and data fed into a computer.

Interface   The meeting point of two or more networks or strings.

Interfering float   The difference between the total float and the free float. Also the slack of the end event.

Internal Rate of Return (IRR)   The discount rate at which the Net Present Value is zero.

Investment appraisal   Procedure for analysing the viability of an investment.

Ladder   A string of activities which repeat themselves in a number of stages.

Lag   The delay period between the end of one activity and the start of another.

Latest finish   The latest time at which an activity can be finished without affecting subsequent activities.

Latest start   The latest time at which an activity can be started without delaying the project.

Lead   The time between the start of one activity and the start of another.

Lester diagram   Network diagram which combines the advantages of arrow and precedence diagrams.

Line of balance   Planning technique used for repetitive projects, sub-projects or operations.

Logic   The realistic interrelationship of the activities on a network.

Logic links   The link line connecting the activities of a precedence diagram.

Loop   A cycle of activities which returns to its origin.

Manual analysis   The method for calculating floats and the critical path without the use of a computer.

Master network   Coordinating network of subnetworks.

Matrix   The table of activities, durations and floats used in arithmetical analysis.

Matrix organization   Management structure where functional departments allocate selected resources to a project.

Menu Screen listing of software functions.

Method statement Narrative or graphical description of the methods envisaged to construct or carry out selected operations.

Milestones Key event in a project which takes zero time.

Milestone slip chart Graph showing and predicting the slippage of milestones over the project period.

Negative float The time by which an activity is late in relation to its required time for meeting the programme.

Net Present Value (NPV) Aggregate of discounted future cash flows.

Network A diagram showing the logical interrelationships of activities.

Network analysis The method used for calculating the floats and critical path of a network.

Network logic The interrelationship of activities of a planning network.

Node The intersection point of activities. An event.

Organization breakdown structure (OBS) Diagrammatic representation of the hierarchical breakdown of management levels for a project.

Organogram Family tree of an organization showing levels of management.

Output The information and data produced by a computer.

P3 Primavera Project Planner.

Path The unbroken sequence of activities of a network.

PERT Programme Evaluation and Review Technique. Another name for **CPA**.

Phase A division of the project life cycle.

Planned cost The estimated (anticipated) cost of a project.

Precedence network A method of network programming in which the activities are written in the node boxes and connected by lines to show their interrelationship.

Preceding event The beginning event of an activity.

Printout *See* **Output**.

Product Breakdown Structure (PBS) Hierarchical decomposition of a project into various levels of products.

Program The set of instructions given to a computer.

Programme A group of related projects.

Programme manager Manager of a group of related projects.

Progress report A report which shows the time and cost status of a project, giving explanations for any deviations from the programme or cost plan.

Project A unique set of co-ordinated and controlled activities to introduce change within defined time, cost and quality/performance parameters.

Project life cycle All the processes and phases between the conception and termination of a project.

Project management   The planning, monitoring and controlling of all aspects of a project.

Project management plan (PMP)   A document which summarizes of all the main features encapsulating the Why, What, When, How, Where and Who of a project.

Project manager   The individual who has the authority, responsibility and accountability to achieve the project objectives.

Project organization   Organization structure in which the project manager has full authority and responsibility of the project team.

Project task force   See Task force.

Quality management   The management of all aspects of quality criteria, control, documentation and assurance.

Quality plan   A plan that sets out the quality standards and criteria of the various tasks of a project.

Random numbering   The numbering method used to identify events (or nodes) in which the numbers follow no set sequence.

Resource   The physical means necessary to carry out an activity.

Resource levelling   *See* **Resource smoothing**.

Resource smoothing   The act of spreading the resources over a project to use the minimum resources at any one time and yet not delay the project.

Responsibility code   Computer coding for sorting data by department.

Responsibility matrix   A tabular presentation showing who or which department is responsible for set work items or packages.

Return on capital employed   Profit (before interest and tax) divided by the capital employed given as a %.

Retentions   Moneys held by employer for period of maintenance (guarantee) period.

Return on Investment (ROI)   Average return over a specified period divided by the investment given as a %.

Risk   The combination of the consequences and likelihood of occurrence of an adverse event or threat.

Risk analysis   The systematic procedures used to determine the consequences or assess the likelihood of occurrence of an adverse event or threat.

Risk identification   Process for finding and determining what could pose a risk.

Risk management   Structured application of policies, procedures and practices for evaluating, monitoring and mitigating risks.

Risk management plan   Document setting out strategic requirements for risk assessment and procedures.

Risk register   Table showing the all identified risks, their owners, degree of P/I, and mitigation strategy.

Schedule   *See* **Programme**.

Schedule Performance Index   The ratio of earned value cost (or time) and the planned cost (or time).

Schedule variance   The arithmetical difference between the earned value cost (or time) and the planned cost (or time).

Sequential numbering   The numbering method in which the numbers follow a pattern to assist in identifying the activities.

Slack   The period between the earliest and latest times of an event.

Slip chart   See milestone slip chart.

SMAC   Site man hour and cost. The name of the computer program developed by Foster Wheeler Power Products Limited for controlling man hours in the field.

Software   The programs used by a computer.

Sponsor   The individual or body who has primary responsibility for the project and is the primary risk taker.

Stakeholder   Person or organization who has a vested interest in the project. This interest can be positive or negative.

Statement of Work (SOW)   Description of a work package which defines the project performance criteria and resources.

Start event   The first event of a project or activity.

Subnetwork   A small network which shows a part of the activities of a main network in greater detail.

Succeeding event   The end event of an activity.

Task   The smallest work unit shown on a network programme (see also Activity).

Task data   The attributes of a task such as duration, start and end date, resource requirement.

Task force   Project organization consisting of a project team which includes all the disciplines and support services under the direction of a project manager.

Time estimate   The time or duration of an activity.

Toolbar   The list of function icons on a computer screen.

Topological numbering   A numbering system where the beginning event of an activity must always have a higher number than the events of any activity preceding it.

Total float   The spare time between the earliest and latest times of an activity.

Updating   The process of changing a network or programme to take into account progress and logic variations.

Value hours   The useful work hours spent on an activity. This figure is the product of the budget hours and the percentage complete of an activity or the whole contract.

Variance   Amount by which a parameter varies from its specified value.

Weightings   The percentage of an activity in terms of man hours or cost of an activity in relation to the contract as a whole, based on the budget values.

Work breakdown structure (WBS)   Hierarchical decomposition of a project into various levels of management and work packages.

Work package   Group of activities within a specified level of a work breakdown structure.

Bibliography

Adair, J., *Effective Leadership*, PAN (1983)

Ahuja, H.N., *Construction Performance Control by Networks*, Wiley (1976)

Andersen, E.S., Grude, K.V. & Haug, Tor, *Goal Directed Project Management*, 2nd edn, Kogan Page (2002)

Antill, J.M. & Woodhead, R., *Critical Path Methods in Construction Practice*, Wiley (1982)

APM, *Body of Knowledge*, Association for Project Management (1996)

APM, *Planning Contracts for Successful Project Management*, APM Group (1998)

APM, *Project Risk Assessment and Management, 'PRAM Guide'*, APM Group (1997)

APM, *Standard Terms for the Appointment of a Project Manager*, APM Group (1998)

Archibald, R.D., *Managing High-Technology Programs and Projects*, John Wiley (1976)

Archibald, R.D. & Villoria, R.L., *Network-based Management Systems*, John Wiley (1967)

Baden-Hellard, R., *Managing Construction Conflict*, Longman Scientific (1988)

Baden-Hellard, R., *Project Partnering: Principle and Practice*, Thomas Telford Publications (1995)

Baden-Hellard, R., *Total Quality in Construction Projects*, Thomas Telford Publications.

Baguly, Phil, *Teach Yourself Project Management*, T.Y. Books (1999)

Bank, J., *The Essence of Total Quality Project Management*, Prentice Hall (1992)

Barnes, N.M.L. (ed.), *Financial Control*, Thomas Telford Publications (1990)

Battersby, A., *Network Analysis*, Macmillan (1970)

Belanger, T.C., *The Complete Planning Guide to Microsoft Project*, Butterworths (1996)

Belbin, M., *Team Roles at Work*, Butterworth-Heinemann (1993)

Boyce, C., *Successful Project Administration*, Hawksmere (1992)

Bradley, K., *Prince: A Practical Handbook*, Butterworth-Heinemann (1992)

Breech, E.F.L., *Construction Management in Principle and Practice*, Longman (1971)

Briner, W., Hastings, C. & Geddes, M., *Project Leadership*, Gower (1996)

British Standards Institution, *BS 6079, Part 1, Guide to Project Management*, BSI (2002)

British Standards Institution, *BS 6079, Part 2, Project Management Vocabulary*, BSI (2000)

British Standards Institution, *BS 6046, Parts 1–4, Use of network techniques in project management*, BSI (1992)

British Standards Institution, *BS 7000, Design Management Systems*, BSI (1995)

British Standards Institution, *BS ISO 10006, Quality Management – Guidelines to Quality in Project Management*, BSI (1997)

Burke, R., *Project Management Planning & Control Techniques, 3rd edn*, John Wiley (1999)

Burman, P.J., *Precedence Networks for Project Planning and Control*, McGraw-Hill (1972)

Buttrick, R., *The Project Management Workout*, Pitman (1997)

Carter, B. *et al.*, *Introducing RISKMAN*, NCC Blackwell (1994)

CCTA, *Guide to Programme Management*, HMSO (1997)

CCTA, *Introduction to Management of Risk*, HMSO (1993)

Chapman, C.B. & Ward, S., *Project Risk Management*, John Wiley (2000)

Cleland, D.I. & Gareis, R., *Global Project Management*, McGraw-Hill (1993)

Cleland, D.I. & King, W.R., *Project Management Handbook*, McGraw-Hill (1993)

Cleland, D.I. & Ireland, L.R., *Project Management*, 4th edn, McGraw-Hill (2002)

Cleland, D.I. & Ireland, L.R., *Project Manager's Portable Handbook*, McGraw Hill (2000)

Clough, Richard H., Sears, Glenn A., and Sears, Keoki, *Construction Project Management*, 4th edn, John Wiley (2000)

Corrie, R.K. (ed.) *Project Evaluations*, Thomas Telford Publications (1994)

Davison-Fram, J., *Managing Projects in Organisations*, Jossey-Bass Publishers (1987)

Dingle, J., *Project Management – Orientation for Decision Makers*, Edward Arnold (1997)

Edwards, L., *Practical Risk Management in the Construction Industry*, Thomas Telford (1995)

Field, Mike & Keller, Laurie, *Project Management*, Thomson (2002)

Figenti, Enzo & Comminos, Dennis, *The Practice of Project Management*, Kogan Page (2002)

Flanaghan & Norman, *Risk Management in Construction*, Blackwell Scientific (1993)

Fleming, Q.W. & Koppelmann, J.M., *Earned Value Project Management Systems*, PMI (1996)

Frame, Davidson, J., *Managing Projects in Organizations*, Rev. edn, Jossey Bass (1995)

Frame, Davidson, J., *The New Project Management*, Jossey Bass (2002)

Geddes, M., Hastings, C. & Briner, W., *Project Leadership*, Gower (1990)

Gentle, Michael, *The CRM Project Management Handbook*, Kogan Page (2000)

Goodlad, J.B., *Accounting for Construction Management: An Introduction*, Heinemann (1974)

Goodman, L.J., *Project Planning and Management*, Van Nostrand Reinhold (1988)

Graham, R.J., *Project Management as if People Mattered*, Prima Vera Press (1987)

Greaseley, A., *Project Planning*, Butterworth-Heinemann (1997)

Gray, C. & Larson, E., *Project Management*, McGraw-Hill (2002)

Grey, S., *Practical Risk Assessment for Project Management*, John Wiley (1995)

Hamilton, A., *Management by Projects*, Thomas Telford Publications (1997)

Harris, F. and McCaffer, R., *Modern Construction Management*, Crosby Lockwood (1977)

Harris, J., *Sharpen your Team's Skills in Project Management*, McGraw-Hill (1997)

Harris, R.B., *Precedence & Arrow Networking Techniques for Construction*, Wiley (1978)

Harrison, F.L., *Advanced Project Management*, Gower (1992)

Heldman, Kim, *PMP Project Management Professional*, Sybex (2001)

Hillebrandt, P.M., *Economic Theory and the Construction Industry*, Macmillan (1974)

Hunt, J.W., *Managing People at Work*, McGraw-Hill (1986)

Johnston, A.K., *A Hacker's Guide to Project Management*, Butterworths (1995)

Kerzner, H., *Project Management*, Van Nostrand Reinhold (1995)

Kliem, R.L. & Ludlin, I.S., *The People Side of Project Management*, Gower (1995)

Kliem, R.L. & Ludlin, I.S., *Reducing Project Risk*, Gower (1997)

Kwakye, A.A., *Construction Project Administration in Practice*, Longman (1997)

Lake, Cathy, *Mastering Project Management*, Thorogood (1997)

Lang, H.J. & Merino, D.L., *Selection Process for Capital Projects*, Wiley (1993)

Lester, A., *Project Planning and Cost Control*, ASM (1988)

Lester, A. and Benning, A., *Procurement in the Process Industry*, Butterworths (1989)

Levine, Harvey, A., *Practical Project Management*, John Wiley (2002)

Levy, Sidney M., *Project Management in Construction*, 4th edn, McGraw-Hill (2002)

Lewin Maish, D., *Better Software Project Management*, AMACOM (2001)

Lewis, James P., *Mastering Project Management*, McGraw-Hill (1997)

Lewis, James P., *Team Based Project Management*, McGraw-Hill (1997)

Lewis, James P., *Fundamentals of Project Management*, 2nd edn, AMACOM (2002)

Lewis, James P., *Project Planning, Scheduling and Control*, 3rd edn, McGraw-Hill (2000)

Lientz, B.P. & Rea, P., *International Project Management*, Academic Press (2003)

Lock, D., *Project Management Handbook*, Gower (1987)

Lock, D., *Project Management*, 7th edn, Gower (2000)

Lock, D., *The Essentials of Project Management*, 2nd edn, Gower (2001)

Lock, D., *Handbook of Engineering Management*, Butterworth-Heinemann (1993)

Lockyer, K., *An Introduction to Critical Path Analysis*, Pitman (1970)

Lockyer, K. and Gordon, J., *Project Management and Project Network Techniques*, 6th edn, Pitman (1996)

Martin, Paula & Tate, Karen, *Getting Started in Project Management*, John Wiley (2001)

Maylor, Harvey, *Project Management*, 3rd edn, Pearson (2003)

Meredith, J.R. & Mantel, S.J., *Project Management: A Managerial Approach*, Wiley (1985)

Merna, A. & Smith, N.J., *Projects Procured by Privately Financed Concession Contracts*, 2 volumes, Asia Law & Practice (1996)

Merrett, A.J. & Sykes, A., *Capital Budgeting and Company Finance*, Longmans (1966)

Moore, David, *Project Management*, Blackwell (2002)

Morris, P.W.G., *The Management of Projects*, Thomas Telford Publications (1997)

Morris, P.W.G. & Hough, G.H., *The Anatomy of Major Projects*, John Wiley (1987)

Neale, R.H. & Neale, D.E., *Construction Planning*, Thomas Telford (1989)

NEDC, *Guidelines for the Management of Major Construction Projects*, HMSO (1991)

Newell, M.W., *Project Management Professional*, 2nd edn, AMACON (2002)

Oaklands, J.S., *Total Quality Management*, Butterworth-Heinemann (1994)

Obeng, E., *The Project Leader's Secret Handbook – All Change*, Pitman (1996)

Obeng, E., *Putting Strategy to Work*, Pitman (1996)

O'Brien, J.J. & Peatnick, F.L., *CPM in Construction Management*, 5th edn, McGraw-Hill (1999)

O'Connell, F., *How to Run Successful Projects II*, Prentice Hall (1996)

O'Neill, J.J., *Management of Industrial Projects*, Butterworths (1989)

Oxley, R. & Paskitt, J., *Management Techniques Applied to the Construction Industry*, 5th edn, Blackwell (1996)

OGC, *Best Practice Guidance*, The Stationery Office (2002)

Parkin, J., *Management Decisions for Engineers*, Thomas Telford

Phillips, J.J., Bothell, T.W. and Snead, C.L., *The Project Management Scorecard*, Butterworth-Heinemann (2002)

Pilcher, R., *Project Cost Control in Construction*, Collins (1985)

PMI, *A Guide to the Project Management Body of Knowledge*, Project Management Institute (USA) (1996)

Reiss, G., *Project Management Demystified*, 2nd edn, Spon (2001)

Reiss, G., *Programme Management Demystified*, Spon (1996)

Ridley, J., *Safety at Work*, Butterworths (2003)

Smith, N.J. (ed.), *Project Cost Estimating*, Thomas Telford Publications (1995)

Smith, N.J. (ed.), *Engineering Project Management*, Blackwell Scientific (1995)

Snell, M., *Cost Benefit Analysis for Engineers, Planners and Decision Makers*, Thomas Telford Publications (1997)

Spender, Stephen, *Managing Projects Well*, Butterworth-Heinemann (2000)

Snowden, M., *Management of Engineering Projects*, Butterworths (1977)

Stevenson, Nancy, *MS Project 2002 for Dummies*, Hungry Minds (2002)

Stone, R. (ed.), *Management of Engineering Projects*, Macmillan (1988)

Thompson, P. & Perry, J., *Engineering Construction Risks*, Thomas Telford

Tobis, Irene & Tobis, Michael, *Managing Multiple Projects*, McGraw-Hill (2002)

Turner, J.R., *The Project Manager as Change Agent*, McGraw-Hill (1996)

Turner, J.R., *The Handbook of Project-based Management*, McGraw-Hill (1998)

Turner, J.R., *The Commercial Project Manager*, McGraw-Hill (1995)

Walker, A., *Project Management in Construction*, Blackwell Science (2002)

Ward, S.A., *Cost Engineering for Effective Project Control*, Wiley (1992)

Wearne, S.H., *Principles of Engineering Organizations*, Thomas Telford Publications (1993)

Winch, Graham M., *Managing Construction Projects*, Blackwell (2002)

Woodward, John F., *Construction Project Management: Getting it Right First Time*, Thomas Telford Publications (1997)

Young, Trevor, *The Handbook of Project Management*, Kogan Page (2001)

Young, Trevor, *Successful Project Management*, Kogan Page (2001)

Index